Righteous Indignation

Righteous Indignation

Christian Philosophical and Theological Perspectives on Anger

Edited by

Gregory L. Bock
Court D. Lewis

LEXINGTON BOOKS/FORTRESS ACADEMIC
Lanham • Boulder • New York • London

Published by Lexington Books/Fortress Academic
Lexington Books is an imprint of The Rowman & Littlefield Publishing Group, Inc.
4501 Forbes Boulevard, Suite 200, Lanham, Maryland 20706
www.rowman.com

6 Tinworth Street, London SE11 5AL, United Kingdom

British Library Cataloguing in Publication Information Available

Library of Congress Cataloging-in-Publication Data

Names: Bock, Gregory L., editor. | Lewis, Court D., editor.
Title: Righteous indignation: Christian philosophical and theological
    perspectives on anger / [edited by] Gregory L. Bock and Court D. Lewis.
Other titles: Righteous indignation (Lexington Books/Fortress Academic)
Description: Lanham: Lexington Books/Fortress Academic, [2021] | Includes
    bibliographical references and index. | Summary: "Righteous Indignation
    explores the philosophy of Christian anger-for example what anger is, what
    it means for God to be angry, and when anger is morally appropriate. The
    contributors examine several dimensions of the topic, including divine
    wrath, imprecatory psalms, and the proper place of anger in the life of
    Christians today."—Provided by publisher.
Identifiers: LCCN 2021015866 (print) | LCCN 2021015867 (ebook) | ISBN
    9781978711525 (cloth) | ISBN 9781978711532 (epub)
Subjects: LCSH: Anger—Religious aspects—Christianity. | God
    (Christianity)—Wrath.
Classification: LCC BT153.W7 R54 2021 (print) | LCC BT153.W7 (ebook) |
    DDC 231.7/6—dc23
LC record available at https://lccn.loc.gov/2021015866
LC ebook record available at https://lccn.loc.gov/2021015867

♾™ The paper used in this publication meets the minimum requirements of American
National Standard for Information Sciences—Permanence of Paper for Printed Library
Materials, ANSI/NISO Z39.48-1992.

Contents

Contributors

Michael W. Austin, Eastern Kentucky University
Michael W. Austin is professor of philosophy at Eastern Kentucky University, senior fellow at the Dietrich Bonhoeffer Institute, and a national advocate for gun violence prevention alongside many of today's most prominent interfaith leaders through Everytown for Gun Safety. He has published twelve books, including his latest, *God and Guns in America* (2020).

Joshua Beckett, Loyola Marymount University
Joshua Beckett is lecturer in theological studies at Loyola Marymount University. His research focuses on the intersection of theological ethics, social theory, and political economy. Joshua has contributed chapters to *Discerning Ethics* (2020) and *Breaking the Marriage Idol* (2018).

Gregory L. Bock, The University of Texas at Tyler
Gregory L. Bock is assistant professor of philosophy and religion and program director of the Philosophy, Religion, and Asian Studies Programs at UT Tyler. He is also director of UT Tyler's Center for Ethics. His areas of research include bioethics, the ethics of forgiveness, and the philosophy of religion. He is editor of volumes III and IV of *The Philosophy of Forgiveness* (2018, 2019).

Matthew R. Boulter, The University of Texas at Tyler
Matthew R. Boulter holds a PhD in philosophy from the National University of Ireland (Maynooth), having recently defended his dissertation, *Repetition and Identity: Ratzinger's Bonaventure and the Meaning of History*. He is an Episcopal priest and teaches philosophy as an adjunct professor at the University of Texas at Tyler.

Jason Cook, Grace Community Church

Jason Cook is pastor of men and theology at Grace Community Church in Tyler, Texas. He is also ninth-grade Bible teacher at Grace Community School. His research interests include biblical Hebrew, Old Testament narrative, and biblical theology.

Tammy W. Cowart, The University of Texas at Tyler

Tammy W. Cowart is associate professor of business law at UT Tyler. She serves as the director of graduate programs for the Soules College of Business and the associate director of UT Tyler's Center for Ethics. Cowart teaches business law and business ethics to undergraduate, graduate, and executive students. Her areas of research include intellectual property law, privacy law, business ethics, and compliance.

Joshua R. Farris, Alpine Christian School

Joshua R. Farris is professor of theology of science, Missional University and part-time lecturer at Auburn University of Montgomery. He is also the director of Trinity School of Theology. Previously he was the Chester and Margaret Paluch Professor at Mundelein Seminary, University of Saint Mary of the Lake, and assistant professor of theology at Houston Baptist University. He has edited and authored several volumes, see the following representative sampling: *Being Saved*; *Idealism and Christian Theology*; *The Routledge Companion to Theological Anthropology*; *An Introduction to Theological Anthropology: Humans, Both Creaturely and Divine*; *The Soul of Theological Anthropology: A Cartesian Exploration*. He is the coeditor of the *Routledge Handbook of Idealism and Immaterialism* (forthcoming in 2021). Finally, he is the international editor of *Perichoresis: The Theological Journal of Emanuel University*; the associate editor of *Journal of Biblical and Theological Studies*; and an international editor for the *European Journal of Philosophy of Religion*.

S. Mark Hamilton, JESociety

S. Mark Hamilton is a research associate at JESociety.org and has published a number of articles, chapters in books, and one monograph. His most recent work includes essays titled "Jonathan Edwards on the Person of Christ" in Douglas A. Sweeney and Jan Stievermann, eds., *The Oxford Handbook of Jonathan Edwards* (2021); "Confessionalism and Causation in Jonathan Edwards (1703–58)," coauthored with C. Layne Hancock, in Joshua R. Farris and Benedikt Paul Göcke, eds., *Routledge Handbook on Idealism and Immaterialism* (forthcoming 2021); and "Jonathan Edwards on Atonement Redux," in Kyle C. Strobel, Phillip Hussey, Christina Larsen, eds., *Jonathan Edwards and the Reformed High Orthodox* (forthcoming

2022). His next monograph is titled *Jonathan Edwards on Spirit Christology* (forthcoming 2021).

Phillip A. Hussey, Saint Louis University
Phillip A. Hussey is a PhD candidate in historical theology at Saint Louis University.

Court D. Lewis, Pellissippi State Community College
Court D. Lewis is associate professor of philosophy at Pellissippi State Community College. Specializing in ethics, forgiveness, and justice, Court is the author of *Repentance and the Right to Forgiveness* (2018); series editor of Vernon Press's series *The Philosophy of Forgiveness*; member of the Concerned Philosophers for Peace; and proud father, volunteer, and musician.

John C. Peckham, Andrews University
John C. Peckham is professor of theology and Christian philosophy at Andrews University in Berrien Springs, Michigan. He is the author of several books, including *The Love of God: A Canonical Model* (2015), *Canonical Theology* (2016), *Theodicy of Love: Cosmic Conflict and the Problem of Evil* (2018), and *The Doctrine of God: Introducing the Big Questions* (2019).

Melissa C. M. Tan, University of Aberdeen
Melissa C. M. Tan is currently pursuing a PhD in divinity at the University of Aberdeen, Scotland, where she is analyzing the theological dimensions of the social dynamics of honor-shame in Paul's writings. Melissa has also contributed the essay "Jesus's Presentation of God's Love and Forgiveness in the Three 'Lost' Parables" in *The Philosophy of Forgiveness*, volume IV.

Charlie Trimm, Talbot School of Theology, Biola University
Charlie Trimm is associate professor of biblical and theological studies at Talbot School of Theology, Biola University. He is the author of *Fighting for the King and the Gods: A Survey of Warfare in the Ancient Near East* (Society of Biblical Literature) and coauthor of *Understanding Old Testament Theology: Mapping the Terrain of Recent Approaches* (Zondervan, with Brittany Kim).

Introduction

Gregory L. Bock and Court D. Lewis

The fact that anger is one of the seven deadly sins might cause one to think that "Christian anger" is an oxymoron. Additionally, the Bible contains many warnings against anger. For example, the Apostle Paul writes, "Let all bitterness and wrath and anger and clamor and slander be put away from you" (Ephesians 4:31), and the book of James says, "The anger of man does not produce the righteousness of God" (James 1:20).

Nevertheless, there are examples of righteous anger in the Bible, too. For instance, in the Old Testament, Moses gets angry with the sins of the people of Israel and breaks the stone tablets (Exodus 32:19), David gets angry with the enemies of God (Psalm 39:20–24), and God himself regularly gets angry with human sin. There are examples of righteous anger in the New Testament, as well, the most famous of which is the incident in the Temple when Jesus throws out the money changers (John 2:13–15).

Some Christian writers down through the centuries have denied that God gets angry in the sense of experiencing emotions like ours (Cassian, Augustine, etc.), and some writers (Calvin, Wesley, etc.) stress the negative aspects of human anger more than others. Yet there is a strong current, even among these writers, that extols anger in its proper place. On this view, human anger is God-given and has an important role to play in the lives of Christians; moreover, many believe that divine anger is both real and justified because God, in the fullness of love, reacts with indignation against injustice and human wickedness.

Recent events in society, such as the #MeToo movement, Black Lives Matter, and the 2020 presidential election cycle, have Christians rethinking the place of anger in a life of discipleship. Is it okay to get angry at social injustice, or should Christians suppress and forswear their anger? Is anger the cause of our social discord, or is it the consequence? Should Christians avoid conflict, or should they be marching along with other protesters on the frontlines? Application questions like these motivate the book.

The book concludes with several chapters of application; however, to get there we feel it is necessary to begin with a theology of anger, in particular an investigation of anger as an attribute of God, because one's theology inevitably shapes one's ethics. Chapters 1 through 4 focus on divine anger. Chapter 5 addresses the difficult question of whether imprecatory prayers in the Bible, instances of praying judgment upon one's enemies, should be disavowed or whether they are still relevant and helpful. Chapters 6 and 7 examine the teachings on anger in the work of two of the most famous theologians in church history: Thomas Aquinas and Jonathan Edwards. Chapters 8, 9, and 10 apply the topic to particular issues, and chapter 11 considers the place of anger in Christian ethics.

This is a multidisciplinary volume. The authors are scholars from philosophy, theology, law, and biblical studies, and their essays investigate the topic using tools from their disciplines. While this may present challenges for editors and readers alike, we feel the rewards are worth the effort because when all is said and done, the picture will be much more complete, and researchers looking for help on the topic may find it from a discipline they had not previously considered. As editors, we have tried our best to direct the project without interfering with the unique voice of each contributor. Where there is disagreement among them, we have allowed this to remain.

In "Divine Anger and Human Love," Joshua Beckett addresses several misunderstandings about the doctrine of divine anger and its effect on human anger, exploring anger from the perspectives of biblical studies, constructive theology, and Christian ethics. First, Beckett describes the biblical emphasis on God's mercy and love. Second, he explores the biblical concept of divine anger. Finally, he shows how these can produce in us a constructive loving anger that will be pleasing to God and a vital force in communities of love and hope. In his view, divine anger is just what we need to bring about change in a society filled with social injustice.

In "The Righteous Anger of the Immutable God of Love," John C. Peckham considers whether the idea of divine anger is compatible with the doctrines of divine immutability, impassibility, and love. First, he makes a distinction between strict immutability and qualified immutability and argues that while divine anger may be inconsistent with the former, it fits well with the latter. For on a qualified account, God's character is unchanging, but his relational properties are not; his changing relational properties are on full display in Scripture. Second, he argues that divine anger is compatible with divine love because such anger is perfect anger, unlike ours, and is directed at human sin and wickedness. God becomes angry in response to evil because he cares so deeply for us. Finally, Peckham argues that God's compassion far outweighs his anger.

In "Quenching Divine Fire: Divine Anger and the Atonement," Joshua R. Farris and S. Mark Hamilton examine divine anger as it relates to the doctrine of the atonement. Approaching the question of the atonement in terms of God's glory being the goal of creation, they consider three accounts: Reformed Anselmianism, Penal Substitution, and Christus Odium. According to Reformed Anselmianism, Jesus Christ's atonement is meant to satisfy a debt that humanity owes, having offended God's honor. In Penal Substitution, the atonement pays a debt of retributive punishment owed because of a public violation of the moral law. In Christus Odium, sin is a private offense against God, but Christ "absorbs the holy, fiery hatred of God." Farris and Hamilton argue that Christus Odium is an inadequate account because it cannot explain the atonement. It either leaves God's hatred unappeased, or it inaccurately describes God's state of anger.

In "The Hidden Face of God: A Visual Depiction of God's Anger in the Old Testament," Melissa C. M. Tan examines the biblical metaphor of the face of God and how the hiding of God's face is used to communicate the idea of anger. She explores the lexical meaning of the term "face" and its honor-shame sociological context. She also discusses various uses of the term "face" in the Old Testament in order to better understand occurrences of the term when it is used to refer to God's anger. She notes that the metaphor of God's hidden face is used both to describe God's anger and care, but in either case, God's disposition toward Israel (and us) remains unchanged: that our relationship with him should be restored and strengthened.

In "Praying against Enemies: Biblical Precedents, Ethical Reflections, and Suggested Guidelines," Charlie Trimm examines the meaning of imprecatory psalms in the Old and New Testaments and explores whether Christians should continue to pray them today. In his discussion of Old Testament occurrences, Trimm stresses the balance between the prayers of judgment and other Old Testament passages that teach care for one's enemies. Next, he balances "love thy enemy" commands in the New Testament with the fact that Jesus and his disciples occasionally call down curses on their enemies. He remarks that while some things have changed between the old and new covenants, God still hates injustice. So, prayers that assume this are still justified. Trimm concludes by describing ways that Christians today can pray imprecatory prayers, and he offers four guidelines to this effect.

In "Aquinas on Anger," Matthew R. Boulter presents the Thomistic account of anger by explaining what Aquinas says about anger as both a passion and a vice. Boulter says that in order to understand anger as a passion we must first understand the difference between concupiscible and irascible passions (both of which, for Aquinas, are necessarily good). Concupiscible passions desire certain objects. Irascible passions are directed toward the same objects but arise in response to obstacles in the way of those objects. Anger is an irascible passion. For Aquinas, anger is also a vice in that it stands opposite of clemency and meekness. It is vicious insofar as it is passion wrongly directed or is excessive.

In "Jonathan Edwards on Divine Justice and Anger," Phillip A. Hussey explores the concept of anger in relation to God's nature in the theology of Edwards, the eighteenth-century pastor and theologian, famously known for his sermon "Sinners in the Hands of an Angry God." First, he considers what Edwards thinks about divine anger in relation to the divine perfections *ad intra* and concludes that anger as vindictive justice is not an internal property of God. Second, he considers the divine anger in relation to the divine perfections *ad extra* and concludes that, though vindictive justice must be expressed in relation to the occurrence of sin in creation, God orders its expression primarily in the crucifixion of Christ. This expression of divine justice enables sinful humanity to better understand the eternal love between the persons of the Trinity.

In "Anger, Humility, and Civil Discourse," Michael W. Austin argues that there are good and bad forms of anger and that humility can help us avoid the bad forms and promote civil discourse. After exploring several cases of vicious anger, he discusses the teachings on humility by C. S. Lewis, Dallas Willard, and Thomas Aquinas, and argues that humility and love should combine to change the way we discuss controversial issues with others, not with anger but with love and respect. Using several personal examples, he shows how discourse on social media can go wrong and explains that Christians ought to adopt an approach he calls "rhetorical nonviolence," which involves taking a stand for the truth in a loving and respectful way.

In "Anger and the Law—Free from Passion?," Tammy W. Cowart considers anger's place in the law. She describes the tradition, which stretches from Aristotle to James Madison, that separates the two, and she considers how Christian warnings against anger have supported the separation. However, she argues that anger has an important role to play in bringing about positive change in the law. Citing examples like Martin Luther and Martin Luther King Jr., she argues that great changes in history have started with anger at injustice, and she makes connections with current events, showing that anger is still doing its work, such as with the #MeToo and Black Lives Matter movements.

In "Racism and the Spiritual Discipline of Righteous Anger," Jason Cook wrestles with being a black Evangelical Christian in America, being angered, on the one hand, by racial injustices, but sharing a faith tradition, on the other, with white Christians who undervalue the emotion of anger. He considers the dangers of anger, for example that anger begets violence and more anger.

State-sanctioned or judicial anger may seem preferable to personal anger, but it is often just a defense of the status quo and is subject to the same abuses as unsanctioned anger. He argues that righteous anger should be thought of as a spiritual discipline, such as loving one's neighbor. It is not something that necessarily comes naturally but must be cultivated with practice. He explores examples of righteous anger in Scripture, such as God's anger at the Israelites and the practice of calling down curses on one's enemies. Godly anger, he claims, should be directed at injustice and should be accompanied by love for one's enemies.

In "Anger in an Ethics of Love," Gregory L. Bock explores the connection between anger and love in the ethical tradition of agapism. After explaining the meaning of love and the theory of agapism, he considers what Joseph Butler has to say about the connection in his eighteenth-century sermons on resentment and forgiveness. Butler argues that anger and love are compatible, but he says very little about any deeper connection. Applying a distinction made by David McNaughton, Bock argues that resentment (bad anger) is anger that takes wrongs personally and excessively. Indignation (good anger) is the loving response to wrongs committed against self and others. In short, godly anger is an expression of love.

We hope you will find this collection as helpful to your own spiritual journey as we have to ours. However, if your thirst for anger is still unquenched, we also recommend our other collection, *The Ethics of Anger,* from Lexington Books, which approaches the topic from a broader range of perspectives, religious and secular.

Chapter 1

Divine Anger and Human Love

Joshua Beckett

A PAINFUL PROBLEM

Despite its long pedigree in the sacred texts of the Abrahamic traditions, the doctrine of the wrath of God has fallen into widespread disfavor. The reasons for this eclipse of divine anger are legion. To begin with, many of its features—including atonement, holy war, and damnation—appear jarringly out of sync with contemporary sensibilities. Additionally, the marred, checkered history of antagonistic interpretations and violent practices by adherents of monotheistic faiths rightly gives us pause—particularly since even up to the present, many have understood themselves as righteous agents of an angry God (in Crusades, Inquisitions, colonial invasions, territorial occupations, and terrorist acts).

Taken together, these features cast a pall over considerations of the constructive value of divine anger, for fear of improper human imitation. American Buddhist scholar Robert A. F. Thurman voices a common concern: "The religious ones don't try that hard to challenge anger, since they believe that God models anger, has done so from the beginning, and that it would be the sin of pride to think they could alter their own nature. They also think that anger can be good when you're righteous" (Thurman 2005, 20). Characterizing Jewish and Christian accounts of divine wrath as God going "on a rampage," he concludes:

> God gets angry with humans again and again. He gets angry on behalf of Israel, and sometimes he gets angry at Israel. He's a real punisher. Anyone who was indoctrinated by sacred texts in the image of such a God as the model of ultimate reality personified could be forgiven if he or she thought that anger was

an excellent energy and manifestation, as long as one was powerful enough to overcome the enmity such anger stirs up in others. (33–34)

However glib Thurman's tone may be in these lines, I nonetheless take his challenge quite seriously. Focusing on the Christian tradition of which I am a part, I must begin by humbly acknowledging and deeply lamenting the painful realities of violence—verbal and physical, racial and sexual, institutional and systemic—done in the name of Christianity, often under the purported cover of righteous indignation. There are simply too many such instances, historical and contemporary, to write them all off as being perpetrated by "bad apples," thus avoiding discernment of a broader pattern leading to a devastating conclusion: Christianity has an anger problem. And our (mis) interpretation of the biblical accounts of God's wrath is partly to blame.

With this in mind, in this chapter I make the case that the wrath of God has, in fact, been too easily dismissed. Far from its inevitably unleashing a flood of human violence, I contend instead that the aforementioned failures can and should be deconstructed as stemming from a profound misunderstanding of divine character, which divorces divine anger from divine love, and delinks divine agency from the human pursuit of justice and mercy in community and society. Furthermore, even as Christians radically repent of our commission of and complicity in violence, the very Scriptures that we have sullied in harming others are still capacious to reorient us to work for the common good and to bear witness to our neighbors, who may also struggle with navigating their own anger. Anger turns out to be a human, not just a Christian, problem.

To develop this thesis, I integrate contributions from three disciplines: biblical studies, constructive theology, and Christian ethics. Ultimately, I argue that the anger of the God of holy love, expressed as righteous wrath against injustice and evil, is not an inherent obstacle to human love and kindness. Rather, when rightly understood, the wrath of God serves both as a safeguard to prevent humans from lashing out in reckless vengeance and as an impetus to liberate humans to use our anger constructively, engaging in creative work with and for the most vulnerable.

DIVINE LOVE AND HUMAN LOVE

Contrary to the caricature expressed above, Scripture accentuates the *mercy* of God, both as more enduring than the wrath of God and as an explicit model for human imitation. On this, the Hebrew Bible and the New Testament are complementary witnesses; the former emphasizes the loving and merciful divine character, and the latter concretizes the mimetic human response.

When God's loving mercy and angry judgment are described together, the former outmatches the latter by orders of magnitude. The Torah's quintessential expression of this asymmetry is the revelation of the Divine Name to Moses: "The Lord, the Lord, the compassionate and gracious God, slow to anger, abounding in love and faithfulness, maintaining love to thousands, and forgiving wickedness, rebellion, and sin. Yet he does not leave the guilty unpunished; he punishes the children and their children for the sin of the parents to the third and fourth generation" (Exod. 34:6–7). Similarly, the psalmists repeatedly trumpet the love of the Lord as steadfast and unfailing, to Israel and to all creation, from everlasting to everlasting—in contrast to the anger of the Lord, which is vastly shorter in duration: "For his anger lasts only a moment, but his favor lasts a lifetime; weeping may stay for the night, but rejoicing comes in the morning" (Ps. 30:5). Likewise, the prophets assure the covenant people that although God's love must not be taken for granted through disobedience, it endures beyond discipline: "Who is a God like you, who pardons sin and forgives the transgression of the remnant of his inheritance? You do not stay angry forever but delight to show mercy" (Mic. 7:18). Glimpses of a divine internal struggle are also revealed: "How can I give you up, Ephraim? How can I hand you over, Israel? . . . My heart is changed within me; all my compassion is aroused. I will not carry out my fierce anger, nor will I devastate Ephraim again. For I am God, and not a man" (Hos. 11:8–9).

In the New Testament, this understanding of God's steadfast love and radical mercy is presupposed by and embodied in Jesus. Furthermore, the Gospels portray Jesus as commending a direct imitation of these divine attributes as a matter of faithful discipleship. He does so by centering the parenthood of God in a sermon to a large crowd ("Love your enemies, do good to them, and lend to them without expecting to get anything back. Then your reward will be great, and you will be children of the Most High, because he is kind to the ungrateful and the wicked. Be merciful, just as your Father is merciful," Luke 6:35–36). Later, at an intimate gathering of his disciples, Jesus references his own example ("A new command I give you: Love one another. As I have loved you, so you must love one another," John 13:34). Paul unites both of these patterns in his letter to the church in Ephesus: "Get rid of all bitterness, rage and anger. . . . Be kind and compassionate to one another, forgiving each other, just as in Christ God forgave you. Follow God's example, therefore, as dearly loved children, and walk in the way of love, just as Christ loved us" (Eph. 4:31-5:2). Other epistles also stress imitative love, in response to the gifts of Jesus' incarnation and atonement, as the ultimate diagnostic of the knowledge of God:

Beloved, let us love one another, for love comes from God. Everyone who loves has been born of God and knows God. Whoever does not love does not know God, because God is love. This is how God showed his love among us: he sent his one and only Son into the world so that we might live through him. This is love: not that we loved God, but that he loved us and sent his Son as an atoning sacrifice for our sins. Beloved, since God so loved us, we also ought to love one another. (1 John 4:7–11)

On this passage, Croatian theologian Miroslav Volf reflects, "Like solidarity with the victims, the atonement for the perpetrators issues forth from the heart of the triune God, whose very being is love" (Volf 1996, 23). God's love spans and surpasses, rather than incites, human violence.

DIVINE ANGER AND HUMAN ANGER

The above account of the consistent biblical emphasis on divine love does not diminish the significant presence of divine anger in Scripture. To the contrary, the wrath of God features prominently in both Testaments, not as an arbitrary or capricious phenomenon, but as a deliberate and proportionate reflection of the divine character and purpose. Throughout the Hebrew Bible, the wrath of God is oriented primarily against idolatry, relatedly against injustice, and derivatively against immorality. Divine anger is presented simultaneously as a deterrent to sin and a goad to repentance ("Circumcise your hearts, you people of Judah and inhabitants of Jerusalem, or my wrath will flare up and burn like fire because of the evil you have done," Jer. 4:4). It is both a fearsome reality to seek refuge from and a ground for epistemic reorientation ("If only we knew the power of your anger! Your wrath is as great as the fear that is your due. Teach us to number our days, that we may gain a heart of wisdom," Ps. 90:11–12). Likewise, the New Testament—often erroneously contrasted with the Hebrew Bible as presenting a God of anger-less love—is unabashed about the wrath of God as part of the fabric of reality and a core feature of redemptive history. The Gospels, epistles, and Apocalypse highlight the various ways that God's wrath takes specific forms of judgment, against: religious leaders' hypocrisy, rejection of God's will, and abdication of responsibility to care for the most vulnerable (Matthew 23–25); humanity's rejection of the knowledge of God through idolatry and lawbreaking (Romans 1–3); and economic exploitation and imperial oppression (Revelation 17–19).

With this overview in place, further treatment of the biblical accounts of divine and human anger (and the relationship between them) is in order. Lutheran Old Testament scholar Terence E. Fretheim discerns a plethora of images for wrath in the Torah and the prophets:

The metaphors used to portray the divine wrath (and its effects) are remarkable in their range, many of them drawn from the sphere of the nonhuman. They include: fire (smoke/oven/melt), water (flood/rain/hail), and storm/clouds. These images in turn lead to the use of certain verbs, such as "consume," "pour out," "come down," and "drinking" from the cup. That such images are so often used to depict wrath and its effects suggests that wrath is commonly understood in natural terms. (Fretheim 2015, 143)

Yet the realm of human agency is also quite significant in relation to the content of divine wrath. After surveying the canonical texts shared by Jews and Christians, Fretheim offers a helpful typology: God's wrath, which can include the use of violence, is "associated with two basic purposes: judgment and salvation" (134).

Regarding the former, Fretheim notes a supervenient relationship between divine and human agency: "Divine violence seems always to be related to human sin. Generally speaking, if there were no human violence, there would be no divine wrath or judgment. . . . Violent human actions lead to violent consequences. *That* there are such consequences to human violence is named divine judgment" (134, emphasis original). Yet Fretheim cautions against extrapolating from the presence of a divine guarantor of justice to a project of its aggressive imposition: "Generally speaking, the relationship between sin and the judgment of violence is conceived in intrinsic rather than forensic terms; consequences grow out of the deed itself. That is, God mediates the consequences of sin that are already present in the situation, rather than through the imposition of a penalty from without" (134–35). As an illustration, Fretheim cites the prophet Ezekiel, who reports this divine speech: "I have consumed them with the fire of my wrath. I have returned their conduct upon their heads" (Ezek. 22:31). This is not to say that the Bible *never* portrays God as actively meting out forensic wrath on people or nations, but rather to recognize that the Bible's general pattern testifies to righteous divine wrath as negotiating the intrinsic relationship between evil human actions and their just recompenses.

If the purpose of judgment in divine wrath is oriented toward constraint of and response to human violence, the purpose of salvation in divine wrath extends even further, including subversion of and liberation from human violence. The paradigmatic example of this is the deliverance from Egypt, when "God uses violence to save Israel from the effects of *other people's sins*"; yet the principle also applies in the Persian conquest of Babylon, as "God uses violence in order to save God's people from the effects of *their own sins*, which got them into exile in the first place. Salvation is thus comprehensively conceived" (136, emphasis original).

Ultimately, Fretheim discerns an organic unity between the purposes of judgment and salvation in divine expressions of wrath: "These two ways . . . may be reduced to one. That is, God's use of violence, inevitable in a violent world, is intended to subvert human violence in order to bring the creation along to a point where violence is no more. . . . In other words, God's violence, whether in judgment or salvation, is never an end in itself, but is always exercised in the service of God's more comprehensive *salvific* purposes for creation," including deliverance of the righteous, the poor, and the needy (136, emphasis original). Indeed, maintaining such relationality is of crucial importance for understanding the connection between the wrath of God and the character of God more broadly. Fretheim explains, "For God or humans, anger is always relational, exercised with respect to others. Even more, as with human anger, the divine anger is a sign that the relationship is taken seriously (apathy is not productive of anger). God is deeply engaged in this relationship and is passionate about what happens to it. As such, anger is always *provoked* from within such relationships, testifying to the affectivity of both human beings and God" (144, emphasis original). Such affectivity is also ubiquitous throughout the psalms of lament, a genre that is less concerned "with theological accuracy, but rather explodes with emotion, wrapping together . . . anger, desperation, grief, and fear" (Beckett 2016, 212). This irreducible relationality further helps to clarify the intrinsic connection between divine wrath and divine grief, especially among the prophets: "Anger accompanied by weeping, while still anger, is different—in motivation and in the understanding of the relationship at stake. God's judgment is not matched by an inner harshness. Words of wrath are proclaimed reluctantly and with great anguish" (Fretheim 2015, 145).

Such prophetic imagery underscores how the divine attributes of love and holiness constitute the deeper realities, of which divine wrath and grief represent contingent expressions. It also shows the limits of the parallel between divine and human anger. In the words of Rabbi Abraham Joshua Heschel, "[Our] sense of injustice is a poor analogy to God's sense of injustice. The exploitation of the poor is to us a misdemeanor; to God, it is a disaster. Our reaction is disapproval; God's reaction is something no language can convey. Is it a sign of cruelty that God's anger is aroused when the rights of the poor are violated, when widows and orphans are oppressed?" Heschel answers his own rhetorical question in the negative; rather, "the anger of God [represents] the end of indifference" (Heschel 1962, 284–85).

In the New Testament, the Gospel of Mark portrays Jesus as stepping into this same pattern: holiness and love expressing anger and grief for the purposes of salvation and judgment. In a synagogue on a Sabbath, Jesus confronts a group of Pharisees who are seeking a reason to accuse him, such as healing at an improper time: "Then he said to them, 'Is it lawful to do good or to do harm on the Sabbath, to save life or to kill?' But they were silent. He looked around at them with anger; he was grieved at their hardness of heart and said to the man [with the withered hand], 'Stretch out your hand.' He stretched it out, and his hand was restored" (Mark 3:4–5). Catholic pastoral counselor Carroll Saussy notes that this is "the single occasion when Jesus is explicitly described as angry," and that it is an "anger that works for change" (Saussy 1995, 95). (Of course, other Gospel passages, especially Jesus" clearing the courts of the temple and denouncing it as a den of robbers, strongly imply the presence of dominical anger.)

Another New Testament passage that similarly draws inspiration from the Hebrew Bible's treatment of divine wrath is the Pauline exhortation to the Christian community in Rome:

Do not repay anyone evil for evil. Be careful to do what is right in the eyes of everyone. If it is possible, as far as it depends on you, live at peace with everyone. Do not take revenge, my dear friends, but leave room for God's wrath, for it is written, "It is mine to avenge; I will repay," says the Lord. On the contrary: "If your enemy is hungry, feed him; if he is thirsty, give him something to drink. In doing this, you will heap burning coals on his head." Do not be overcome by evil, but overcome evil with good. (Rom. 12:17–21)

British New Testament scholar Stephen H. Travis argues that the first quotation (from Deut. 32:35) "suggests that he is thinking of the future judgment. But the timing is not the main point. Whenever wrath may occur, says Paul, it is God's business, not ours" (Travis 2008, 66). The second quotation (from Prov. 25:21–22) may refer to an ancient "ritual in which an offender came back to the person whom he had wronged and evidenced the genuineness of his repentance by carrying a tray of burning coals on his head" (66). Therefore, the force of bringing these two quotations together means that Paul seeks "to urge his readers not merely to practice non-resistance but actively to show love to their enemies in the hope of delivering them from their condition as objects of wrath. The implication remains, of course, that those who do not repent will remain under wrath. . . . Yet the thrust of the passage is not retributive or vindictive, but positive and creative" (67). Similarly, the book of James explicitly warns about the dangers of merely human anger: "Everyone should be quick to listen, slow to speak and slow to become angry, because human anger does not produce the righteousness that God desires" (Jas. 1:19–20).

Thus, both the Hebrew Bible and the New Testament present a complex, nuanced portrait of divine wrath and its relationship to human anger. Far removed from the distorted image of a destructive deity losing control and smiting everyone (and ushering forth violent human imitators), divine anger flows from divine love for human beings and all creation, is joined together with divine grief at human evil and pain, and remains a divine prerogative oriented toward divine purposes of judgment and salvation in concert with faithful human responses.

HUMAN ANGER AND HUMAN LOVE

But will human beings respect this divine prerogative, yielding vengeance and judgment to the God of holy love? Volf articulates the high stakes of the matter:

> There is a duty prior to the duty of imitating God, and that is the duty of *not wanting to be God*, of letting God be God and humans be humans. Without such a duty guarding the divinity of God the duty to imitate God would be empty because our concept of God would be nothing more than the mirror image of ourselves. Preserving the fundamental difference between God and nonGod, the biblical tradition insists that there are things which only God may do. One of them is to use violence. (301, emphasis original)

There are certainly many examples of self-proclaimed Christians who have transgressed this licit boundary, becoming indirect aiders and abettors (or direct perpetrators and exacerbators) of violent, vengeful wrath. Partially for this reason, patristic and medieval monastics identified wrath as one of the capital vices (also known as deadly sins). Reformed ethicist Rebecca Konyndyk DeYoung notes that this tradition is "careful to distinguish anger, the *passion*, a part of normal human emotional makeup, from wrath, the *vice*, which is anger in its sinful, excessive, misdirected form" (DeYoung 2009, 118, emphasis original). In God, wrath flows faithfully from and toward justice; in human beings, however, wrath "is self-promoting—but in a dressed-up, self-righteous way" (123). Even appropriate anger can perversely devolve into the vice of wrath, such that "it twists any real concern about sin or injustice into service of the self—protecting our own ego, demanding something from the world we would not reasonably expect for anyone else, feeding our own reputations for righteousness instead of admitting our complicity" (119).

Righteous anger and vicious wrath have one major commonality: "In both cases, we acknowledge justice—whether real or apparent—to be a great and greatly motivating good, and the banner under which our anger marches" (120). Despite this shared source, however, they soon diverge in aim, direction, and effect. Again, DeYoung clarifies, "Anger turns vicious . . . when it fights for its own selfish cause, not for justice, and when it fights dirty. That is, anger becomes a vice when there are problems with its target—whatever it is that makes us angry—or with the way we try to hit that target—how we express our anger" (122). Thus, paradoxically, when anger is most appropriate, it requires the most caution: "If anger is in for a fight, then to stay clear of being a vice, it must fight the good fight. This means fighting for a good cause *and* fighting well. Anger must serve the cause, not the other way around" (121, emphasis original).

In light of these theological apprehensions about the ways that anger can go wrathfully wrong, can human anger ever legitimately partner with, or even lead to human love? DeYoung is cautiously hopeful, provided that divine love and justice remain central: "Anger, when it is a *holy* emotion, has *justice* as its object and *love* at its root. Both love and justice are focused on the good of others" (130, emphasis original). As a diagnostic rubric and prescriptive rule, she proffers the Bible's oft-repeated refrain ("The Lord is merciful and gracious, slow to anger and abounding in steadfast love"). DeYoung summarizes the upshot for human beings seeking to link their anger to divine justice and love, while eschewing wrath and violence, in this way: "Wariness over the temptation to wrath should *not* temper our passion for justice now; rather, it *should* keep our anger and its frustration focused on God's agenda. Keeping our anger under control allows us to keep a clear view of the goal—justice, the need of the people for whom we will it, and the humanness of those who currently thwart it" (132, emphasis original). Indeed, concludes DeYoung, such disciplined, God-centered, others-oriented anger is marked by "gentleness and humility [which] get their strength from trusting God's power and will. . . . With confidence that we do indeed have a role to play in addressing injustice, but acknowledging that our role is not God's role, our anger can find its rightful, effective place—helping rather than hindering our response to a world that persistently yearns for justice and restoration" (138). Human anger can thus directly serve the purposes of divine love.

DIVINE ANGER AND HUMAN LOVE

Potential expressions of such projects of justice-oriented anger and God-inspired love abound, each necessarily rooted in concrete contexts. In the United States, there have been a wealth of historical movements for gender and racial justice—in pursuit of equal voting rights and economic opportunities for women, and the abolition of slavery and advancement of civil rights for African Americans—as well as contemporary appeals for reform and protests of resistance. These evince admirable models of anger linked to interpersonal love and social transformation, in contrast with relationship-destroying, community-eroding, self-centered wrath. Here we would do well to pay careful attention to some constructive methodological reflections made by seasoned theological voices in the struggle for gender and racial justice.

To begin with, the late feminist ethicist Beverly Wildung Harrison—particularly the analysis and advice she gave in her inaugural lecture at Union Theological Seminary nearly four decades ago—retains remarkable relevance for today. For Harrison, embodied ethics entail engagement with, not withdrawal from, struggle: "The deepest danger to our cause is that our anger will turn inward and lead us to portray ourselves and other women chiefly as victims rather than those who have struggled for the gift of life against incredible odds. The creative power of anger is shaped by owning this great strength of women and of others who have struggled for the full gift of life against structures of oppression" (Harrison 1990, 198–99). Here, human agency has a significant role in striving for the full enjoyment of divine gift. Relatedly, both the historical experience of women and the Great Commandment of Scripture converge in the centrality of love and justice for liberative, feminist ethics: "That the locus of divine revelation is in the concrete struggles of groups and communities to lay hold of the gift of life . . . means, among other things, that we must learn what we are to know of love from immersion in the struggle for justice" (Harrison 1990, 200). Formation in the way of love unfolds through action.

Additionally, this human struggle is linked to divine agency and leads to interdependent, mutually reciprocal community. Harrison writes:

> The fateful choice is ours, either to set free the power of God's love in the world or to deprive each other of the very basis of personhood and community. This power of human activity, so crucial to the divine-human drama, is *not* the power of world conquest or empire building, nor is it control of one person by another. . . . The most basic of all the works of love [is] the work of human communication, of caring and nurturance, of tending to the personal bonds of community. (203)

Furthermore, these communal bonds help illuminate the relationship between love and anger. Harrison is clear on this point: "Anger is not the opposite of love. It is better understood as a feeling-signal that all is not well in our relation to other persons or groups or to the world around us. Anger is a mode of connectedness to others and it is always a vivid form of caring. . . . We must never lose touch with the fact that all serious human moral activity, *especially action for social change*, takes its bearings from the rising power of human anger" (206, emphasis added). Thus, far from being in conflict with one another, anger and love become inextricable partners for communal and social transformation.

Finally, and most importantly, is "the centrality of relationship. . . . a feminist moral theology celebrates the power of *our* human praxis as an intrinsic aspect of the work of *God's* love" (207, emphasis original). Harrison links this human solidarity directly to Jesus' example:

> Like Jesus, we are called to a radical activity of love, to a way of being in the world that deepens relation, embodies and extends community, passes on the gift of life. Like Jesus, we must live out this calling in a place and time where the distortions of loveless power stand in conflict with the power of love. We are called to confront, as Jesus did, that which thwarts the power of human personal and communal becoming, that which twists relationship, which denies human well-being, community, and human solidarity to so many in our world. (210)

Thwarted potential, twisted relationships, and denied communities are indeed legitimate grounds for an anger that, once aroused, provokes and confronts in order to transform and restore.

More recently, with a similar logic to Harrison and an acute pathos all his own, African American theologian Willie James Jennings has shared reflections on the relationship between anger and hope. Regarding the current moment of national reckoning with the historical roots and ongoing realities of systemic racial injustice—especially the hopelessness and rage catalyzed by police killings of unarmed black men and women—Jennings explains, "Hope is a discipline; it is not a sentiment. But . . . living the discipline of hope in this racial world, in this white supremacist-infested country called the United States of America, requires anger" (Jennings 2020). Indeed, Jennings perceives an intrinsic connection between human anger and divine anger, while acknowledging "that it is very dangerous to suggest the connection between human anger and God's righteous indignation. All kinds of mischief can happen with such a connection. There is great danger and great power in saying, 'What I am angry about God is angry about.'"

Jennings offers "two abiding characteristics" for communal discernment about whether human anger can make legitimate claim to divine solidarity. First, the anger "must be about the destruction of life," the illegitimate theft of God's gift by idolatrous human presumption. Second, the anger "must be shareable; in fact, it must be shared. I don't think enough people, especially enough Christians, understand that the righteous indignation of God is to be shared. . . . God wants us to hate what God hates. God invites us into a shared fury, but only the kind that we creatures can handle." The human temptation to trespass beyond the bounds of righteous indignation into hatred and violence remains powerful, and it cannot be overcome through denial. Instead, Jennings centers divine agency both for the prevention of illegitimate human violence ("What keeps anger from touching hatred is not the cunning of reason or the power of will. It is simply Jesus") and the unleashing of human efforts for social change: "For the Christian, Jesus stands between anger and hatred, prohibiting the reach, blocking the touch, and saying to us, 'Don't go there. There is nothing there but death.' Anger bound to God's righteous indignation has a different purpose for us that points us to the change that must happen, that is the overturning of an unjust world order, this racial order." Jennings closes by proposing three practices toward this end: "take hold of the anger," "address the shape of communities," and "rethink the formation of police officers, the shape of policing, and the processes of criminalization." Such transformation is marked both by a sharing of hope in God and a sharing in the anger of God.

CONCLUSION

In light of these methodological contributions by Harrison and Jennings, and against the earlier backdrop provided by Fretheim, DeYoung, and others, a couple of final comments are in order. Love and hope, like their sibling theological virtue of faith, abide eternally. Although anger is never promised the same kind of permanence, it does play a critical partnering role in the face of evil and injustice this side of the Eschaton. Indeed, when carefully tethered to divine anger, and rooted in communities of love and hope, human anger can be a constructive force for good. Furthermore, human beings, far from being driven inexorably to violence and vengeance, will actually find themselves more deeply supported in their hopeful pursuit of love and justice, of creativity and liberation, when they recognize that the God of holy love is angry too.

REFERENCES

Beckett, Joshua. 2016. "Lament in Three Movements: The Implications of Psalm 13 for Justice and Reconciliation." *Journal of Spiritual Formation & Soul Care* 9, no. 2 (Fall): 207–18.

DeYoung, Rebecca Konyndyk. 2009. *Glittering Vices: A New Look at the Seven Deadly Sins and Their Remedies*. Grand Rapids, MI: Brazos.

Fretheim, Terence E. 2015. *What Kind of God? Collected Essays of Terence E. Fretheim*, edited by Michael J. Chan and Brent A. Strawn. Winona Lake, IN: Eisenbrauns.

Harrison, Beverly Wildung. 1990. "The Power of Anger in the Work of Love: Christian Ethics for Women and Other Strangers." In *Feminist Theology: A Reader*, edited by Ann Loades, 194–213. London: SPCK.

Heschel, Abraham Joshua. 1962. *The Prophets*. New York: Harper & Row.

Jennings, Willie James. 2020. "My Anger, God's Righteous Indignation." *For the Life of the World* Podcast, June 2, 2020.

Saussy, Carroll. 1995. *The Gift of Anger: A Call to Faithful Action.* Louisville, KY: Westminster John Knox.

Thurman, Robert A. F. 2005. *Anger: The Seven Deadly Sins.* New York: Oxford University Press.

Travis, Stephen H. 2008. *Christ and the Judgment of God: The Limits of Divine Retribution in New Testament Thought.* Peabody, MA: Hendrickson Publishers.

Volf, Miroslav. 1996. *Exclusion and Embrace: A Theological Exploration of Identity, Otherness, and Reconciliation.* Nashville: Abingdon.

Chapter 2

The Righteous Anger of the Immutable God of Love

John C. Peckham

To many minds, divine anger is scandalous. Anger, some suppose, is incompatible with God's nature and opposed to God's character of love. Yet, even a cursory reading of the Bible manifests that biblical authors repeatedly depict God as becoming angry. What, then, should Christian theologians conclude regarding whether anger is appropriate to divinity? For the purposes of this essay, I will frame the issue in terms of two overarching questions. First, is divine anger compatible with God's nature (e.g., divine immutability)? Second, is divine anger consistent with God's character (e.g., divine love)?

Toward addressing these two questions, this chapter offers a brief theological consideration of some implications of divine anger as depicted throughout Scripture, particularly relative to the debate among Christian theists over divine immutability and how divine anger may relate to God's character. In brief, this chapter outlines the view that divine anger is God's holy, just, and rational response to evil, consistent with the immutability of God's essential nature and character of perfect love.

DIVINE ANGER AND DIVINE IMMUTABILITY

We turn first to the question of whether divine anger is compatible with God's nature, focusing particularly on ongoing debates about divine immutability and divine impassibility.[1] Broadly speaking, to say God is immutable is to say God does not change (in some or all respects) and to say God is impassible is to say God is without passions (in some or all respects). In Christian theology, both immutability and impassibility may be understood in strict or qualified senses. Understood in their strict senses, *strict* immutability maintains that God cannot change in any way whatsoever and *strict* impassibility maintains that God cannot be affected by creatures and cannot experience emotional change.[2]

Strict conceptions of immutability and impassibility, however, appear to conflict with the many biblical depictions of God becoming angry.[3] Given that "Christian theologians have almost universally assumed" the standard of biblical warrant, namely "that a theological claim can be true only insofar as it is drawn from or at least coheres with Scripture" (Anizor 2018, 60), biblical depictions of God becoming angry present difficulties for Christian theologies that claim God does not change at all.[4]

On one hand, an abundance of biblical material depicts God *becoming* angry in response to evil and otherwise undergoing emotional change. On the other hand, Scripture claims that God does not change (Mal 3:6). At least at first glance, this juxtaposition by itself presents a problem for Christian theologians committed to the standard of biblical warrant. Initially, it might seem that one must choose between two biblical claims, affirming either that: (1) God does not change or (2) God is angered by evil. In my view, however, one can consistently affirm both claims. To see how, let us briefly consider a representative sample of biblical passages regarding both claims.

Divine Anger in Scripture

Regarding divine anger, according to Deuteronomy 9:7–8, the people "provoked the LORD your God to wrath in the wilderness" by being "rebellious against the LORD" and "provoked the LORD to wrath" at Horeb such that "the LORD was so angry with you that He would have destroyed you."[5] The Hebrew word translated "provoked . . . to wrath" (*qāṣap,* "to be angry") is in a form that typically indicates causation (the hiphil stem), indicating that the people (in some sense) *caused* God to be angry. Similarly, according to Deuteronomy 32:16, the people "made Him jealous with strange gods; with abominations they provoked Him to anger" (cf. 32:21).[6] The word translated "provoked . . . to anger" here is a different Hebrew term (*kā'as,* "to be vexed, angry"), but is also in the typically causative hiphil stem. Psalm 78:58 likewise adds, "they provoked him to anger [*kā'as,* hiphil] with their high places; they moved him to jealousy with their idols" (NRSV). Further, according to Zechariah 1:15, God states: "I am very angry with the nations who are at ease; for while I was only a little angry, they furthered the disaster."

In these instances and others throughout Scripture, God's anger is consistently in response to evil.[7] As Romans 1:18 explains, "the wrath of God is revealed from heaven against all ungodliness and unrighteousness of men."

Many other passages also teach that God becomes angry in response to evil, but the verses surveyed above suffice to show this biblical pattern, which relates closely to judgment. As Psalm 7:11 puts it, "God is a righteous judge, and a God who has indignation every day."[8] Romans 5:9 adds, those "justified by" Christ's "blood" are "saved from the wrath of God through Him" (cf. 1 Thess 1:10). Conversely, one "who does not obey the Son will not see life, but the wrath of God abides on him" (John 3:36; cf. Rom 2:5–8; Eph 5:6; Col 3:6). In sum, Scripture repeatedly depicts God being angered by evil and consistently teaches that God's anger or wrath is God's judgment in response to evil.

Divine Immutability in Scripture

Yet, how can such claims that God *becomes* angry in response to evil be reconciled with divine immutability? Scripture repeatedly emphasizes the immutability of God's character (moral changelessness). For example, Deuteronomy 32:4 teaches, God's "work is perfect, for all His ways are just; a God of faithfulness and without injustice, righteous and upright is He" (cf. Ps 100:5; 117:2; 1 John 1:5). 2 Timothy 2:13 adds, "If we are faithless, He remains faithful, for He cannot deny Himself" (cf. Num 23:19; Isa 25:1; Tit 1:2; Heb 6:17–18). Whatever else one concludes regarding divine immutability, Scripture consistently claims God is changeless with respect to his perfect character.

This is also affirmed by the text most often cited in support of divine immutability, Malachi 3:6, which states (in part): "I, the LORD, do not change." Likewise, James 1:17 affirms: "Every good thing given and every perfect gift is from above, coming down from the Father of lights, with whom there is no variation or shifting shadow." While some claim these passages support the view that God is *strictly* immutable (changeless in *every* respect), the passages themselves highlight God's *moral* changelessness in the context of relationship.[9]

Indeed, Malachi 3 itself indicates that God may change relationally. Specifically, just after stating, "I, the LORD, do not change," God goes on to say, "therefore you, O sons of Jacob, are not consumed" (Mal 3:6). Then, in the very next verse, God urges: "Return to Me, and I will return to you" (Mal 3:7). This verse, like many others (e.g., Jer 15:19; Zech 1:3; Ps 81:13–14), indicates God will change course relationally if humans will do so. Malachi 3:6–7, then, highlights the immutability of God's character while also depicting God as capable of relational change in response to humans (contrary to *strict* immutability).[10] Similarly, in describing God as without variation relative to giving perfect gifts, James 1:17 does not make the claim that God is *strictly* immutable, but highlights God's *moral* changelessness. As Nicholas

Wolterstorff puts it, James 1:17 teaches "that God is unchangeable in that God is never the source of evil" but "only and always of good" (2010, 163). These and other passages indicate that God is *morally* immutable, but neither these nor any other passages in Scripture teach that God is *strictly* immutable. On the other hand, an abundance of biblical passages attribute relational change to God, including Malachi 3 itself.[11] The evidence of Scripture, then, seems to provide biblical warrant to conclude that God is immutable in some significant sense or senses (e.g., *at least* moral changelessness), but also that God changes relationally—consistent with a qualified conception of divine immutability (defined further below).

With regard to divine anger specifically, the situation with respect to the biblical data is much the same. Scripture repeatedly depicts God being angered by evil (as seen earlier), but I am not aware of any biblical passages that indicate God does not become angry or contradict the conclusion that God *becomes* angry. Accordingly, there seems to be biblical warrant for the conclusion that, in some sense appropriate to divinity, God becomes angry at evil.[12]

Some Thoughts on Theological Interpretation of Scripture

That Scripture depicts God becoming angry is not a matter of dispute. What is contested, however, is how such depictions should be interpreted theologically. To reconcile their position that God cannot change in any way whatsoever with the many biblical depictions of God becoming angry or otherwise undergoing relational changes, advocates of *strict* immutability often appeal to the accommodative nature of theological language. To say language is accommodative is to say language accommodates human understanding by communicating at a level humans can understand—analogous to the way I can teach my nine-year-old son about God at a level he can understand.

Based on the conclusion that biblical language is accommodative, some argue that language depicting God *becoming* angry—and other language indicating divine change—merely portrays God in limited human language, through which God "communicates the truth about his infinite and unchanging existence under the form of what is finite and changeable" (Dolezal 2014, 135). As such, the claim goes, biblical language depicting divine change should not be understood to mean God actually changes—biblical depictions of God becoming angry should not be interpreted as conveying God actually becomes angry. Coupled with such claims, many theologians emphasize that theological language is unavoidably analogical, meaning there is some correspondence or analogy between language as it applies to God and language as it applies to creatures, but also great dissimilarity because God is the utterly unique Creator of all.

I agree that biblical language of divine anger (and other language about God) is accommodative and analogical.[13] It is crucial to recognize this and, in so doing, be careful to avoid conceptually reducing God to what can be conveyed in human language. However, *all* theological language that humans can understand is accommodative and analogical.[14] Accordingly, merely recognizing that biblical (or other) language about God is accommodative and analogical neither tells us to what extent such language applies to God nor provides warrant for negating what biblical depictions convey about God.[15] Metaphors and other analogical language convey meaning and, if there is analogy, there must be some correspondence.[16]

If so, the question remains as to what biblical passages depicting divine change (such as divine anger) convey about God. Some theologians appeal to the Christian tradition as a way to decide what elements of biblical depictions of God should be understood as appropriate to God and what elements of such depictions should be negated. However, appeal to the Christian tradition does not seem to provide an avenue to settle the debate regarding immutability (and related predications) because theologians on various sides of the question appeal to the Christian tradition as supportive of their position.[17] While some argue that strict immutability and impassibility are the traditional Christian view (e.g., Dolezal 2019; Weinandy 2000), others argue for more qualified conceptions (e.g., Gavrilyuk 2006; Castelo 2009; Lister 2013; cf. Scrutton 2011).[18]

Conclusions regarding what predications are appropriate to God are bound up with a host of other commitments, adequate discussion of which extends far beyond this chapter's scope.[19] In my view, theological judgments about which predicates apply to God should be continually subjected to the standard of biblical warrant, alongside the standard of systematic coherence. Accordingly, I believe such judgments should be formed and (when appropriate) reformed by careful consideration of the biblical material as a whole, understood in a way that is systematically coherent relative to other biblically warranted claims about God.[20]

In this brief chapter I can neither make an adequate case for my methodological commitments to these standards nor sufficiently demonstrate why I believe my conclusions meet these standards.[21] Accordingly, I make no attempt in this chapter to dogmatically exclude the possibility that other positions might be preferable. Instead, I will simply proceed to outline the way of approaching the compatibility of divine anger and the divine nature that I find most helpful given my own commitments and studies, beginning with a model of qualified immutability.

Qualified Immutability: A Theological Model

Qualified immutability maintains that God's essential nature and character are changeless, but God changes relationally. That is, God is immutable with respect to his essential nature and character, but such immutability is consistent with relational changes such as being pleased or displeased by creaturely actions. However, as creator and sustainer of all, God need not experience any relational change. The world (all of creation) is not essential to God, but God *freely* relates to the world. God freely "created all things, and because of [God's] will they existed and were created" (Rev. 4:11; cf. Heb 1:3). In this regard, Alan Padgett contends, "God is immutable relative to essential divine attributes," but the "ability to change in response to others is part of what makes God a perfect Being" (2001, 109).[22]

This understanding of qualified immutability affirms divine aseity and self-sufficiency, meaning God exists of himself and does not depend on anything relative to his existence or essential nature. As Creator, God is "before all things" and thus existed prior to any creation (Col 1:17). Being self-existent, God does not need anything (Acts 17:25; cf. John 5:26) and could enjoy eternal Trinitarian relationship without any world (cf. John 17:24), but freely created the world (Rev 4:11), freely decided to enter into relationship with creatures, and thus voluntarily opened himself up to relational change consistent with his essential nature and the Creator-creature distinction. As J.P. Moreland and William Lane Craig put it, "God could have remained [utterly] changeless had he wished to; the fact that he did not is testimony to both his love and freedom" (2003, 527).

No creature could affect God had God not enabled creatures to do so. However, because God freely opened himself to being affected by creatures, God may have emotions responsive to creaturely actions, including being pleased or displeased—delighting in goodness and angered by evil. Yet, divine "emotions" are perfect and, as such, differ in many significant ways from those of humans—divine emotions are always appropriately evaluative, perfectly rational, and otherwise in accord with God's perfect nature, character, and will. Accordingly, when speaking of divine anger or wrath, we should remember such words apply to God analogically—only in ways appropriate to God's perfection (*mutatis mutandis*). If God is immutable in this qualified sense, there is no inconsistency between divine immutability and God becoming angry at evil.

DIVINE ANGER AND DIVINE LOVE

Is divine anger, however, consistent with God's character of love? Although some believe a loving God should not become angry, throughout Scripture love and justice are intertwined such that love requires justice (e.g., Ps 33:5; 89:14; 119:149; Isa 61:8; Jer. 9:24; Hosea 2:19; Mi. 6:8; Luke 11:42). As such, I am convinced divine anger is the appropriate response of divine love against injustice and evil.

Divine Anger as Righteous Indignation at Evil

God becomes angry at evil because evil always harms at least one of God's children, even when self-inflicted. As Peter Craigie explains, God is "a loving Father [who] finds it hard to look on while his children invite disaster by their sinful behavior" (1976, 383). Likewise, Jordan Wessling concludes, "Because God loves His wayward children, He refuses merely to standby when they hurt themselves and others" (2020, 218). Indeed, what manner of "love" would not be angered by the atrocities humans inflict on one another? Imagine a mother seeing a man attack her three-year-old daughter. Should she not be angry? Even as a mother would be justified in being angered by such an attack, God is always righteous in his indignation against evil. Yet, unlike human anger, God's anger is always the expression of the perfect purity of his compassionate love for *everyone*.

Throughout Scripture, humans repeatedly commit immense atrocities such as child sacrifice (cf. 2 Chron 33:6), alongside all manner of depravity, oppression, and injustice. Precisely *because* God loves intensely, evil and injustice provoke God to intense, but always appropriate, anger. Accordingly, Gordon Wenham comments, the God of Scripture exhibits "the anger of someone who loves deeply" (1987, 146). Tony Lane adds, "Failure to hate evil implies a deficiency in love" and "lack of wrath against wickedness is a lack of caring, which is a lack of love" (2001, 160).

However, many kinds of anger are incompatible with love (cf. Matt 5:22; 1 Cor 13:4–7; Gal 5:20; James 1:19–20). Accordingly, it is crucial to distinguish between God's righteous indignation against evil and the misplaced, selfish, irrational, and/or petty anger that humans often exhibit. While human anger is sometimes arbitrary, God's anger is never arbitrary; God only becomes angry in response to evil. While human anger is sometimes irrational, God's anger is always perfectly rational. While human anger is often illegitimate and immoral, God is never angry without cause or in a way that is immoral or less than fully and perfectly loving. While humans are often quick to anger, God is slow to anger and long-suffering (Exod 34:6–7). While humans are sometimes controlled by anger and overreact, God willingly restrains his anger against evil according to his exceedingly great compassion, mercy, and grace (Ps 78:38; Isa 48:9). While human anger tends to exceed human mercy and compassion, God's compassionate grace far exceeds his wrath; God's "anger is but for a moment," while "his favor is for a lifetime" (Ps 30:5). While human compassion often fails—relative to anger and otherwise— God's compassions never fail (Lam 3:22).[23]

In these and many other ways, Scripture depicts God's anger as perfect— always *righteous* indignation motivated by love. In this regard, defining "God's wrath as his opposition to sin and evil," which "involves an emotive state of anger as well as God's actions on the basis of that emotion," Eric T. Yang and Stephen T. Davis conclude that "[g]iven the existence of sin and evil, the possession of such an emotion seems necessarily to follow from any being that has a morally perfect nature" (2015, 155).

God's righteous anger is prominently displayed and affirmed in the OT and NT alike. The popular claim that the OT God is a God of wrath and the NT God is a God of love does not hold up under scrutiny. In the OT *and* NT, God is love and, because he is love, becomes angry at evil. Even a cursory reading of the NT manifests that Jesus himself expressed deep anger against evil. For example, Jesus expressed righteous indignation against those who used the temple system to take advantage of widows, orphans, and the poor (Matt. 21:12–13). While this display of Jesus' anger troubles some, Gerald Borchert comments, "spineless love is hardly love" and "anger and judgment can in fact be the obverse side of the coin of love" (2001, 164). Further, in Mark 3:4–5, when some spoke against Jesus healing on Sabbath, Jesus declared it is "lawful to do good" on Sabbath and looked "at them with anger, grieved at their hardness of heart." Later, when "the disciples rebuked" people bringing children to Jesus, Jesus "was indignant and said to them, 'Permit the children to come to Me' (Mark 10:13–14; cf. Matt 18:6). Elsewhere, Jesus repeatedly teaches about the coming wrath of God, describing the righteous final judgment of God against evil and attributing this judgment to himself (e.g., Matt 13:41–42; 25:41–43; cf. 8:12; 10:28; 22:5–6, 13; 23:16–33; 24:50–51; Luke 13:28).

Many other NT instances likewise highlight God's righteous anger against wickedness (e.g., Rom 1:18; 2:4–9; 3:5–6; 9:22; cf. Col 3:5–6; Eph 5:5; 1 Thess 2:15–16; Heb 3:10–11, 17; 4:3). And, Paul explicitly rejects the idea that divine anger and wrath is unjust, saying: "The God who inflicts wrath is not unrighteous, is He? (I am speaking in human terms.) May it never be! For otherwise, how will God judge the world?" (Rom 3:5–6). Yet, contrary to the worry that recognition of divine wrath might license humans to exact retribution from people, Scripture explicitly reserves vengeance for God (Deut 32:35; Rom 12:19; Heb 10:30; cf. Ps 37:7–9).

Wrath, however, is not an *essential* attribute of God. Divine wrath is the appropriate response of divine love against evil.[24] Yet, because divine wrath is the righteous response of love against evil, "where there is no sin [or evil], there is no wrath, but there will always be love in God" (Carson 2000, 67). As Thomas McCall puts it: "God's righteous wrath is always portrayed in Scripture as God's antagonism toward sin. . . . It is the contingent [yet natural] expression of the holy love that is shared between Father, Son, and Holy Spirit" (2019, 334). The God of Scripture becomes angry and wrathful at evil precisely because God is love.

Divine Anger and Justice

Far from pitting love against justice, Scripture connects the two such that love requires justice. As Psalm 89:14 declares, "Righteousness and justice are the foundation of [God's] throne; lovingkindness and truth go before" God (cf. Jer 9:24). Accordingly, evil rightly provokes God to anger in favor of victims, the oppressed and abused. Voices throughout Scripture highly anticipate divine judgment as a very good thing because it brings justice and judgment against the oppressors and corresponding deliverance of the victims of injustice.

While people today commonly question why the God of Scripture becomes angry at evil and brings judgment, biblical authors instead often questioned why God did not bring judgment more rapidly and decisively, crying: "How long, O Lord?" (e.g., Hab 1:2; cf. Rom 3:25–26). Many in the West seem to be desensitized to the magnitude and devastating impact of injustice and evil and thus find God's righteous anger more alarming and scandalous than the injustice and evil that provokes God to anger. This particularly plagues those of privilege—those of us in the Laodicean condition who say, "I am rich, and have become wealthy, and have need of nothing" (Rev 3:17).

The God of Scripture, however, is deeply concerned about injustice and continually commands humans to act toward bringing justice. For instance, God commands: "Learn to do good; Seek justice, reprove the ruthless, defend the orphan, plead for the widow" (Isa 1:17; cf. Mic 6:8). Likewise, God declares: "Dispense true justice and practice kindness and compassion each to his brother; and do not oppress the widow or the orphan, the stranger or the poor; and do not devise evil in your hearts against one another (Zech 7:9–10; cf. Matt 23:23). Many other texts display God's profound concern for justice and indignation against injustice, with some highlighting the execution and distribution of justice as a facet of divine love (e.g., Deut 10:18; Isa 61:8; Luke 11:42). As Bruce Baloian comments, throughout Scripture "God is passionately concerned about the lives of human beings and whether justice takes place among them" (1997, 381).

God's anger stems from God's righteous love, which *requires* appropriate response against evil. Divine anger is not the opposite of love; it is the proper response of love against evil of every kind. Justice may be delayed, but love cannot permit injustice to continue forever unabated. Thus, while some emphasize divine grace in a way that effectively minimizes God's concern for justice, the God of Scripture does not turn a blind eye to injustice—because he is love. The God of Scripture is the God of love and justice and, accordingly, the God of the oppressed (see Cone 1975) who will save repentant oppressors, but whose "judgment will be merciless to one who has shown no mercy" (James 2:13).

In this regard, writing about reaction to the case of Botham Jean, a black man murdered by a police officer while he was minding his own business in his own apartment in 2018, Dorena Williamson highlights the mistake of emphasizing grace and forgiveness to the exclusion of justice. After the police officer was convicted of murder, Jean's brother publicly forgave and hugged the police offer—a moment of grace and forgiveness that quickly went viral. Conversely, the response of Jean's mother that highlighted systemic injustice did not go viral. On this juxtaposition of a brother's forgiveness going viral, while a mother's pain and cry for justice went largely overlooked, Williamson wrote: "When a black person extends radical forgiveness, we see the grace of the gospel. But when we ignore a black person's call for justice, we cheapen that grace. Both are acting like the God we serve; we need to listen to them both" (2019).[25]

As Miroslav Volf explains, God is concerned for justice and wrathful at evil and injustice *because* he is love. Specifically, Volf writes:

I used to think that wrath was unworthy of God. Isn't God love? Shouldn't divine love be beyond wrath? God is love, and God loves every person and every creature. That's exactly why God is wrathful against some of them. My last resistance to the idea of God's wrath was a casualty of the war in former Yugoslavia, the region from which I come. According to some estimates, 200,000 people were killed and over 3,000,000 were displaced. My villages and cities were destroyed, my people shelled day in and day out, some of them brutalized beyond imagination, and I could not imagine God not being angry. Or think of Rwanda in the last decade of the past century, where 800,000 people were hacked to death in one hundred days! How did God react to the carnage? By doting on the perpetrators in a grandparently fashion? By refusing to condemn the bloodbath but instead affirming the perpetrators basic goodness? Wasn't God fiercely angry with them? Though I used to complain about the indecency of the idea of God's wrath, I came to think that I would have to rebel against a

God who wasn't wrathful at the sight of the world's evil. God isn't wrathful in spite of being love. God is wrathful because God is love. (2006, 138–39)

Both God's compassionate mercy and righteous indignation against evil are integral to God's perfect and immutable character of love.

Divine Compassion Far Exceeds Anger

Yet, God's compassion and grace far exceed divine anger, extending beyond all reasonable expectations. God always retains self-control and often restrains his anger, bearing long with rebellious people before bringing judgment. Indeed, despite his people's incessant rebellion, "being compassionate, [God] forgave their iniquity and did not destroy them; and often He restrained His anger and did not arouse all His wrath" (Ps 78:38; cf. Isa 48:9). Further, even when God finally brings judgment against evil, God "does not afflict willingly" but "if He causes grief, then He will have compassion" (Lam 3:32–33; cf. Judg 10:16; Ps. 81: 11–14; Hosea 11:8–9). God has no pleasure in the death of anyone (Ezek 18:23; 33:11) and God does not want anyone to perish (2 Pet 3:9), yet love requires eventual judgment against evil, which God brings only when there is no preferable alternative available to him. And, throughout Scripture God first warns people of coming judgment, consistently provides some way of escape, and delays the execution of judgment until there is "no remedy" (2 Chron 36:16; cf. Isa 5:1–7). In this regard, Kevin Kinghorn concludes that God's wrath is a function of God's love, always motivated by God's concern for the long-term well-being of others, limited, provisional, "always a last resort," and responsive to repentance (2019, 63, 82).[26]

Far exceeding divine anger, God's compassion is exponentially greater than even the exceedingly great love of a mother love for her newborn. Indeed, God states, "Can a woman forget her nursing child and have not compassion on the son of her womb? Even these may forget, but I will not forget you" (Isa 49:15). Although human compassion often fails, God's "compassions never fail" (Lam 3:22). While God's "anger is but for a moment, His favor is for a lifetime. Weeping may last for the night, but a shout of joy comes in the morning" (Ps 30:5; cf. Exod 34:6; Judg 10:16; Isa 30:18; 54:7–10; Luke 13:34).

The unfathomable depth of God's compassionate love is supremely demonstrated in Jesus: "God demonstrates His own love toward us, in that while we were yet sinners, Christ died for us" (Rom 5:8; cf. John 3:16; Eph 5:2). There is no greater love than this (John 15:13) and, amazingly, even as humans tortured and killed him, Jesus prayed, "Father, forgive them" (Luke 23:34).

However, although divine compassion far surpasses divine anger, it does not cancel the execution of divine judgment. While God "is slow to anger," God "will by no means leave the guilty unpunished" (Nah 1:3; cf. Jer 30:11). This should not be understood as if God's love and divine anger are set in opposition—as if to be angry is to be unloving. Rather, Scripture depicts divine anger as the proper response of perfect love against evil—the righteous anger of the immutable God of love.

CONCLUSION

This brief chapter has only scratched the surface of the many issues concerning the nature of divine anger. While much more should be said, this chapter offered a brief theological consideration of divine anger as depicted throughout Scripture, particularly relative to whether divine anger is consistent with God's unchanging nature and character of love and justice, outlining the view that divine anger is God's holy, just, and rational response to evil, consistent with the immutability of God's essential nature and character of perfect love and justice.

NOTES

1. The debates over divine immutability and impassibility are bound up with larger debates over God's nature and the God-world relationship. For the sake of brevity, here I focus on immutability and impassibility. For more on the constellation of views in which these debates are embedded, see Peckham 2019a.

2. Strict impassibility aligns with a strict form of aseity, which James Dolezal defines as the view that "God is wholly self-sufficient in all that he is and thus exists independently of all causal influence from his creatures" (Dolezal 2019, 18). There is also a significant relationship to divine timelessness (God is without temporal succession), strict simplicity (God has no parts), and divine blessedness (the claim that God always enjoys perfect bliss). See, further, Peckham 2019a.

3. In this regard and more broadly, R. T. Mullins makes a case that (strict) immutability and impassibility are incompatible with God being angry (Mullins 2020).

4. For example, Gregory of Nyssa wrote, "we make the Holy Scriptures the rule and measure of every tenet; we necessarily fix our eyes upon that, and approve that alone which may be made to harmonize with the intention of those writings" (*On the Soul and the Resurrection, NPNF* 5:439).

5. Unless otherwise noted, all biblical quotations are from the NASB.

6. Notably, while "jealousy" is often viewed today as a pejorative characteristic, Scripture depicts divine "jealousy" (better translated as "passion") in a way that sharply differentiates it from the adverse connotations of human jealousy (e.g., envy).

The God of Scripture's passion or "jealousy" is always loving and righteous passion for exclusive relationship with his people, akin to the passion of a loving husband for exclusive relationship with his spouse. As Paul House explains, this kind of "jealousy is a good and normal trait. God's jealousy is equally positive." It "is no character flaw" but "magnifies God's righteousness, concern, and covenant loyalty" (House 1995, 194). For more on this, see Peckham 2015, 156–59.

7. See, further, Heschel 2001.

8. This verse uses yet another Hebrew term, *zāʿam*, "to be indignant."

9. Ps 102:27 also emphasizes God's immutability in some respect, but does not specify in what way(s) God remains "the same."

10. Nicholas Wolterstorff comments, this passage affirms "covenant fidelity, not [strict] ontological immutability" (2010, 161). Likewise, see Moreland and Craig 2003, 526.

11. See the discussion in Peckham 2021, chapter 2; Peckham 2015, chapter 6.

12. I do not mean to claim this is the only conclusion that could be consistent with Scripture, but that a qualified conception of immutability allowing for relational change such as God becoming angry at evil seems to meet the standard of biblical warrant. See, further, Peckham 2019b; Peckham 2021. See also Ware 1984.

13. See the discussion in Peckham 2015, 172–76. Cf. the discussion in Thomas Aquinas, *Summa Theologiae* I.1.13.

14. In Justo L. González's words, "all speech about God is anthropomorphic" (2005, 9; so, also, Hinlicky 2016, 200).

15. For more on this, see Peckham 2015, chapter 6; Peckham 2021, chapters 1–2.

16. Indeed, at least some biblical scholars maintain "there are always literal realities behind the figures of speech in the Scriptures" (Duvall and Hays 2019, 8).

17. For more on this, see Peckham 2019a, chapter 2; Peckham 2021. For an illuminating article on patristic understandings of divine wrath as very different from human anger, see McCarthy 2009.

18. Relative to divine anger specifically, Gavrilyuk contends that some Church Fathers offered "a purely subjectivist interpretation" wherein God is not actually angry, but humans merely perceive him to be angry while others (e.g., Tertullian, Lactantius, Novatian, and Cyril of Alexandria) claimed God "indeed experiences anger," but "in a carefully qualified sense" (2006, 58). For example, Lactantius wrote: "But God is not angry for a short time, because He is eternal and of perfect virtue, and He is never angry unless deservedly" and "He who commands us to be angry is manifestly Himself angry; He who enjoins us to be quickly appeased is manifestly Himself easy to be appeased" and "because He is endued with the greatest excellence, He controls His anger, and is not ruled by it, but that He regulates it according to His will," *On the Anger of God* 21 (*ANF* 7:277). On the other hand, Gavrilyuk maintains that Augustine affirmed a subjective account of divine anger, though not consistently (2006, 57). See, e.g., Augustine, *Against Faustus the Manichaean* 22.18 (*NPNF* 4:278); Augustine, *On Patience* 1 (*NPNF* 3:527).

19. For an introduction to various competing approaches to the doctrine of God, see Peckham 2019a.

20. For much more on the way I approach the theological interpretation of Scripture, see Peckham 2016; Peckham 2017.

21. For my case, in this regard, see Peckham 2021. See also Peckham 2019b.

22. Many other theologians affirm some form of qualified immutability. See, e.g., Oden 2009, 68; González 1990, 92; Horton 2011, 247–48; Feinberg 2001, 271; Wolterstorff 2010, 134; Moreland and Craig 2003, 527; Richards 2003, 195; Ware 2004, 141; cf. Sonderegger 2015, 491–95.

23. On the biblical warrant for the claims in this list, see Peckham 2015, chapter 6.

24. See, further, Peckham 2015, 156–61.

25. See also the discussion of anger against injustice alongside hope for the salvation of even the oppressors in McCaulley 2020. Cf. Isaiah 49.

26. It is beyond the scope of this chapter to take up the related debate over divine violence in Scripture. For one helpful treatment of this topic, see Copan and Flannagan 2014.

REFERENCES

Anizor, Uche. 2018. *How to Read Theology: Engaging Doctrine Critically and Charitably*. Grand Rapids: Baker Academic.

The Ante-Nicene Fathers (ANF). 1885–1887. Edited by Alexander Roberts and James Donaldson. 10 vols. Buffalo: The Christian Literature Company.

Aquinas, Thomas. *Summa Theologiae*. Translated by the English Dominican Fathers. London: Burns Oates & Washbourne, 1920.

Baloian, Bruce. 1997. "Anger." In *New International Dictionary of Old Testament Theology & Exegesis*, vol. 4, edited by Willem A. VanGemeren. Grand Rapids: Zondervan.

Borchert, Gerald. 2001. *John 1–11*. New American Commentary 25A. Nashville: B&H.

Carson, D .A. 2000. *The Difficult Doctrine of the Love of God*. Wheaton, IL: Crossway.

Castelo, Daniel. 2009. *Apathetic God: Exploring the Contemporary Relevance of Divine Impassibility*. Paternoster Theological Monographs. Colorado Springs, CO: Paternoster.

Cone, James. 1975. *God of the Oppressed*. New York: Seabury.

Copan, Paul, and Matthew Flannagan. 2014. *Did God Really Command Genocide?* Grand Rapids: Baker.

Craigie, Peter C. 1976. *The Book of Deuteronomy*. New International Commentary on the Old Testament. Grand Rapids: Eerdmans.

Dolezal, James E. 2014. "Still Impassible: Confessing God without Passions." *Journal of the Institute of Reformed Baptist Studies* 1: 125–51.

———. 2019. "Strong Impassibility." In *Divine Impassibility: Four Views*, edited by Robert Matz and A. Chadwick Thornhill, 13–37. Downers Grove, IL: IVP Academic.

Duvall, J. Scott, and J. Daniel Hays. 2019. *God's Relational Presence: The Cohesive Center of Biblical Theology*. Grand Rapids: Baker Academic.

Feinberg, John. 2001. *No One Like Him: The Doctrine of God*. Wheaton, IL: Crossway.

Gavrilyuk, Paul L. 2006. *The Suffering of the Impassible God: The Dialectics of Patristic Thought*. New York: Oxford University Press.

González, Justo L. 1990. *Mañana: Christian Theology from a Hispanic Perspective*. Nashville: Abingdon.

———. 2005. *Essential Theological Terms*. Louisville, KY: Westminster John Knox.

Heschel, Abraham. 2001. *The Prophets*. New York: Perennial.

Hinlicky, Paul. 2016. *Divine Simplicity: Christ the Crisis of Metaphysics*. Grand Rapids: Baker Academic.

Horton, Michael. 2011. *The Christian Faith: A Systematic Theology for Pilgrims on the Way*. Grand Rapids: Zondervan.

House, Paul. 1995. *1, 2 Kings*. New American Commentary 8. Nashville: B&H, 1995.

Kinghorn, Kevin S., with Steven Travis. 2019. *But What About God's Wrath? The Compelling Love Story of Divine Anger*. Downers Grove, IL: IVP Academic.

Lane, Tony. 2001. "The Wrath of God as an Aspect of the Love of God." In *Nothing Greater, Nothing Better: Theological Essays on the Love of God*, edited by Kevin J. Vanhoozer, 138–67. Grand Rapids: Eerdmans.

Lister, Rob. 2013. *God Is Impassible and Impassioned: Toward a Theology of Divine Emotion*. Wheaton, IL: Crossway.

McCall, Thomas H. 2019. *Against God and Nature: The Doctrine of Sin*. Wheaton, IL: Crossway.

McCarthy, Michael. 2009. "Divine Wrath and Human Anger: Embarrassment Ancient and New." *Theological Studies* 70: 845–74.

McCaulley, Esau. 2020. *Reading While Black: African American Biblical Interpretation as an Exercise in Hope*. Downers Grove, IL: IVP Academic.

Moreland, J. P., and William Lane Craig. 2003. *Philosophical Foundations for a Christian Worldview*. Downers Grove, IL: IVP Academic.

Mullins, R. T. 2020. *God and Emotion*. Cambridge: Cambridge University Press.

The Nicene and Post-Nicene Fathers (NPNF). 1885–1887. Edited by Philip Schaff. 14 vols. Buffalo: The Christian Literature Company.

Oden, Thomas. 2009. *Classic Christianity: A Systematic Theology*. San Francisco: HarperOne.

Padgett, Alan. 2001. "Eternity as Relative Timelessness." In *God and Time: Four Views*, edited by Gregory Ganssle, 92–110. Downers Grove, IL: InterVarsity.

Peckham, John C. 2015. *The Love of God: A Canonical Model*. Downers Grove, IL: IVP Academic.

———. 2016. *Canonical Theology: The Biblical Canon, Sola Scriptura, and Theological Method*. Grand Rapids: Eerdmans.

———. 2017. "The Rationale for Canonical Theology: An Approach to Systematic Theology After Modernism." *Andrews University Seminary Studies* 55, no. 1: 83–105.

———. 2019a. *The Doctrine of God: Introducing the Big Questions*. London: T&T Clark.

———. 2019b. "Qualified Possibility." In *Divine Impassibility: Four Views*, edited by Robert Matz and A. Chadwick Thornhill, 87–113. Downers Grove, IL: IVP Academic.

———. 2021. *Divine Attributes: Knowing the Covenantal God of Scripture*. Grand Rapids: Baker Academic.

Richards, Jay Wesley. 2003. *The Untamed God: A Philosophical Exploration of Divine Perfection, Simplicity, and Immutability*. Downers Grove, IL: InterVarsity.

Scrutton, Anastasia Philippa. 2011. *Thinking Through Feeling: God, Emotion, and Passibility*. London: Continuum.

Sonderegger, Katherine. 2015. *Systematic Theology: The Doctrine of God*. Minneapolis: Fortress.

Volf, Miroslav. 2006. *Free of Charge: Giving and Forgiving in a Culture Stripped of Grace*. Grand Rapids: Zondervan.

Ware, Bruce A. 1984. "An Evangelical Reexamination of the Doctrine of the Immutability of God." PhD Dissertation. Fuller Theological Seminary.

———. 2004. *God's Greater Glory: The Exalted God of Scripture and the Christian Faith*. Wheaton, IL: Crossway.

Weinandy, Thomas. 2000. *Does God Suffer?* Notre Dame: University of Notre Dame Press.

Wenham, Gordon. 1987. *Genesis 1–15*. Word Biblical Commentary 1. Dallas: Word.

Wessling, Jordan. 2020. *Love Divine: A Systematic Account of God's Love for Humanity*. Oxford: Oxford University Press.

Williamson, Dorena. 2019. "Botham Jean's Brother's Offer of Forgiveness Went Viral. His Mother's Calls for Justice Should Too." Accessed 10/7/19: https://www.christianitytoday.com/ct/2019/october-web-only/botham-jean-forgiveness-amber-guyger.html.

Wolterstorff, Nicholas. 2010. *Inquiring About God: Selected Essays*, volume 1. Cambridge: Cambridge University Press.

Yang, Eric T., and Stephen T. Davis. 2015. "Atonement and the Wrath of God." In *Locating Atonement: Explorations in Constructive Dogmatics*, edited by Oliver D. Crisp and Fred Sanders, 154–67. Grand Rapids: Zondervan.

Chapter 3

Quenching Divine Fire

Divine Anger and the Atonement

Joshua R. Farris and S. Mark Hamilton

As unpleasant as it may be to contemporary thinkers, anger (or wrath) is characteristic of God's relationship to human moral corruption.[1] The Scriptures are replete with descriptions of God's anger toward those who have violated his moral law (e.g., Deuteronomy 9.8; Exodus 15.7; Exodus 32.10–11; Numbers 11.1–2; Job 4.9; Isaiah 13.5; Jeremiah 32.29; Lamentations 2.2; Numbers 32.13; Ezekiel 7.8; Isaiah 13.9; Daniel 8.19; Deuteronomy 31.17; 2 Kings 17.18; Psalm 78.59; Matthew 3.7). However much the subject of Divine anger is a prominent theme in the Scriptures, it is, by contrast, not a prominent theme in contemporary theological literature. Some notable exceptions notwithstanding, in this chapter we engage the subject of Divine anger as it relates specifically to the work of Christ and the demands of God's moral law. In what follows, we provide an account of Divine anger from a distinctively Reformed theological perspective. For it seems to us that Divine anger is an emotive state that must be described in the context of *covenantal relations* between God and humans (and humans with other humans) that is ruled or governed by human obligations of Divine justice.

Following some brief engagement with one principal (and profitable) source from among the literature on Divine emotions, we set out three objectives. First, and by way of laying some necessary groundwork, we consider God's relation to the end for which he is said to have created the world; what we will later refer to as an account of Divine egoism. Second, we develop three accounts of Divine anger in relation to human creatures, prompted by differing conceptions of God's moral law in the atonement literature. Third, we argue against a view—a view popular among evangelicals—that Divine anger is somehow equivalent to God's *hatred* of human creatures and that that is somehow necessary to Christ's sacrificial work (Farris and Hamilton 2020).[2]

ANALYTIC THEOLOGY AND THE MEANING OF DIVINE ANGER

Conceptual clarity in this discussion depends chiefly on what we mean by Divine anger. And, for our part, the surest move toward achieving said clarity is an appeal to contemporary analytic theological literature (Spiegel 2018).[3] Some of the most useful light on the subject of Divine anger is found in the literature on emotions (i.e., briefly described as some internal motive or state that presupposes propositional content). To date, analytic philosopher of religion Anastasia Scrutton has provided one of the most thorough treatments of emotion in a broadly "Christian" frame. Scrutton describes emotion in two ways: (1) passion and (2) affections. She describes passion as those emotions that are involuntary and irrational internal states. She describes affections, by contrast, as those emotive states that are voluntary and rational. They are not reactive (thinking along the lines of theistic personalism; or speaking analogously) so much as they are under the direct deliberation of the Divine mind's control. Passion is not a fitting description of God's internal states—if in fact he has internal states, for on a classical view God's internal states do not change (Scrutton 2011).[4]

As an affection of God, anger might be described as a negative emotion toward sin. Divine anger, then, is an emotive state directed toward covenant lawbreakers who have violated obligations given to humanity by God in order to maintain one's (or a people's) good standing with God. When it comes to divine wrath, we mean something quite similar. The two are closely related terms that have a shared semantic domain. Wrath seems to carry with it the additional meaning of anger *in action*, as when the Scriptures describe God as if he were literally boiling with anger, culminating in his dispensation of that anger on an unjust nation. This language is, arguably, metaphorical, but it provides some context for reflection on the nature of Divine anger to human sin.

There is another concept that is related to anger and wrath, namely divine *hatred*. Perhaps the most straightforward example of this is when the Scripture speaks of God's love for those who obey and his hatred (the contrast of love), found in Deuteronomy 7.12–15 and 28.2–12, where we find an explicit reference to God loving and blessing obedience and cursing disobedience. So, you might think of God being angry toward his covenant children, as a parent is at times angry with her disobedient child, yet not seeking to bring about the end of the child. By way of contrast, it is conceivable that Divine hatred is directed toward unrepentant sinners with the intent of punishing individuals, as Deuteronomy clearly states.

There is a further distinction in this discussion that needs to be made. Following Romans 3.25, some take it that justice is manifested by God eschatologically, that is, at the end of time rather than in the immediate present. Accordingly, one might take it that God directs his hatred toward sinners who have entered the eschatological state and have failed to repent. Rather than see God's declaration of humans in relation to him as an immediate present reality, the Scriptures describe this as an eschatological judgment.

There is another sense of the term hatred recently advanced by Eleonore Stump (Stump 2010, ch. 5, end. 74). In her classically Thomistic way, she describes hatred as the contrast of love, that is, as an earnestness for the good/benefits of another and, more specifically, the desire to be united with that someone for their good. She describes hatred as having two possible meanings. One possible meaning is that hatred is compatible with love. On such a view, God desires that some harm befall the sinner in hopes that she will turn and be united to God. This, we believe, is satisfyingly captured by the term wrath, which might more fittingly represent the relationship between God and some humans, as a Father relates to his children when he disciplines them. The other possible meaning she describes in terms of a person who desires final separation with another—in the case of the Divine-human relation, this would be realized in the destruction of those who ultimately reject God. As it impinges on the nature of atonement, we are strongly inclined to think that Divine hatred does not factor into the nature of Christ's atonement, as we shall discuss below.

Given that the atonement discussion has to do with uniting God and humans, Divine anger either becomes the motivation for atonement, the problem that needs solving, or the manifestation of that atonement. Atonement is, to put it simply, the doctrine according to which God and humans are set at one. The whole discussion around Divine anger, wrath, and hatred raises this most important question: How are God and humans set at one? This question has to do with models of God that ultimately impact what we mean by Divine emotions. It is here where the objective state of affairs that separates the Divine from human union prompted by human sin (i.e., once again, the violation of covenantal obligations) is met. And it is the death of

Christ where we find a mechanism for reconciling the state of affairs that all humans find themselves in before God's moral law. For Divine emotions in general, and Divine anger in particular, raise an important discussion about the nature of God.

For our purposes, there are two models for thinking about God. Much of our thinking falls, historically speaking, along the lines of what is often called *Classical Theism*, which is the view that God is not, strictly speaking, a creature among other creatures, as with individual human persons. God is of a class all to himself, which prevents us from predicating strict univocal properties to him. On this classical picture then, God is said to be impassible, which means that, strictly speaking, emotions cannot be predicated of him in the way that we predicate emotions to humans (i.e., they would be called by some theologians as "Cambridge" properties[5]). So it would be inaccurate to say that God internally experiences a change from jollity to anger. God experiences no change in his passions. Rather, he experiences goodness and the distinction is one in which creatures experience his goodness in a different way.

The alternative model for thinking about God, and one which has become commonplace among many analytic theologians and philosophers, is the view called *Theistic Personalism*. This is basically the view that God is analogous to human persons in that he is a mind or a soul of which certain properties may be predicated of him univocally. So, on this view, we can literally say of God that he experiences a change from jollity to anger. So also, we can still ascribe those maximal properties that make him a perfect being that are inclusive of affections, as described earlier, rather than passions.

In order to spell out the relation of different versions of Divine anger to the atonement that we have discussed here, we must consider the nature and purpose of God's creation. What is the final goal or object of Divine interaction with human creatures? On some models, the nature and purpose is wrapped up in Divine love, yet on other accounts it is Divine glory (also see Crisp, Arcadi, and Wessling 2019).[6] In what follows, we develop Divine anger in relation to the atonement along the lines of Divine egoism and a glory model of creation's purpose. We do so because this is in keeping with what we see as the common dogmatic frame in the Reformed theological tradition (Manton 1669, Q.1, Q.2).[7]

DIVINE EGOISM AND DIVINE GLORY

What precipitates God's anger toward humanity is something prompted by God's purpose for human creation. So, understanding the final end for which

God created the world, and human creatures in particular, is important to providing an account of Divine anger in the atonement. Divine egoism is the idea that God's moral end is self-interest; God's (*ad extra*) acts are guided by his own self-interest (Moseley 2020). Ethical demands have as their aim God's interest in his own glory. Divine egoist accounts stand in contrast to anthropocentric models that describe all of Divine action as somehow centered on love for humans. This is so because all of God's acts are directed toward glory and the motivation for human action is unified by how it is that our acts are related to Divine glory (Crisp, Arcadi, and Wessling 2019). God acts in creation and redemption out of his self-interest, which culminates in his glory. The reason or rationale for understanding what prompts Divine anger, then, must be understood in this broader context. When Divine glory is not fulfilled, then God's anger is the result of the failure to maintain or satisfy God's intended end for his own glory. Hence, by violating the moral law, humans ultimately fail to fulfill the means by which God has designed the governance of his world ultimately expressing his glory in creation and redemption. Following a common tradition within Christian history and exemplified (though not by the name Divine egoism) perhaps most clearly in the writings of Jonathan Edwards (1703–1758), in this next section, we explore the nature of Divine anger in relation to law and atonement in the broader context of Divine egoism. How this relates to the atonement can be worked out as expressions of Divine glory where Christ manifests God's glory in the achievement of redemption by satisfying human debt. But it is here that we can gain a clearer sense of what it is that causally results in Divine anger toward human sin.

Three Views of Divine Anger in the Atonement

There are three distinct, albeit closely related, Reformed theories of the atonement that give us different understandings of both what prompts Divine anger, and the means that God employs for satisfying that anger. These include a *Reformed Anselmianism* (what we call Reparative Substitution), *Penal Substitution*, and what we elsewhere call *Christus Odium*. What is clear about all Reformed theories of the atonement is that Divine anger is precipitated by the violation of the moral law. When the Old Testament speaks of Divine anger toward humans, it always does so in the context of covenant violators of God's moral commands, but this is, arguably, distinct from Divine hatred. For one might take it that Divine anger is not synonymous with Divine hatred. We will discuss this in a moment when we discuss Christus Odium. When creatures violate God's moral commands, God relates to those creatures via his moral law. Insofar as creatures violate the moral law, that violation brings about a change in how it is that God relates to his creatures. In other words, a debt accrues, arguably, first to the moral law (what we will later call the public demands) of which Divine anger follows (the private demands of the law that change between God and creatures). The nature of the debt that ensues from the moral law and the satisfaction of that debt is distinct on each theory of the atonement. Divine anger, then, is an affective state and distinct from passionate states. According to the passions view, again, God is reactive and subject to the imperfection of human fragility. God is a perfect being who exemplifies all the attributes completely whether we conceive his states and actions along theistic personalist lines or along the lines of classical theism. Thus, God's emotive states are directed toward lawbreaking. According to classical theism, this means that we experience Divine goodness as Divine anger rather than this being an actual intrinsic change in God's emotional states. On theistic personalism, however, God actually experiences these emotive states as affections that occur in the context of lawbreaking.

Let us begin with Reformed Anselmianism. At the heart of Reformed Anselmianism is the concept of honor (which for present purposes we will assume is suitably equivalent to the concept of glory): Divine honor and the honor of his moral law. On this view, the moral law is designed to govern the moral order of human beings. Humans being set under this moral order have obligations to this moral order as covenantal participants. When they disobey Divine commands, as in the case of the primal sin (and all this thereafter), they incur debt; a debt that if left unpaid precipitates Divine anger toward humans. Here is the breakdown of Reformed Anselmianism.

a. Christ's atonement is necessary to his work.
b. Christ's death is an act of divine love.
c. Christ's death procures an infinite merit (i.e., a merit of holiness).
d. The infinite merit of Christ's death pays a debt of honor to God.
e. The infinite merit of Christ's death pays a debt of honor to God's moral law.
f. Christ's death is sufficient for all humanity (what we might call a global substitute).
g. Christ death efficiently sways divine wrath for all until the eschaton.
h. Christ's death is efficient for those who by faith are united to Christ.

Notice that the nature of the law being centrally focused on honor—honor to both God and the honor of the moral law itself—governs the human moral order. Notice also that Divine honor is impacted eschatologically in one of two ways. It is impacted by Christ's paying the debt of honor owed to God on our behalf (representation) and in our place (substitution). By so doing, those who by faith are united to Christ's merit that is paid first to the honor of the moral law then to the honor of the Father (Bates 2017).[8] Christ's sacrifice quells the anger toward the faithful whereas those who are not found united by faith to Christ, they will experience divine anger in its fullness following the judgment. This probably sounds a lot different than the more familiar penal substitutionary terms that contemporary Reformed evangelicals make so much of.

Penal substitution is a theory of atonement that conjoins the substitutionary work of Christ with the debt of punishment due to humans. On this theory, humans are reckoned covenant lawbreakers, having violated Divine commands and in so doing become debtors to the moral law (at least one way of cashing out penal substitution).[9] According to this way of construing penal substitution, Divine anger is distinct from the punitive demands of the moral law designed by God for moral governance. Divine anger is a private state and an emotive state, following Anastasia Scrutton, that exemplifies Divine dissatisfaction with and opposition to lawful violators, which naturally corresponds or fits with the private-public distinction concerning offenses. Divided up into constituent parts, here is a breakdown of penal substitution:

a. Christ's atonement is necessary to his redemptive work.
b. Christ's death is sufficient to assuage divine retribution for all humanity.
c. Christ dies as a penal substitute for individual persons.
d. Christ dies in order to absorb the retributive (penal) consequences of divine justice precipitated by human sin, being treated by God as if he were those individuals to whom the punishment were due (i.e., the mechanism).
e. Christ's death pays a debt of punishment.
f. Christ's death is a vicarious sacrifice.

Notice the centrality of retributive justice. As covenant lawbreakers, we, humans, become debtors to the moral law. Divine anger is precipitated by disobedience to the covenant demands, but as we have been developing penal substitution it should not be conflated with the punitive demands of the law because the two are distinct. What Christ pays is the debt to the moral law on our behalf (representation) in our place (substitution). For Christ does not directly satisfy the personal offense (i.e., private offense to Divine anger) of sin against God, but he pays the public debt to the moral law that is owed by each individual sinner.[10] By doing this, Christ effectively satisfies Divine anger as the next logical step in the redemption that he secures by his death.[11] Yet, there is a distinct type of penal substitution-ary theory that has gained some ground among evangelicals (of a mostly neo-Calvinist variety) simply as *the* doctrine of penal substitution.[12] This theory isolates the moral law as synonymous with the Divine nature and often pictures God as a reactive passionate being to human violation of the moral law.

Christus Odium, as the name suggests, explicitly takes into account the nature of Divine anger as hatred. God's manifest hatred toward sinners just is the penalty owed to human sinners. In short, Christ takes that penalty on himself in our place (substitution) and on our behalf (representation). Building on the foundation of more standard accounts of penal substitution, advocates for Christus Odium take the curious (and frankly, dangerous) step toward pressing into service for a more exotic version of Divine anger. On Christus Odium, Divine anger is equivalent to Divine hatred. Additionally, the satisfaction of Divine hatred just is the problem that needs solving in Christ's atonement of human sinfulness. Assuming (a.)–(f.), Christus Odium goes like this:

g. Exercises of divine retribution are equivalent the exercises of divine hatred.
h. Paying a debt of punishment, the Son becomes the object of the Father's hatred.
i. When Christ dies on the cross, the Son of God himself (and/or the human nature of Christ) dies.

There are two important distinctions between the first version of penal substitution and Christus Odium. Each centrally locates a distinct notion of justice at the heart of their conception of law and punishment. The distinction between public notions of justice and private notions of justice are important here. The first notion of penal substitution, as we define it, contains within it a public notion of justice and Christus Odium a private notion of justice (or at least the conflation of public with private). A public notion of justice high-lights the fact of the nature of moral law as something that is due to the gov-erning order of human beings. A private notion of justice in the moral law is conceived of between persons, for example, like the debt one owes to another after slapping the person in the face. Along these lines, Christus Odium is the view that collapses the public notion into the private notion of justice and makes equivalent the violation of moral law with dishonoring a person directly. The two are synonymous, that is, there is no distinction between the public demands and the private demands of the law. The second difference is that Divine anger is equivalent to Divine hatred on Christus Odium, which on the version of Penal Substitution we describe there are sufficient distinctions between anger and hatred. First, there is the distinction between the anger a Father experiences toward his children. Second, there is the distinction of anger as hatred being in effect the reality that is only meted out at the end of time in the eschatological judgment.

Coming back around to the alternative conceptions of Divine anger to Christus Odium, here's a summary. First, it is the case that on Reformed Anselmianism and the version of Penal Substitution we advanced that God the Father's anger is not directed toward sinners due to Christ's work on the cross—which pushes the judgment of God toward sinners eschatologically forward (see Romans 3.25, where God is said to forebear sin until the eschaton).[13] In this way, there is not an emotive state of anger directly aimed at sinners in this present time of redemptive history.

Second, anger as hatred (which we defined as the desire for ultimate and final destruction of sinners or the separation from those lawbreakers) is not an accurate reflection of God's relation to human sinners until the end of time, in eschatological separation, with both Reformed Anselmianism and Penal Substitution. If we work backward from the fact that Christus Odium falsely represents God's relation to human sinners as eschatologically conceived, then it appears to give a false picture of God's relation to human violations. What this means is that the private demands of Divine anger are meted out on sinners at the end of time, but Divine anger does not meet those sinners who are united to Christ and experience his atoning work.

Christus Odium advocates hold to the notion that human sinners incur a debt of punishment, but that debt of punishment is equivalent to Divine hatred poured out on those sinners. As we have shown, this suggests that the public demands of the law are identical to or equivalent to the private demands that are owed by sinners to their Creator. And the only solution for redemption is that Christ would stand on our behalf and in our place. What this means is that Christ not only absorbs the punitive demands of the law, but that he absorbs the holy, fiery hatred of God. The logic is actually quite simple. God hates sinners, so in order for that debt to be taken away Christ (as our substitute) must stand in the place of sinners—a place that God the Father finds utterly revolting. But Christ cannot do this. First, this would mean that God the Father was anything but pleased with his beloved Son. Second, Christ's representative work in redemptive history fully satisfied and pleased his Father. In fact, we have no indication in Scripture that God the Father is ever dissatisfied with Christ's representative work of humans. Third, God the Father could not experience eschatological separation from the Son (which is effectively the definition we assigned to the term "hatred") because that would create a rift in the Trinity, one that would be unorthodox and logically impossible.[14] If we are right about this, then it would stand to reason that the debt presumed in Christ's atoning work is not that of God's hatred. Hence, we are left with two options. One option has it that Divine hatred is the debt required of sinners—that must be absorbed by them. A debt that Christ could not take for us, effectively leaving us in our sins and requiring that you and I absorb that debt. A second option has it that Divine hatred does not adequately describe Divine anger in redemptive history as the debt required of sinners. We take it that there are alternative ways of understanding human sinners in relation to the law in addition to Christ's atoning work on the cross, which gives us a different picture of Divine anger toward human lawlessness.

CONCLUDING THOUGHTS

Divine anger is an important theme in Scripture, yet it receives little attention in contemporary theology. What we have hoped to contribute is not to the deficit of literature on Divine anger, but to the small, albeit growing, set of literature on the subject. We have covered a lot of ground. We have done so by carving out a description of Divine anger through a brief survey of the literature, situating it in a macroethical vantage point (i.e., Divine egoism), and exploring it in relation to the moral law and three different conceptions of the atonement. We have also shown that one version of Penal Substitution, namely Christus Odium, inaccurately portrays Divine anger toward human sinners. We have suggested that the reader reject Christus Odium and take up one of the alternative Reformed theories of the atonement as a way of conceiving Divine anger now and in the eschaton.

NOTES

1. We prefer to use the terms *feature* or *characteristic* because anger refers to a contingent activity and potentially an internal state in contrast to attribute. Attribute, at times, carries with it the connotation of a stable character or an essential property. We are loathe to consider this an attribute that is stable or essential, but rather an activity or character that is prompted by God's love or goodness. Some contemporary authors use the term *attribute*, see the useful article Yang and Davis 2015 (155–57).

2. For more on atonement and contemporary accounts of Divine hatred, see Farris and Hamilton 2020.

3. One recent analytic treatment of the subject that attempts to lay out criteria for determining Divine wrath is seen in Spiegel 2018 (301–16). See also a forthcoming response from Gregory L. Bock.

4. For this way of defining concepts, see Scrutton 2011.

5. Cambridge properties are often used in the contemporary theological literature to describe God's characteristics that appear to change, but they only change relative to his human creatures. There is no actual change in God.

6. For a helpful treatment of Divine love that overlaps with the discussion of anger here, see Crisp, Arcadi, and Wessling 2019.

7. For example, see specifically Q.1 and Q.2 in Manton 1669, which makes this claim clear.

8. Consider that this fits quite well in a view of soteriology that takes human creatures along the lines of "allegiance" to the King in his moral order (see e.g., Bates 2017).

9. Most supporters of PSA conflate God's internal state that needs satisfying with the public demands of the moral law. However, these are not necessarily identical and can be distinguished. We have argued elsewhere that they should be distinguished. We are convinced that a more satisfying coherent option does distinguish the two. For one instance in the recent analytic atonement literature, see Craig 2020.

10. In the following article, we advance an alternative version of Penal Substitution and one for which we believe is a coherent and plausible theory. See Farris and Hamilton 2020. We make a distinction here between Christ taking on a penal debt, yet not for us (i.e., substitution), which amounts to the Moral Government theory of atonement. Instead, on the version of PSA we advance Christ assumes our (or "my") debt of punishment that follows from the public demands concerning the moral.

11. See Crisp's helpful work (Crisp 2020, ch. 6). Also see Vidu's excellent work (Vidu 2014). Crisp edges in the direction of making a distinction between the moral law and the Divine nature, but it is not as explicit as Vidu, who makes a distinction between the moral law and the Divine nature in relation to his creation. This is an important distinction that is often lost on contemporary neo-Calvinist theologians who often conflate God's nature in relation to his creatures and the moral law itself.

12. For some of the more explicit examples of Christus Odium, see Setser 2015. See also Chou 2010. See also Allender and Longman (1999) 2015 (184–85); David Platt 2019. There are, however, several accounts that come very close to Christus Odium. One might call this the Owen version of PSA (following the Reformed theologian John Owen).

13. This is also the case on another restitution theory of the atonement that we have not addressed in any detail here, namely the Moral Government atonement. On the Moral Government theory of the atonement, the basic idea is that Christ on the cross assumes not our debt in our place (i.e., nonsubstitutionary), but he does take the punitive consequences of the moral law on our behalf (i.e., representational). In this way, some have called the theory (or versions of it) penal but nonsubstitutionary because Christ in his representative work takes on a penalty as the one who sets aright the moral government.

14. See McCall 2012 for a discussion on this. Those who try and salvage Christus Odium might take one additional step by arguing that it was not the Son that the Father poured out his hateful derision, but the human nature of Christ. Assuming this

sort of move presses one's Christology dangerously close to Nestorianism (i.e., the view that the Logos assumes not just a human nature but a human person). The first problem: the debt is explicitly between persons, but on the view that God the Father pours out his wrath on a human nature does not seem to coherently make sense of the private demands of lawbreakers to a personal God. The second problem: God the Father is never dissatisfied with Christ in his humanity, but he is instead pleased with Christ's perfect representation of humanity.

REFERENCE LIST

Allender, Dan B., and Tremper Longman. [1999] 2015. *In the Cry of the Soul: How Our Emotions Reveal Our Deepest Questions About God.* Colorado Springs, CO: NavPress.

Bates, Matthew W. 2017. *Salvation by Allegiance Alone.* Grand Rapids: Baker Academic.

Chou, Abner. 2010. "The King, the Curse, and the Cross: OT Intertextuality, Paul's Logic, and Justification." Unpublished paper, *Evangelical Theological Society.*

Craig, William Lane. 2020. *Atonement and the Death of Christ.* Waco: Baylor University Press.

Crisp, Oliver. 2020. *Approaching the Atonement.* Downers Grove: IVP.

Crisp, Oliver, James Arcadi, and Jordan Wessling, eds. 2019. *Love, Divine and Human: Contemporary Essays in Systematic and Philosophical Theology.* New York: Bloomsbury Press.

Farris, Joshua R., and S. Mark Hamilton. 2020. "Which Penalty? Whose Atonement? Revisiting Christus Odium." *Journal of Biblical and Theological Studies.*

Manton, Thomas, ed. 1669. *Westminster Shorter Catechism.* In *The Westminster Confession of Faither: Edinburgh Edition*, 2015, 531–618. Accessed August 5, 2020. https://www.monergism.com/thethreshold/sdg/westminster/The%20 Westminster%20Confession%20of%20F%20-%20Westminster%20Assembly%20 Ministers.pdf.

McCall, Thomas. 2012. *Forsaken.* Downers: IVP Academic Press.

Moseley, Alexander. 2020. "Egoism." *Internet Encyclopedia of Philosophy.* Accessed July 7, 2002. https://www.iep.utm.edu/egoism/.

Platt, David. 2019 "Does God Hate Sin but Love the Sinner." *Radical.* Accessed on May 5, 2020. https://radical.net/does-god-hate-sin-but-love-the-sinner/.

Scrutton, Anastasia. 2011. *Thinking Through Feeling: God, Emotion and Passibility.* New York: Continuum.

Setser, Adam. 2015. "Big Picture of God's Mission." *Adam Setser Blog.* Accessed May 5, 2020. https://www.adamsetser.com/blog/2015/7/25/the-big-picture-of-gods-mission-a-concise-overview-of-the-entire-bible-by-dr-abner-chou.

Spiegel, James S. 2018. "'It's the Wrath of God': Reflections on Inferring Divine Punishment," *Journal of Biblical and Theological Studies* 4, no. 2: 301–16.

Stump, Eleonore. 2010. *Wandering in Darkness.* Oxford: Oxford University Press.

Yang, Eric T., and Stephen T. Davis. 2015. "Atonement and the Wrath of God." In *Locating Atonement*, edited by Oliver D. Crisp and Fred Sanders, 154–67. Grand Rapids: Zondervan.

Vidu, Adonis. 2014. *Atonement, Law, and Justice: The Cross in Historical and Cultural Contexts*. Grand Rapids: Baker Academic.

Chapter 4

The Hidden Face of God

A Visual Depiction of God's Anger in the Old Testament

Melissa C. M. Tan

In Christianity, professing believers are taught that their belief manifests itself in having a relationship with God. However, what does it mean to relate to a being who is abstract and noncorporal? How does a Christian discern God's presence or interpret his perceived absence? This fascination with perceiving or relating to the God of Christianity has also manifested itself in various scholarly conversations. These debates have sought to organize and interpret the evidence for the modes in which God relates to human beings, but their conclusions are unsatisfactory.[1]

With these questions as a backdrop, this essay seeks to understand a reoccurring metaphor in the Old Testament regarding the depiction of God's face.[2] This metaphor appears in multiple guises to describe various dimensions of God's embodiment, his presence, and his relationship with the people of Israel. One particular guise appears in the context of righteous indignation, or anger, at the sins of Israel, where God hides his face from Israel. What is the significance of this gesture? Is God denying relationship with Israel in those instances? Is he withdrawing his presence as a punishment to them? What is one supposed to understand from a metaphor that suggests God as an embodied being? Finally, what is the nature of God's anger toward Israel?

This essay will draw upon insights related to the social dynamics of honor-shame and the related concept of the face in cultural anthropology as heuristic tools of analysis, alongside the traditional critical tools of biblical studies.[3] It will probe beyond the literal dimensions of the face, as an embedded metaphor, to investigate possible underlying significance regarding the depiction of God's anger—expressed through his face—in the Old Testament. Focus will be placed on the narrative context of the gesture, possible reasons for this gesture, and reflections on its impact on the relationship between God and Israel.

LEXICAL CONSIDERATIONS

The Hebrew term for *face* (*pānîm*) occurs 2,128 times in the Old Testament.[4] This term is commonly used to denote the face of a human being (e.g., Gen. 43:31; Exod. 10:29) or animal (e.g., Ezek. 10:14) in its anatomical sense, or the surface of an inanimate object such as the face of the earth (e.g., Gen. 1:29) or the front or side of a building (e.g., 1 Kings 6:3). The term is also frequently used as a synecdoche, where it functions synonymously as the whole person whom the term is referencing. In these cases, since the term itself is redundant, translations will choose to omit the term in the rendering of the phrase. For example, in Exodus 2:15, the author describes Moses fleeing, literally "from the face of Pharaoh," but translations will simplify the phrase to "from Pharaoh." Also, just over half of those occurrences (1,128 times) appear in conjunction with the preposition *ly* to form the compound prepositional phrase "before" or "in the presence of." This continues the usage of *face* to synonymously represent the person, being, or object referenced.

The term *pānîm* is also used anthropomorphically of God, both denoting his face and synonymously denoting his being or presence, such as in the phrase "before the face of the LORD," commonly rendered "in the presence of the LORD."[5] For example, the first time *pānîm* is used to denote the face of God occurs in Genesis 3:8, when Adam and Eve hid themselves, *literally* "from the face of the LORD," but usually translated "from the presence of the LORD." Adam and Eve's behavior here occurs soon after they had eaten the fruit and then realized they were both naked.[6] But instead of showing any pride or victory in their actions, upon detecting his presence in the garden, they both instinctively hid from him. We will return to this passage later in the essay to consider the significance and reasons for their actions.

SOCIAL CONSIDERATIONS

In cultural anthropology, the concept of *face* falls under the larger category of honor-shame. As a social dynamic, honor-shame pertains to a person's evaluation of their self-worth or value within their social group. An oft-quoted definition is: "Honor is the value of a person in his or her own eyes (that is, one's claim to worth) *plus* that person's value in the eyes of his or her social group" (Malina 1981, 30). A person's perception of self-worth is influenced by the evaluation of worth from the members of their social group (their community, their neighbors, friends, family). Thus, where the concept of honor represents worth, value, and high regard within a community, the concept of shame represents the lack of worth and value, and low regard.

In cultures where communities play a central role (known as collectivistic or group-oriented cultures), they also have a loud voice in speaking about a person's self-worth. This "voice" is commonly known as the court of public opinion or reputation. It can either be a group of people or an individual person of high regard or standing and reputation within the community. The higher the reputation of the "court," the more honor is given to the person being evaluated.

Significantly, honor also represents acceptance within a community. Someone with honor is accepted by the "court" and by the community as a whole. Someone with shame is either marginalized within the community or, more drastically, ostracized by the community. A truly shameful person may no longer be accepted by the community and is thus rejected or excluded from it.

A related concept is gift- or favor-giving.[7] Either requesting or assigning honor is not limited to verbal expressions. It can also be expressed via requesting a favor or bestowing a favor. The act of favor-giving can signify an offer of friendship, to bring a person into a community. An ongoing bestowal of a favor signifies a person's continued acceptance within a community. Notably, giving *a favor* (either in the form of an actual object, or an action such as a blessing, aid, or protection) is not the same as giving *favor in general*, which is simply another way of expressing the idea to give honor or show partiality to a person. But the two concepts are closely related, especially where the giving of *a favor* implies showing favor to a person.

The concept of *face* is relevant in honor-shame considerations because of the public dimension of honor-shame. The "court" can only evaluate a person by looking at their appearance, behavior, and actions. Thus, a person's status, reputation, or level of honor can be represented in any description of their outward appearance, to the extent that the person's face has become the emblem of status, honor, or reputation. An honorable person would proudly show their face. Conversely, a shameful person would hide their face (because they did not feel worthy of showing their face). This act of hiding is a response to having an awareness of their shame. Also, a person of high standing (such as the person regarded as the "court" of that community) can choose to give or deny access to their face as another way of assessing a person's level of honor or acceptance. Notably, in contrast to the earlier hiding of one's face, here the honorable person can choose to hide his face as the expression of denying access to someone who is shamed or not accepted. Where the shameful person's hiding is a response, here, the honorable person's hiding is not a response, but is the initial action. In this last aspect, the face functions as synecdoche or represents the person's presence. Therefore, to give access to one's face equates to giving access to one's being or presence.

The cultures represented in the Old Testament are defined as collectivistic cultures, for their strong community ties and close-knit families. The Israelites displayed many collectivistic behaviors and experienced much honor or shame before the LORD, their God, who also functioned as their highest "court" of public opinion. For these reasons, the social dimension of the concept of *face*, as understood through cultural anthropology and the concepts of honor-shame, will be applied to this discussion of the patterns of *face* usage observed in the Old Testament.

OLD TESTAMENT DEPICTIONS
OF "THE FACE OF GOD"

Before focusing on the passages depicting God's hidden face in relation to his anger, some survey and consideration is required regarding other depictions of his face in the Old Testament, in order to build a framework within which to understand the significance of the hidden face. Also, because of the social dimensions of *face*, the face of God cannot be analyzed in isolation, but must be done in relation to the face of the human being with whom God is interacting. Therefore, as we begin to survey the various expressions of *face* in the Old Testament, observations will be made regarding the interactions with the face of God and the respective human beings described in each passage, whether they are described explicitly or implicitly.

Face to Face

This survey begins with the ultimate expression of a close, intimate relationship between God and man: *pānîm 'el-pānîm ("face to face"). Occurring just five times in the Old Testament, this idiomatic phrase is reserved for a very select number of people who have been granted this special privilege of access to the presence of God at this level of intimacy. It is worth looking at all five occurrences to establish a baseline understanding of what it means to have full access to the face of God.*[8]

The first occurrence of this idiom is found in Genesis 32:30 [MT 32:31],[9] at a point of transition in the Jacob narrative, between Jacob's departure from Laban and his return to Canaan. During the night, Jacob wrestled with a man he later realized was God (32:24). While there is much mystery and debate surrounding this passage regarding the actual identity of the man and his motivations for this encounter with Jacob (Mathews 2005, 556), what is important is that Jacob himself was convinced that it was God himself with whom he had wrestled, and still lived (32:28, 30 [MT 32:29, 31]). Reading this encounter through the anthropological lens, a few important observations can be made. First, given the evenness of the wrestling match, God had lowered himself to the level of Jacob, so that he essentially came face to face with Jacob, a fact that Jacob acknowledges after the encounter. This access to God's face implies access to his presence. Second, God granted Jacob's request for a blessing. Implicit in the granting of this request—itself a form of favor-giving—is an offer of relationship (Mauss 1954, 10–14; Chavel 2012, 20). By granting Jacob his requested blessing (or favor), God was establishing a relationship between himself and Jacob. By receiving the blessing, Jacob reciprocated that relationship. Third, the sum total of access to God's presence and favor-giving implies an overall granting of honor and acceptance to Jacob. This connection between access to God's face and favor-giving will prove to be a reoccurring motif. Thus in Gen. 32:30 [MT 32:31], to acknowledge and memorialize the significance of this theophany, Jacob declared that he had seen God "face to face" and survived, and thus named the place Peniel, literally "Face of God."[10]

The next two occurrences of this idiom both concern Moses.[11] The first appears in Exodus 33:7–11, a passage that functions as an excursus or sidebar of sorts (Childs 1974, 584–85), describing how Moses would set up the tent to meet with the LORD at a distance from the main camp. In contrast to the ritual lengths required by the Israelites to maintain a distance from the LORD (33:8–10), 33:11 plainly describes how the LORD spoke to Moses "face to face." The author even adds that the interaction was "as a man speaks to his friend." There is no doubt God and Moses had a close relationship. The placement of this excursus is significant, located in the middle of a lengthy narrative about the unfaithfulness and rebellion of Israel. It sits directly *after* the golden calf incident where the Israelites egregiously rebelled and jeopardized the covenantal relationship with the LORD (32:1–33:6) and *before* the lead-up to the renewal of the covenant (33:12–34:35). In 33:12–23, the LORD assured Moses that he and Israel still had the LORD's favor as evidenced by his presence among them, but now, he (Moses) was unable to see his face directly and survive. And so, the LORD instructed Moses to hide in the cleft of a rock, where the LORD would shield him with his hand (another expression of embodiment) until he (the LORD) had passed by, and Moses only saw his back. On this occasion, the denial of access is only restricted to his face, not his presence itself. Close proximity to Moses is required in order for the LORD to reach out to cover Moses with his hand. Thus, the purpose of this act is not for rejection or shame, but is possibly protection and care. In 34:1 onward, the LORD renewed the covenant, which involved replacing the stone tablets containing the laws (themselves emblematic of the gift that was the covenant) that Moses broke, in his own anger at the unfaithfulness of the Israelites (32:19).

The second of the two *pānîm 'el-pānîm* occurrences related to Moses is found in Deuteronomy 34:10. His close relationship with God is referenced at the end of his life when he is remembered as the prophet whom the LORD knew "face to face." That description of their relationship also includes a statement on the significant work accomplished by Moses, on behalf of the LORD, for Israel. Thus, even though no explicit references to a specific favor are found in the vicinity of this particular occurrence, the descriptions of Moses' accomplishments themselves represent the *favor in general* he found in the Lord, represented in holding the responsibilities of mediator and servant (Craigie 1976, 406).

The fourth occurrence is found in Judges 6:11–24, when the angel of the LORD made the first of a series of appearances to Gideon, to call him to help deliver Israel from the Midianites.[12] In 6:17, Gideon acknowledged the connection between seeing the LORD and being granted favor. Then, at the end of the encounter, Gideon declared that he had just seen the angel of the LORD "face to face."

The final occurrence is an unusual one because it appears in Ezekiel 20:33–38, within a pronouncement of judgment upon Israel from God, as the highest "court of public opinion." The occurrence itself appears in Ezekiel 20:35, during the LORD's lament on the state of Israel's rebelliousness. Here, *pānîm 'el-pānîm* is used to describe the manner in which he would judge Israel. In this situation, the idiom seems to function with a double emphasis: the intimate relationship between the LORD and Israel *and* the directness of the judgment with nothing to shield or mitigate its severity. The fact that this phrase alludes to the intimate relationship between God and Israel emphasizes the level of anger God felt toward Israel for their rebellion, that not even a cloud is used to mitigate God's majesty (Block 1997, 651). This anger shows that God regarded the sin of idolatry—Israel's act of turning away from God—particularly severely. However, this anger was one that arose out of intense love and commitment to Israel. For despite the negative pronouncement, the LORD still did not withhold his favor from Israel. In the verses immediately surrounding the occurrence, the LORD acknowledges that he is still king over them (20:33), he will bring them back from where they were scattered (20:34),[13] he will bring them back into the covenant (20:37), until ultimately Israel will acknowledge him as their LORD again (20:38). The LORD still showed his protection and care over Israel in the midst of their rebellion and his judgment. As with Deut 34:10, while the explicit term for favor is not used, these verses describe favor-giving from the Lord.

In summary, Ezekiel 20:33–38 is a passage of contrasting themes. God is depicted as both a judge and a shepherd, offering both judgment and salvation, and shows both anger and kindness at the same time (Allen 1990, 14). These contrasts depicted simultaneously make this passage an enigmatic one that portrays the relationship between God and Israel as a relationship of complexity and nuance. Further discussion around these insights will be made later in this essay.

"To Lift the Face"

Another idiomatic use of the term *pānîm* appears in the phrase *nāśā' pānîm,* "to lift the face," where this action itself conveys the meaning "to grant favor."[14] With this idiom it does not matter whether God is lifting his own face or the face of the human being, but the meaning is still the same: it is God, as the "court," who does the favor-granting. For example, in Genesis 19:21, the angel of the LORD said to Lot, literally "I lift your face" meaning "I grant your favor (or request)" not to destroy the city. Here, *pānîm* refers to the face of Lot because he was the one asking for the favor. But it is still the angel of the LORD who grants the favor itself. Meanwhile, in the priestly blessing of Numbers 6:25–26, it is the LORD's face being referenced, in "to make his face shine" and "to lift up his face," with the recipient of the blessing being Israel.

Access to the Face of God

On multiple occasions, human beings seek or entreat the face of God (e.g., 2 Kings 13:4; 2 Chron. 33:12; Jer. 26:19; Zech. 8:21; Ps. 119:58). The context of each instance makes it clear that it is some favor, such as protection or help from God, that is being requested, to the extent that *face* can also be synonymous with *favor*.[15] More broadly, some observations can also be made regarding the behavior of human beings before the face of God (the "court") as it relates to their perception of their acceptance by him. This behavior before God can also be discerned through honor-shame dynamics, expressed either explicitly or implicitly. We shall consider two passages that contain these dynamics.

In Ezra 9:1, the full extent of the disobedience and unfaithfulness of the Israelites is reported to him. Upon hearing this report, Ezra tore his clothes, pulled his hair from his head and beard, and mourned until the evening (9:3–5). Where honor-shame dynamics relate to how one is perceived outwardly by one's social group, Ezra's appearance would be considered shameful.

This outward expression of shame reflects his inner sense of shame, as he articulates in 9:6 onward. He cries out to the LORD, expressing his shame and inability to lift his face to him. Ezra knows that he is not worthy to look at the face of the LORD. He denies himself access to God's face. This is an excellent example of the strong connections and sense of identity that are derived from within a collectivistic culture because while the unfaithfulness was Israel's not Ezra's, he still felt that shame intensely, as if it were his own.

Another passage that highlights the connections between the concepts of *face* and honor-shame is Isaiah 50:4–9. In this third Servant Song, the servant speaks about his own obedience and close relationship with the LORD. In 50:6–7, he describes how others struck him and pulled on his beard. The pulling of the beard recalls what Ezra did to himself in Ezra 9:3. But in this passage, it was others who subjected the servant to this humiliation. Further, they even shamed and spat on him (50:6). However, he does not hide his face from those acts of shaming because he knows that before the LORD he is not actually shamed. In fact, he proudly holds his face up high ("I have set my face like a flint") because he knows that ultimately he will not be shamed. While his enemies (the human "court") have pronounced him shameful, the servant knows that only the LORD's pronouncement counted (the divine "court"). Before the LORD, the servant is not shamed.

Returning to Genesis 3:8, these two examples help provide a better understanding of Adam and Eve's behavior in the Garden of Eden. By discerning the underlying honor-shame dynamics, we can now understand that their instinct to hide from the face of God was a reaction to the realization of their sin, their shame and unworthiness to be face to face with God. They were preempting what they were afraid God would do, which is to deny them access to his presence by hiding his face from them.

There are also instances of humans hiding their faces from God to express their respect for him. In Exodus 3:6, Moses is described as hiding his own face from God because he is afraid, namely that he is showing respect and awe of him. Exactly in what manner he hid his face is unknown. Another expression of respect for God also appears in the falling on one's face. In Joshua 5:14, Joshua is described falling on his face as a sign of respect for the LORD. In Judges 13:20, Manoah and his wife also fall on their faces out of respect and awe for the LORD.

Related to the falling on one's face is the metaphor of the fallen face. One noteworthy occurrence of this metaphor used of a human being—not out of respect, but anger—is the example of Cain in Genesis 4:5. After he has realized the LORD has not accepted his offering, his face falls in anger at the rejection of his offering. This is a human being who is angry with God. This is also an example of a human being offering a gift to God, but it is not accepted, and by inference, Cain is not honored. After Cain kills his brother

Abel in anger, he realizes his sin and its implications for his relationship with the LORD from that point onward. In 4:14, Cain realizes that he no longer deserves this relationship, saying "from your face I shall be hidden," and then declares himself a fugitive who will be killed. While the LORD does not contradict Cain's first statement, he does still care for Cain and will continue to protect him. The LORD grants him mercy (it is a partial favor), but no longer allows him access to his face, as is stated at the conclusion of this part of the narrative: Cain went away from the presence [literally, the face] of the LORD and settled in the land of Nod, east of Eden (Gen. 4:16).

This same use of *face* is also found in Jeremiah 3:12, but in reference to the face of God. Here, the opening words of the first speech from the LORD are: "Return, faithless Israel, declares the LORD. I will not look on you in anger," literally, "I will not make my face fall on you." Here, it is the LORD's face that falls in anger at Israel.

THE HIDDEN FACE OF GOD

With this understanding of the significance of access to God's face in relation to honor-shame dynamics, we shall now look at the depictions of God hiding his face in anger.[16] First we will look at two occurrences in one particular passage in Deuteronomy, and then we will focus on the Prophets, where this metaphor appears numerous times.

Deuteronomy 31:16–22

At the end of Moses' life, the LORD calls Moses and Joshua to meet with him in the tent of meeting (Deut. 31:14–15). In 31:16, the LORD then begins to describe what will happen to the Israelites after Moses' death. He describes their worship of other gods (idolatry), their abandoning of him, and their breaking of the covenant yet again. He recognizes their propensity toward unfaithfulness (Craigie 1976, 372). It is in 31:17–18 that he describes the extent of his anger at this. The LORD's anger is so great that he will not protect them from any future evils and troubles that they may encounter, but will "hide [his] face from them" (31:17). This point is repeated again in 31:18 for emphasis. Also, there is interesting wordplay in 31:18 between face (*pānîm*) and the verb "to turn" (*pānâ*). The LORD will turn his face away because the Israelites have turned their own faces to other gods.

The LORD then instructs Moses to teach the Israelites a song that will remind them that despite their turning away and breaking of the covenant, he still gave them abundant blessings (31:19–20). And thus, whenever they encounter those future evils and troubles, this song would act as a witness and reminder of their disobedience and rebellion (31:21–22). This song serves as a warning to Israel of what would happen if they turned away from God again (Craigie 1976, 372). It is in these verses that the theme of favor appears in conjunction with the face metaphor.

The Prophets

In the prophetic literature, the term *pānîm* appears 444 times, with the majority of these occurrences located in the books of Isaiah, Jeremiah, and Ezekiel.[17] The metaphor of God hiding his face appears numerous times in all three books.

The opening oracle in Isaiah 2 begins with a command to hide from the "terror [lit. of the face] of the LORD and from the splendor of his majesty." In Isaiah 8:17, 54:8, 59:2, and 64:7 [MT 64:6], the LORD hides his face from Israel. In 54:8, it is also stated that the hiding of his face happened in his anger, and yet the LORD still had compassion on them because of his love for them. In 59:2, interestingly it is the sins that are the grammatical subjects of the sentence, and thus responsibility for the separation between Israel and God resides in Israel's sins. Also, it is the sins that have hidden God's face from them so that he does not hear their prayers. This verse emphatically locates the reason for God's absence from Israel in their sins. This connection is repeated again in 64:7, which states that no one is praying to God ("There is no one who calls upon your name") because he has hidden his face from Israel and did not protect them from their enemies because of their sins.

In the book of Jeremiah, the metaphor of God—as the divine "court"—hiding his face is expressed in a number of ways. In Jeremiah 33:1–9, the LORD expresses his anger and wrath at the evil of Israel, citing this as his reason for his hidden face (33:5). But he also immediately follows this expression of anger with a promise of restoration, healing, and blessings (33:6–9). In 33:8, the verb "to cleanse" is used to describe the removing of all the guilt felt by the Israelites for their sins. This image relates to the social dynamic of clean-unclean, where cleanliness signifies honor and acceptance, but uncleanliness signifies shame and rejection (Douglas 1966, 114). Thus, the act of cleansing is symbolically a means of getting rid of shame.

A related metaphor of God turning or removing Israel away from his face—thus a more drastic version of denying access than simply hiding—appears in a number of passages: Jer. 15:1, 32:31, and 52:3. In 15:1, Jeremiah makes a plea on behalf of Israel for the LORD not to turn away from them. But the LORD is unrelenting, instead declaring that they should be sent away from his face. The reference to favor occurs later in the speech (15:19–21), where the LORD speaks again of protection, deliverance, and most importantly restoration of his presence and relationship.

In 32:31, the LORD also expresses his anger and wrath at Israel, to the extent that he will turn them away from his face. This verse is part of 32:26–35, where the LORD expresses his anger and frustration at the numerous ways that Israel disobeyed and rebelled, resulting in the destruction of the city of Jerusalem. But he immediately continues in 32:36–41 describing the ways in which he will restore the city, provide protection, and restore the covenant with them again, so that they will return to him. The theme of favor is nearby again, showing that it is not far from the LORD's mind even in the midst of his anger.

Finally, in Jeremiah 52:3, the reign of Zedekiah is described as evil, where the anger of the LORD was so great that he "cast them from his face." What then follows is a lengthy description of the extent of the evil and rebellion that characterized Zedekiah's reign, leading to the Babylonian capture of Jerusalem.

Ezekiel 39:21–29

Located in one of the final prophecies against the enemies of Israel, Ezekiel 39:21–29 contains three occurrences of the hidden face metaphor and is the final passage analyzed in this essay. Beginning in 39:21, the LORD describes the public dimension of his judgment upon Israel. His glory will be known among the nations who will witness his judgment. In 39:23, he summarizes the consequences—including the hiding of his face (the first occurrence of the metaphor)—that the LORD meted out to Israel as a result of their unfaithfulness.[18] He repeats the public nature of the consequences, to make Israel a witness of the covenantal relationship—not just the favor that comes with it, but in this case the consequences of turning away from it—for the other nations to see. In 39:24, the LORD cites Israel's resultant uncleanliness as a reason for hiding his face, the second occurrence of the metaphor. His anger is expressed in this second occurrence.

In 39:25, the LORD continues his declaration, now focusing on the eventual restoration of Israel, a demonstration of his power, mercy, and grace, *and* constitutes the favor-giving aspect of this interaction. But even after this return to their land and deliverance from their enemies, the LORD wants the people of Israel to carry the shame of their prior unfaithfulness as a reminder that it was the LORD who was responsible for everything—both their exile and their return (39:26–7).[19] "Far from being a source of pride at having been selected as the objects of divine compassion, the experience of grace will lead to a recognition of their unworthiness" (Block 1998, 486). Verse 28 clarifies further the reason for still remembering their shame and unworthiness. The LORD states, "Then they shall know that I am the LORD their God." The prophecy concludes with the final occurrence of the metaphor: "And I will not hide my face anymore from them, when I pour out my Spirit upon the house of Israel, declares the LORD God" (Ezek. 39:29). Access to the LORD's face is restored. The honor of Israel is restored too. This action is ratified with the pouring out of the Spirit, itself acting as a "permanent seal" of the covenantal relationship between Israel and the LORD (Block 1998, 488).

This passage contains all the relevant aspects to understanding how the hiding of his face relates to the relationship between God and Israel. By paying attention to the honor-shame dynamics present (both explicitly and implicitly) in the passage, the themes of acceptance and relationship are highlighted. In this passage, God makes it clear that being denied access to his presence (expressed via the hiding of his face) is the consequence of Israel's sin and rebellion. Their exile is also part of that consequence. They had turned away from God, which angered him. In this public judgment, Israel's sins were exposed for all the nations to see. Their reputation was completely destroyed. There was no honor to be gained, only shame. However, God also revealed that the purpose of Israel's exile and the public shame that accompanied it was to remind Israel that he was their LORD God. Even if they had turned away from him, he had not turned away from them permanently. Upon the restoration of the relationship, God restored their land and fortunes back to them, and restored access to his presence again.[20]

CONCLUSION: THE (IN)VISIBLE GOD

This essay analyzed and reflected on the metaphor of the face of God in the Old Testament. By paying attention to the social dynamics of honor-shame and the related concept of *face* in a number of passages, the meaning and significance of God hiding his face in anger were uncovered, along with important insights about the nature of the relationship between God and Israel. The face metaphor was used in multiple ways, to represent God himself, his presence, and his regard (positive or negative) toward Israel.

Revealing or granting access to his face generally signaled acceptance, approval, and ultimately a close relationship with Israel. Hiding or denying access to his face generally signaled anger and disapproval. However, there were exceptions to this pattern. God hid his face from Moses as an act of protection and care in Exodus 33:20. God also revealed his face during his act of judgment to Israel in Ezekiel 20:33–8. But regardless of whether the face was hidden or revealed, God's love for Israel was always apparent through his protection and care of them, even while hidden. The juxtaposition of the two passages Exodus 33:7–11 (where God came face-to-face with Moses) and 33:12–23 (where God covered Moses with his hand as he passed by) is also a good example of this. Herein lies the complexity of the hiddenness issue in theological discussions, where attempts to understanding these instances according to simple binary categories do not suffice.

However, the covenantal relationship with God and Israel is a key to understanding God's seemingly contradictory actions. God established a formal covenant with Israel that represented a specific commitment to relationship from both parties. In the passages discussed, aspects of this covenant appeared via the theme of favor-giving, whether it be God's bestowing of favor, Israel's receiving of that favor, or Israel's request for favor in the form of blessing or protection. While this covenant has frequently been understood as a formal contract, it is a vibrant, living relationship that cannot be reduced to a simple contract. Conversely, it is more than a simple relationship, but as a covenantal one, it signified God's deep, unwavering love for Israel, a love beyond anything capable in a human relationship. As seen in multiple passages, God's commitment to this relationship was unconditional, where even in his anger, God still provided some (albeit only partial) protection or blessing. It was because of his commitment to Israel through the covenant, that God was so grieved and disappointed when Israel did not reciprocate with the same level of commitment, as evidenced by their sin of idolatry. In essence this was the act of being unfaithful to the covenantal relationship. This was where his anger was directed.

Ultimately, God's desire was for Israel to return to him. His desire was for reconciliation and restoration of the covenantal relationship. He strategically adapted his actions toward Israel depending on the circumstances, to get their attention in the best way possible. So whether it was to stare at them directly or to hide his face, the purpose was the same: to draw Israel's attention and prompt them to turn back to him.

God still seems to hide his face from Christians today. The analysis conducted in this essay prompts reflection on this question: Could the hiddenness of God still be related to mankind's sin of idolatry today? God was visible to the Israelites when they were in obedience and in relationship with God, but he became invisible when they turned away and worshipped idols. Some idols of the twenty-first-century that seem directly related to the hiddenness of God are secularism and modernity. As legacies of the Enlightenment, secularism and modernity compete with Christianity to provide alternative worldviews. They both have also taught Christians to accept an invisible God as an assumed fact. Furthermore, they have taught Christians to privilege cognitive, abstract knowledge of God over personal, experiential knowledge. Ironically, these "idols" have led to an inability to see God.

Theologian Stephen Pattison has made this same observation, citing post-Enlightenment thought as the root cause of this issue. Regarding Christians who promote this way of thinking, he reflects, "God was then abstract and non-personal, without real presence in the natural material world.

The irrationality and the intrinsic religious reasoning that accompanies thick, revealed religion was eliminated. Figured as invisible, God was easily considered to be non-existent, not a part of the common material world of science and experience" (Pattison 2013, 131). Not pulling any punches, Pattison continues with his sobering assessment of the church's inability to see God: "The upshot of these, and other trends, including widespread secularization, is that God's face has been almost completely lost to sight and to reason. The abstract God of contemporary academic Western theology cannot and never will be seen" (Pattison 2013,133).

But if God still hides his face for the same reasons today as he did for Israel, then the purpose remains the same: his desire for Christians to return and pursue him. "It can be argued that this ambiguity of absence and presence helped create the faith of the Hebrews. Thus it is no longer the presence, but the absence of God that adduces the vision of faith and reassures humans" (Pattison 2013, 157). The frequent depiction of God as an embodied being who relates to humans in the scriptures is hard to ignore. If the pursuit of God and relationship with him is still desired, then God's hidden face should motivate Christians today to seek him even more.

NOTES

1. In the disciplines of theology and biblical studies, debates on the precise nature of God's presence (in contrast to his absence) in the biblical text abound. See Samuel Terrien's 1978 *The Elusive Presence* for an in-depth discussion of presence. For a more recent survey of the debate on presence, see MacDonald and de Hulster 2013. Meanwhile, the problem of divine hiddenness as an obstacle to God's goodness and existence has concerned philosophers and Christian apologists for decades. J. L. Schellenberg's 1993 work *Divine Hiddenness and Human Reason* is considered the landmark book on this topic. Also see Michael Rea's more recent 2018 *The Hiddenness of God* for a more nuanced treatment of the issues at stake.

2. This essay itself will not directly address any of the aforementioned debates because while they have clear overlaps in topic to this essay, the questions being asked are not the same. Rather, the hope is for the reader to hold my essay in tandem with each debate, to see how my conclusions may provide a way forward or even cast a new light on the overlapping issues at stake.

3. The use of analytical tools and insights from the social sciences—mostly in cultural anthropology—has become a dominant feature in biblical studies over the past forty years (see Keady, Klutz, and Strine 2018 discussing the state of social-scientific criticism in biblical studies today). Additionally, Cognitive Metaphor Theory from the social-scientific discipline of cognitive linguistics has also gained interest in biblical studies, particularly in OT studies (see Howe and Green 2014 for the extent to which cognitive linguistics have impacted biblical studies; also see Lakoff and Johnson 1980

on the theory itself). This theory recognizes the extent to which a concept such as *face* is a cognitive metaphor embedded in the Hebrew language. The interest in utilizing social-scientific disciplines such as these in biblical studies has come as a reaction to a growing awareness of the extent to which modern western-centric presuppositions have subconsciously accompanied academic engagement with the biblical text. This is where cultural anthropology and cognitive linguistics have become increasingly successful in mitigating those presuppositions, resulting in new perspectives and insights regarding the biblical text.

4. While *pānîm* is morphologically plural, it is conceptually singular, and thus is the form commonly used to denote its conceptual idea (as opposed to the singular form).

5. This most likely arose from a physicalist understanding of God in early, prebiblical Hebraic tradition.

6. Note: In this essay, "LORD" will be used to translate the tetragrammaton, and "God" will be used for referring to God in general.

7. French sociologist Marcel Mauss' seminal 1954 work *Essai sur le Don* (*The Gift*) is considered the original authority on the concepts of gift-giving in anthropology, still being referenced today in scholarly discussions on social interactions. Specifically, his identification of the three obligatory elements of gift-giving (the obligation to give, to receive, and to repay) have been incorporated into the understanding of God's grace in theological discussions. Cf. Barclay 2015.

8. There is technically one more occurrence of "face to face," but it uses the preposition *bᵉ* instead of *ʿel*. In Deut 5:4, Moses speaks to the Israelites, saying that the LORD spoke to them *pānîm bᵉpānîm*, but that Moses himself still needed to stand between them and the LORD as mediator in that moment because they were afraid of the fire. Thus, this occurrence does not officially count as a true face-to-face occurrence (Chavel 2012, 45).

9. Where the English translation and Masoretic Text versifications differ, the MT verse numbers will be provided in brackets.

10. Later when Jacob reunites with Esau (Gen 33:10), Jacob mentions this divine encounter, referencing the fact that he saw "the face of God." In this conversation with Esau, Jacob acknowledges a connection between his ability to see God's face and being granted his favor and acceptance.

11. Numbers 12:8 is also occasionally cited as a passage where Moses is described being "face to face" with the LORD. Technically, the phrase used here is "mouth to mouth," which is the only time *mouth* is used in a similarly idiomatic manner, and therefore is essentially synonymous with "face to face."

12. Similar to the Jacob narrative discussed earlier, this appearance is considered to be a theophany (Niditch 2008, 90).

13. Incidentally, God's hand and arm are mentioned in 20:33, both descriptions of his embodiment, which lead into the "face to face" reference in 20:35.

14. This idiom is carried over into the New Testament (via the LXX) in Luke 20:21 and Galatians 2:6, where *prosōpon lambanō* becomes the Greek rendering of *nāśāʾ pānîm*. This idiom is even found implicitly in the compound noun *prosōpolēmpsia* meaning partiality (cf. Acts 10:34; Rom. 2:11; Eph. 6:9).

15. The "favor" meaning of *pānîm* was sufficiently widespread that it was also used frequently in interactions between human beings. For example, in both Deut 1:17 and 16:19, *pānîm* is used in Moses' instructions to the Israelites not to show favor or partiality in matters of judgment. In 1 Samuel 25:35, David grants Abigail's request to forgive her husband his transgressions, saying "I lift your face." Here, it is a specific favor being granted, rather than favor in general. Note: In my analysis of these passages, I am assuming the unity of the final form of the text.

16. See Balentine 1983 for an in-depth analysis of the phrase "hide the face" in relation to God in the Old Testament and Fretheim 2002 for a discussion on the wrath of God in the Old Testament. However, the focus of both scholars is on the theological dimensions, with little attention paid to the social dimensions.

17. Isaiah: 89 times; Jeremiah: 128 times; Ezekiel: 155 times, totaling 372 times.

18. The verb used here is *ma'al*, to act unfaithfully. It is also used in Numbers 5:12, 27 regarding marital infidelity.

19. While the majority of English translations render the phrase "forget their shame," the Hebrew verb is *nāśā'* "to lift, carry," which is supported by *lambanō* in the LXX.

20. Balentine also reaches a similar conclusion in his own analysis of Ezekiel 39. "The lament about God's hiddenness is here interpreted as a temporary period of divine judgment, justified because of Israel's unfaithfulness, and followed by forgiveness and restoration" (Balentine 1983, 73).

REFERENCES

Allen, Leslie C. 1990. Ezekiel 20–48. *Word Biblical Commentary*. Dallas: Word Inc.

Balentine, Samuel E. 1983. *The Hidden God.* Oxford: Oxford University Press.

Barclay, John M. G. 2015. *Paul and the Gift.* Grand Rapids: Eerdmans.

Block, Daniel. 1997. The Book of Ezekiel: Chapters 1–24. *The New International Commentary on the Old Testament.* Grand Rapids: Eerdmans.

———. 1998. The Book of Ezekiel: Chapters 25–48. *The New International Commentary on the Old Testament.* Grand Rapids: Eerdmans.

Chavel, Simeon. 2012. "The Face of God and the Etiquette of Eye-Contact: Visitation, Pilgrimage, and Prophetic Vision in Ancient Israelite and Early Jewish Imagination." *Jewish Studies Quarterly* 19: 1–55.

Childs, Brevard. 1974. Exodus: A Commentary. *Old Testament Library.* London: SCM Press Ltd.

Craigie, Peter C. 1976. The Book of Deuteronomy. *The New International Commentary on the Old Testament.* Grand Rapids: Eerdmans.

Douglas, Mary. 1966. *Collected Works, Vol 2: Purity and Danger: An Analysis of Concepts of Pollution and Taboo.* New York: Routledge.

Fretheim, Samuel. 2002. "Theological Reflections on the Wrath of God in the Old Testament." *Horizons in Biblical Theology* 24: 1–26.

Howe, Bonnie, and Joel B. Green, eds. 2014. *Cognitive Linguistic Explorations in Biblical Studies.* Berlin: Walter de Gruyter GmbH & Co KG.

Keady, Jessica M., Todd E. Klutz, and C. A. Strine, eds. 2018. *Scripture as Social Discourse: Social-Scientific Perspectives on Early Jewish and Christian Writings.* London: T&T Clark Biblical Series.

Lakoff, George, and Mark Johnson. 1980. *Metaphors We Live By.* Chicago: University of Chicago Press.

MacDonald, Nathan, and Izaak J. de Hulster, eds. 2013. *Divine Presence and Absence in Exilic and Post-Exilic Judaism.* Tübingen: Mohr Siebeck.

Malina, Bruce. 1981. *The New Testament World: Insights in Cultural Anthropology.* Louisville: Westminster John Knox Press.

Mathews, Kenneth. 2005. Genesis 11:27–50:26. *New American Commentary.* Nashville: B&H Publishing Group.

Mauss, Marcel. 1954. *The Gift.* Translated by Ian Cunnison. London: Cohen & West Ltd.

Niditch, Susan. 2008. Judges: A Commentary. *Old Testament Library.* Louisville: Westminster John Knox Press.

Pattison, Stephen. 2013. *Saving Face: Enfacement, Shame, Theology.* Farnham: Ashgate Publishing Ltd.

Rea, Michael. 2018. *The Hiddenness of God.* Oxford: Oxford University Press.

Schellenberg, J. L. 1993. *Divine Hiddenness and Human Reason.* Ithaca, NY: Cornell University Press.

Terrien, Samuel. 1978. *The Elusive Presence: The Heart of Biblical Theology.* San Francisco: Harper & Row.

Chapter 5

Praying against Enemies

Biblical Precedents, Ethical Reflections, and Suggested Guidelines

Charlie Trimm

Anger is a common topic in the Old Testament, especially divine anger against Israel's enemies and Israel itself. However, in this essay I will examine human anger, specifically the imprecatory psalms that call down divine judgment against an enemy. The first part of this essay will briefly examine these prayers for divine judgment in the Old Testament. The next part of the essay will examine imprecatory psalms in the New Testament to discover if they play any role in the life of Jesus and the early church or if they were condemned. Finally, I will argue for the legitimacy of praying imprecatory psalms today based on the desire to end evildoing in extreme circumstances, offer guidelines for imprecatory prayers, and provide two examples of contemporary imprecatory prayers.[1]

OLD TESTAMENT AND CURSING

Cursing is a common phenomenon in the Old Testament (Trimm 2020). In some cases curses were used as a judgment for a past action. For example, Joshua cursed the people of Gibeon after they deceived the Israelites (Joshua 9:23).[2] However, even in these cases, the curse is also preventative in the sense that the one cursed was separated so as to avoid causing further harm (Scharbert 1974, 408). Anne Marie Kitz describes unconditional curses—her term for judgmental curses—as seeking to "drive away and destroy hostile forces so as to safeguard what is left behind" (Kitz 2014, 246). For example, since the people of Gibeon remained idolaters, the curse separated them from the people of Israel and marked their religion as unauthorized from an Israelite perspective.

However, more commonly curses functioned in a primarily preventive way. For example, a key part of the Mosaic covenant was the blessings and curses, detailing the consequences of the two paths available to the people (Leviticus 26; Deuteronomy 28). If the people followed YHWH, then he promised to prosper them and protect them from their enemies. However, if they rejected YHWH by their actions and attitudes, then he promised to decimate them through nature and their enemies.[3]

Moving on to look at the imprecatory psalms themselves, we see that while their structure varies, they generally include the following parts:

1. A statement of the psalmist's innocence
2. An acknowledgment of the psalmist's weakness
3. A description of the evildoer's actions
4. A call for judgment on the evildoer
5. The rationale for the judgment
6. The goal of the judgment

Several of these aspects are important for comprehending the imprecatory psalms. The acknowledgment of the *psalmist's weakness* reveals dependence upon YHWH: the imprecatory psalms are not a code for a military attack or other kinds of human action undertaken by the psalmist. The *actions of the evildoers* emphasize the basis of the psalmist's anger and the real damage that has been done, both to humans and to the reputation of God. The *rationale for the judgment* is often based in God's promises. For example, in Psalm 74 the psalmist calls on YHWH to destroy the enemy with his right hand (Psalm 74:11) because YHWH should regard the covenant (Psalm 74:20). YHWH had promised to curse those who cursed the Israelites (Genesis 12:3); therefore psalmists were calling on God to keep his promise. Most importantly, the *goal of the judgment* sometimes involves the knowledge of YHWH. While this might entail merely a recognition of a greater power rather than true worship, the goals are suggestive that imprecatory psalms can lead in some cases to the repentance of the evildoer due to their acknowledgment of YHWH.

In spite of what one might initially think, the imprecatory psalms should not be used to demonstrate a general lack of enemy love in the Old Testament, because the Old Testament itself speaks against hating enemies in a variety of places:

You shall not take vengeance or bear a grudge against the sons of your own people, but you shall love your neighbor as yourself: I am the LORD. (Leviticus 19:18)

If you meet your enemy's ox or his donkey going astray, you shall bring it back to him. If you see the donkey of one who hates you lying down under its burden, you shall refrain from leaving him with it; you shall rescue it with him. (Exodus 23:4)

If your enemy is hungry, give him bread to eat, and if he is thirsty, give him water to drink. (Proverbs 25:21)

But seek the welfare of the city where I have sent you into exile, and pray to the LORD on its behalf, for in its welfare you will find your welfare. (Jeremiah 29:7)

These verses raise the question of how imprecatory psalms fit with calls for enemy love. The most conspicuous conflict between imprecatory psalms and enemy love is found in the call to pray for the welfare of Babylon (Jeremiah 29:7) and the prayer for judgment against Babylon (Psalm 137). These two texts are from almost the same time period, but seem completely contradictory. How should they pray for Babylon? Rejecting one or the other options seems unsatisfactory, as does trying to create different audiences or time periods for the texts. In an earlier article I proposed that the ancient Israelite was free to pray both prayers simultaneously.

> The call to pray on behalf of Babylon in Jeremiah 29 that implies a rescue from judgment provides the most likely way to correlate the two texts: the people of Babylon are to turn from their wickedness so as to avoid judgment and live in peace with Judah; if they do not then judgments like those expressed in the imprecatory psalm will come upon them. The exiles were to pray two different kinds of prayers simultaneously and put the matter into God's hands. (Trimm 2020, 33)

NEW TESTAMENT AND CURSING

The topic of imprecatory psalms becomes even more complicated when thinking about the New Testament and contemporary life. Has the coming of Jesus changed the way we pray when we are angry? Should contemporary Christians pray imprecatory prayers? Although many Christians have accepted the ethics of the imprecatory psalms in their Old Testament context, they are more reticent about employing them today.

I will begin by looking at the argument that the New Testament prohibits imprecatory prayers. With the coming of Jesus, Christians have a different relationship with the Old Testament covenants and no longer possess the promise that God will curse their enemies.[4] Jesus also calls on us on to love and pray for our enemies, not curse them. "You have heard that it was said, 'You shall love your neighbor and hate your enemy.' But I say to you, Love your enemies and pray for those who persecute you" (Matthew 5:43–44).[5] Paul expresses a similar thought: "Bless those who persecute you; bless and do not curse them" (Romans 12:14). Jesus and his followers exhibited this attitude in their own life. Jesus prevented an opportunity for an imprecatory prayer when he prohibited James and John from calling for fire from heaven to judge a Samaritan village (Luke 9:54–55). Indeed, he presented a different model when he prayed for forgiveness for those tormenting him on the cross rather than their destruction (Luke 23:34).[6] Stephen prays in a similar fashion at his own death (Acts 7:60). A more theological argument, associated with Dietrich Bonheoffer, views the Old Testament christocentrically and sees the curses of the imprecatory psalms taken on Jesus at the cross. As Paul said, Jesus became a curse for us (Galatians 3:13). Therefore, we have entered a new time in which imprecatory psalms are no longer valid after the cross.

However, others have found that these arguments are not as strong as they first appear (Day 2007; Barker 2016, 127–57). First, while the covenant for Christians has changed with the coming of Christ and the church no longer has a promise that God will curse our enemies, this does not necessarily mean that the principle has changed. The Old Testament covenants reveal to us what YHWH values; in this case the imprecatory psalms remind us that YHWH cares about justice for the powerless. Christians should still be angry with injustice in the world. Second, the mere presence of the enemy love commands does not preclude the employment of imprecatory prayers. As we saw earlier the Old Testament itself contains many references to enemy love, including even praying for the enemy. When Jesus commanded his followers to love their enemies, this should not have been a shocking new teaching for them.

Third, the New Testament itself contains imprecatory prayers. While Jesus avoided imprecatory prayers at times, on other occasions he called down woes and accepted the imprecatory prayers of his followers (Nehrbass 2013, 138–39). During the Passion Week, Jesus cursed a fig tree; while it was only a fig tree, it symbolically works at a higher level in the narrative because it represents Israel (Matthew 21:18–19). Later, Jesus called down a series of woes on the scribes and Pharisees (Matthew 23). When the disciples went to a city that would not listen to them, they were to symbolize their rejection of the city by shaking the dust off their feet when they left the city, and Jesus pronounced a curse on the city by stating that it would be worse for them than for Sodom and Gomorrah (Matthew 10:14–15). Closer to the form of an Old Testament imprecatory prayer is Paul's prayer against Elymas the magician, who was struck with blindness (Acts 13:10–11). More generically, Paul calls down a curse on those who would corrupt the gospel (Galatians 1:8–9) and promises that God would repay Alexander the coppersmith for his evil deeds (2 Timothy 4:14). Jude records the odd story of Michael calling on God to rebuke the Devil (Jude 9). Finally, the martyred saints in Revelation call down vengeance on those who killed them: "O Sovereign Lord, holy and true, how long before you will judge and avenge our blood on those who dwell on the earth?" (Revelation 6:9–11).

Fourth, Paul's prohibition of cursing is also not as straightforward as it first appears. Later in the same chapter he encourages his readers to leave vengeance to God, which is precisely the call of an imprecatory prayer: "Beloved, never avenge yourselves, but leave it to the wrath of God, for it is written, 'Vengeance is mine, I will repay, says the Lord'" (Romans 12:19). The word Paul uses for curse can be employed both positively and negatively; for example, it is the word used in the LXX (the Greek translation of the Old Testament) for the cursing YHWH promised he would do to Israel's enemies in the Abrahamic covenant (Genesis 12:1–3). Therefore, Paul is prohibiting selfish and ungodly cursing (Proverbs 30:11; James 3:9), not all cursing.[7]

Fifth, seeing Jesus as becoming the curse for us is a helpful way to connect the work of Jesus with some of the more difficult parts of the Old Testament, similar to the connection some have made between Jesus and *herem*, the dedication of something or someone to God, such as the Canaanites, often through destruction (Park 2007). However, such a reading is made less likely when it is noted that the New Testament itself does not make such a connection. It also might overuse the practice of seeing Jesus in various texts—perhaps not every single text is about Jesus—or ignore other ways of seeing Jesus in them, such as seeing Jesus in the imprecatory psalms as YHWH who is bringing justice.

In conclusion, I believe that imprecatory prayers can continue to be prayed even after the incarnation of Jesus. YHWH's anger over injustice has not diminished and we should continue to request that YHWH act on behalf of the oppressed.

CONTEMPORARY IMPRECATORY PRAYERS

The final portion of the essay will deal with the question of contemporary imprecatory prayers. Are they a valid way to express anger today? Following the church fathers, C. S. Lewis provides one way forward through his suggestion that we read them by interpreting the wicked as our own wickedness.[8]

From this point of view I can use even the horrible passage in [Psalm] 137 about dashing the Babylonian babies against the stones. I know things in the inner world which are like babies; the infantile beginnings of small indulgences, small resentments, which may one day become dipsomania or settled hatred, but which woo us and wheedle us with special pleadings and seem so tiny, so helpless that in resisting them we feel we are being cruel to animals. They begin whimpering to us "I don't ask much, but," or "I had at least hoped," or "you owe yourself *some* consideration." Against all such pretty infants (the dears have such winning ways) the advice of the Psalm is the best. Knock the little bastards' brains out. And "blessed" he who can, for it's easier said than done. (Lewis 1958, 136)[9]

I think that this is a valid reading of the imprecatory psalms: before we pray an imprecatory prayer against someone else, the initial part of the imprecatory psalms in which the psalmist proclaims their innocence must be taken seriously, following a common biblical theme of examining ourselves before we address the sins of others (Matthew 7:1–5). The literary context of the church discipline passage in Matthew 18 nicely illustrates this as well: a call to humility and self-examination (18:1–9) before church discipline (18:15–20).

However, can we go further than an allegorical reading and pray an imprecatory psalm against another person? John Goldingay has argued that an allegorical view has the potential to tame the imprecatory psalm and prevent us from seeing injustice, especially injustice done by us and "our group." For example, he highlights the imperial actions being done by the British empire at the time Lewis was writing: "There is a link between Lewis' avoidance of the literal meaning of Psalm 137 and the postcolonial implications of the psalm (as we would now put it), but an allegorical interpretation of the psalm avoids these implications" (Goldingay 2015, 115–16).

What we can say without hesitation is that God still cares about justice and that Christians should pray that justice be done in the world. Where it gets more complicated is how that justice is brought about. I propose that imprecatory prayer is a viable option for Christians today: in cases of extreme evil, Christians should pray that God stop the evildoer from committing further evil. As part of this prayer, we can provide God with a variety of ways of accomplishing this goal: either through divine judgment or through conversion of the evil person.[10] This would follow my proposal for understanding the imprecatory prayer against Babylon in Psalm 137 in the context of Jeremiah's call for the peace of Babylon in Jeremiah 29: the exiles could pray for both and leave the matter in God's hands.

I realize that this prayer appears two-faced: we are requesting that God either judge someone or save them. But these two seemingly diametrically opposed options are held together by the core request that the evildoing be stopped. We do not dictate to God how that should be accomplished, but we implore him, whatever he decides, to stop the evil from continuing. This kind of "methodological ambivalence" also helps to calm the concerns some have about praying imprecatory psalms against individuals. For example, while he sees a place for the imprecatory psalm today, Jerome Creach prohibits us from praying them against individuals because the individual might repent and be saved (Creach 2013, 215). This would also account for the unease of Sunday Bobai Agang, who rebuked the imprecatory prayer of his teacher by immediately praying for the salvation of those enemies (Agang 2017, 42–43).

GOALS FOR IMPRECATORY PRAYERS

When thinking about contemporary imprecatory prayers, we need to articulate the goals of such prayers. First, one goal is the honest expression of one's anger through the form of an imprecatory psalm. When dealing with trauma it can be beneficial to voice one's emotions instead of keeping it bottled up inside (Silva 2001; Hankle 2010; Nehrbass 2013, 147–73). In a conversation with Bono, the lead singer of U2, about the Psalms, Eugene Peterson refers to praying the imprecatory psalms as "cussing without cussing" (*Bono and Eugene Peterson: The Psalms* [2016]). In psychological terms, this point can be related to attachment theory.[11] The divine covenants provided a context for God to assume the role of a secure base for explorative behavior. The imprecatory psalms keenly illustrate, in its full stark reality, what a deeply secure attachment might look like between God and his child. Because of God's uninhibited and longstanding commitment to his people as evidenced by the covenants, God's people enjoy both the privilege of maintaining relational proximity with him and the freedom to explore and make sense of the world around them—which evidently includes the full spectrum of their emotional landscape, regardless of how repulsive these emotions may seem at the moment.[12]

The one praying can reflect honestly on their feelings to YHWH, even if they find such feelings reprehensible. In some cases, verbalizing the imprecatory prayer will help us become conscious of the evil of our own hearts, and a further prayer should be offered that God would change the feelings of the one praying (Volf 2019, 124–25). Naturally, an imprecatory prayer should not necessarily be offered every time one has a negative thought about someone: many psalms, such as Psalm 62, refer to the evil deeds of the enemies without also calling for YHWH to curse them (Pemberton 2012, 126–27). If verbalizing anger through an imprecatory prayer will make the one praying bitter, then it should be avoided.

Second, the other possible goal of praying imprecatory psalms is for inspiring anger during those times when one does not feel angry about injustice. The psalms not only reflect our emotions, but also teach us about how we should feel. Especially for those who live in a privileged sociocultural context, praying the imprecatory psalms teaches them to remember that other Christians face injustice and that as part of the body of Christ they should participate in some limited way in their pain. Given the complicity of the Western church in racism, Esau McCaulley has appealed to the imprecatory psalms in his call for the church to contend for justice.

> Psalm 137 is trauma literature, the rage of those who lived. The question isn't why the Psalmist wrote this. The question is what kind of song would the families of Ahmaud Arbery, George Floyd and Eric Garner be tempted to write after watching the video of their deaths? It would be raw and unfiltered. But more than an expression of rage, this psalm is a written record in time. It is a call to remember. This psalm, and the other psalms of rage, require us to remember the trauma that led to their composition. (McCaulley 2020)

The imprecatory psalms can also remind the privileged that many throughout the world might view them as the enemy, and thus cause them to examine themselves (Pemberton 2012, 130–32, 144–46). This would particularly be the case for white evangelicals who are complicit in allowing systemic racism to continue by not addressing the issue.[13]

GUIDELINES FOR IMPRECATORY PRAYERS

If it is legitimate to pray imprecatory psalms today, it will be helpful to provide a few general guidelines for thinking about the appropriate times to pray such prayers and how to pray them. These guidelines would be relevant for all imprecatory prayers, but especially for public imprecatory psalms because of their influence on those listening. The Old Testament gives some precedence for offering public imprecatory prayers since the imprecatory psalms appear to be public statements, but not every occasion is appropriate for a public imprecatory psalm. On the one hand, those who can make a prayer public are typically the ones who have power, precisely the kind of people who should not be praying imprecatory psalms. On the other hand, one can have a certain kind of power but still be powerless in a particular situation or system of oppression (many civil rights leaders are good examples). The two goals mentioned above of expressing anger and inspiring anger would be equally valid for both private and public imprecatory psalms.

I will propose four guidelines. First, *we must be careful with analyzing our motives*. Since a common theme throughout the Bible is dealing seriously with our own sin before addressing the sins of others, we must carefully examine ourselves (though we must also avoid the danger of excessive self-introspection). We should also be cautious about our goal of praying an imprecatory prayer. On the one hand, we must remember that God desires justice and that evildoers must be punished. This theme can be found in many places throughout the Bible, but the book of Nahum is a good example of a serious evildoer—the Assyrian empire in this case—punished by God. However, God might decide to save the evildoer, and we must rejoice with God at that kind of answer to prayer as well. Jonah would have loved to have written the book of Nahum, but YHWH had other plans for the Assyrians at that time. When we pray imprecatory prayers, we must be ready for either answer that God might provide us with. Since our own motives are sometimes difficult for us to analyze, it is good to get counsel from trusted advisors before praying an imprecatory prayer publicly (LeMon 2010). It would be particularly beneficial to gather input from those in other cultural situations—preferably in less powerful situations than our own—to help remove our own blind spots. As noted above, sometimes praying an imprecatory prayer also helps us to see the fault in our own motives.

Second, churches need to *read and preach on the imprecatory psalms* before one is prayed publicly. Since they are little-known in most churches in the United States, a pastor cannot pray an imprecatory prayer on a Sunday morning without instructing the people beforehand about the historical context of imprecatory psalms and their use today (DeClaissé-Walford 2010, 90–92). Cultural background might play a role in this decision; one study of a group of evangelical Africans found that 71 percent of them had considered calling down a curse on someone when they were mistreated (Broadhurst 2004, 61–62). Likewise, David Adamo argues that in an African context many people will go to a witch doctor or an herbalist when faced with oppression; the use of an imprecatory psalm would perform the same function within a Christian worldview (Adamo 2008).[14]

Third, imprecatory prayers—especially those expressed publicly—should be *focused on serious and ongoing sin*. These prayers are to be prayed for evildoers who continue to commit serious sin against other humans, what John Day calls "extreme ethics" (Day 2007, 14–15). These prayers are not for those who have been captured by the authorities or who have already confessed their wrongdoing. Since many in the Western world occupy a privileged sociocultural position, they must be cautious about their own definition of what is an injustice worthy of an imprecatory prayer (Nehrbass 2013, 53–74).

Within the guidelines enumerated here, the category of serious and ongoing sin that we should be angry about include a wide variety of sins. Obvious examples would include terrorism, violence and corruption perpetuated by the mob, brutal acts of racism, and murder and rape perpetrated by people who remain at large and continue to practice their evil deeds. Leaders of foreign nations who consistently mistreat their people in horrific ways would qualify, though we must become increasingly more cautious about motives as we interact with international politics. Powerful men who abuse their positions of authority in our own country could potentially be in this category, such as those who commit blatant war crimes or employ torture.[15]

The use of imprecatory prayers in areas of serious institutional and systemic evil is less clear. These sins are not centered in a few individuals, but are perpetuated by a general culture-wide attitude. In these cases perhaps the judgment in the imprecatory prayer would focus on an oppressive institution, matching the kind of sin being challenged. For example, an imprecatory prayer could be about a racist police department, asking God to bring peace to the community by either judging the department in some way or reforming it out of its racism. Whatever form these imprecatory prayers might take, their ability to focus appropriate anger on injustice is invaluable.

Fourth, these prayers are to be *prayed from a position of powerlessness* (Creach 2013, 214). The prayers are not a request that God would empower the one praying to judge the evildoer themselves, as the prayer itself is a renunciation of personal violence against the evildoer. Zenger frames the issue this way: "these psalms are contextually legitimate on the lips of the victims, but a blasphemy in the mouths of the executioners" (Zenger 1996, 85). One of the dangers of public imprecatory psalms is that they could potentially inspire others to attempt to achieve the goal of the imprecatory psalm violently themselves, when it is not their place to do so.[16] However, church leaders should emphasize how a focus on one's own weakness entails Christians restraining themselves from violent reactions against the evil-doers.

CONCLUSION

In sum, the imprecatory psalms in the Old Testament remind readers of YHWH's promises to protect his people and his anger against injustice. On a human level, they provide a script for bringing our own anger over injustice to God. The New Testament continues the call for injustice to be stopped and provides further grounds for praying imprecatory prayers. Based on the biblical precedents I propose that we as Christians today are permitted to pray imprecatory prayers against cases of extreme evil, but with the important caveat that we must leave the matter in YHWH's hands. If YHWH brings repentance to the enemy and thus stops the injustice, then we must not react with anger as Jonah did, but praise God for answering our prayer. In a world full of injustice, we are to bring the things that make us angry to him and allow him to act as he deems best.

EXAMPLE IMPRECATORY PRAYERS

I will close the essay with two examples of contemporary imprecatory prayers. The first prayer was written in 2014 by someone who interacted with refugees affected by ISIS.

An Iraqi family huddles in their living room with curtains drawn. The parents hold their children close, and their stomachs ache because death is in the street and they want to run but they are trapped and it is just a matter of when and how. Their outer gate is marked with a swipe of paint, a single Arabic letter. They are the marked ones. Pure evil is seeping through their city—black flags bringing executions in public squares, this done by men to whom such actions bring happy sneers, their life goal somehow brought closer. My stomach feels sick and I weep, for the Body is bleeding and what else can I do when part of me is being hacked off?

God, I have prayed that you would smite these evildoers as you once did 185,000 Assyrians who came against Israel. You sent the angel of the LORD on a manhunt and exterminated a deadly threat without your people lifting a finger. Won't you do that now? Don't you love these Iraqi brothers and sisters just as much? Aren't they as precious in your sight?

How long, O LORD? Will you forget your Arab church? You say you will right all wrongs someday, but what about intervening now? Will you allow your church to be destroyed in Iraq? Is there any way a human institution or government can be your just sword and strike on your behalf?

Or must we simply weep with them and pray that they will die well and stay faithful to the end? Christ, have mercy. Give them grace—supernatural grace and peace. I don't know how it's possible to have peace in the face of this, but give your people the ability to stand firm, to forgive and even to love their enemies. And if need be, give them grace to go like lambs to the slaughter, for the glory of the Lamb.

Father, I pray for each man of the Islamic State. You have commanded us, your followers, to live differently than the world. You tell us to love and pray for even men like these. So I pray that you will reveal the deception they are bound by, that you will work powerfully to disarm them—perhaps even through the witness of these they kill. Stop them with the power of your love.

Are these perhaps the last days, Jesus? Even so, come quickly.[17]

The second prayer comes from a series of psalms that have been rewritten from the perspective of a pastor from Namibia. The psalms date to the mid-1980s, when South Africa had recently begun employing apartheid principles in the country (Kameeta 1986, 33, 37–38).

Psalm 54

Save Africa by your power, O God; set her free by your might.

Hear our prayer, O God; listen to our words.

People who regard themselves as superior to us are coming to attack us;

Cruel men are killing our sons and daughters and our old people—

Men who call themselves Christians, yet do not care about God.

But God is our helper; the Lord is our defender;

He will destroy their evil plans because of his faithfulness.

I will gladly offer my life in your service for the liberation of those who suffer.

I will give you thanks because you are good.

You will rescue us from our troubles and we will see our enemies defeated!

Psalm 68 (portion)

Show your power, O God, the power you have used on our behalf.

Rebuke the regime that works evil and destruction;

Rebuke those nations who supply it with weapons to kill the people,

Until they bow down before you and repent.

NOTES

1. This essay began as a research project during spring 2016 for the Center for Christian Thought at Biola University. My thanks to the John Templeton Foundation for the funding to make this research possible.

2. Other examples include Noah's cursing of Canaan (Genesis 9:25), the curse on Meroz for not helping the other tribes (Judges 5:23), and Elisha's curse involving the bears (2 Kings 2:24).

3. Other preventative curses include Joshua's curse on the one who would rebuild Jericho (Joshua 6:26), the curse on the one who would give a wife to Benjamin (Judges 21:18), and Saul's curse on the one who ate before evening (1 Samuel 14:24).

4. Older dispensationalists could easily solve the ethical problem of the imprecatory psalms by assigning them to the old dispensation that we are no longer under as Christians. However, more recent dispensationalists have rejected this solution; for example, see Laney 1981 in the journal *Bibliotheca Sacra*, published by the dispensational school Dallas Theological Seminary.

5. As an example of this view, Christopher Hays concludes his article about the imprecatory psalm in Psalm 137 in this way: "And what are the Beatitudes, then, if not a divine reassessment of Psalm 137:8–9?" (Hays 2005, 55).

6. However, the manuscript evidence for this clause is suspect.

7. This parallels the difference between legitimate and illegitimate curses in the ancient Near East. The former were public and designed to prevent or stop harm, while the latter were private and sought only private advantage; see Althann 1992 (3–4).

8. For a brief survey of this reading of the imprecatory psalms among the church fathers, see Thompson 2007 (54–56). For a contemporary defense of this position from an Eastern Orthodox scholar, see Mihăilă 2012. See also the defense of an allegorical reading (while at the same time condemning their violence directed against humans) in Boyd 2017 (1095–97).

9. See the theme also in Zenger 1996 (84–86); Hays 2005 (54–55).

10. For more on including requests for conversion in contemporary imprecatory psalms, see Nehrbass 2013 (64–65).

11. The material here on attachment theory draws on Wang and Trimm 2013.

12. This call for honest prayer is emphasized in Carney 1983.

13. For an overview of the history of complicity in this area in the church in the United States, see Tisby 2019.

14. However, this should not be seen as unanimous; for a recent argument against the contemporary use of imprecatory psalms from an African perspective, see Agang 2017.

15. However, counsel would be needed in such cases when dealing with government officials in light of such texts as Romans 13:1–4 and 1 Peter 2:13–15, which call for submission to government, especially given the terrible atrocities committed by the Roman government leaders at the time of the writing of these books.

16. For example, after Gordon Klingenschmitt prayed an imprecatory psalm against Mikey Weinstein (who was seeking to remove religion from the United States military), Weinstein received a series of threats. For details, see Brayton 2009; Zubeck 2014.

17. Prayer used with permission of author.

REFERENCES

Adamo, David Tuesday. 2008. "Reading Psalm 109 in African Christianity." *Old Testament Essays* 21: 575–92.

Althann, Robert. 1992. "The Psalms of Vengeance against Their Ancient Near Eastern Background." *Journal of Northwest Semitic Languages* 18: 1–11.

Agang, Sunday Bobai. 2017. *No More Cheeks to Turn?* Bukuru: Hippo.

Barker, Kit. 2016. *Imprecation as Divine Discourse: Speech Act Theory, Dual Authorship, and Theological Interpretation.* JTISup 16. Winona Lake: Eisenbrauns.

Bono and Eugene Peterson: The Psalms. 2016. Fuller Studio. https://www.youtube.com/watch?v=-l40S5e90KY.

Boyd, Gregory A. 2017. *Crucifixion of the Warrior God: Interpreting the Old Testament's Violent Portraits of God in Light of the Cross.* 2 vols. Minneapolis: Fortress.

Brayton, Ed. 2009. "Klingenschmitt Prays for Death of Weinstein, Lynn." *Dispatches from the Creation Wars* (blog). April 27, 2009. http://scienceblogs.com/dispatches/2009/04/27/klingenschmitt-prays-for-death/.

Broadhurst, Jace R. 2004. "Should Cursing Continue? An Argument for Imprecatory Psalms in Biblical Theology." *Africa Journal of Evangelical Theology* 23: 61–89.

Carney, Sheila. 1983. "God Damn God: A Reflection on Expressing Anger in Prayer." *Biblical Theology Bulletin* 13: 116–20.

Creach, Jerome F. D. 2013. *Violence in Scripture.* Interpretation. Louisville: Westminster John Knox.

Day, John N. 2007. *Crying for Justice: What the Psalms Teach Us about Mercy and Vengeance in an Age of Terrorism.* Grand Rapids: Kregel.

DeClaissé-Walford, Nancy L. 2010. "The Theology of the Imprecatory Psalms." In *Soundings in the Theology of Psalms*, edited by Rolf Jacobson, 77–92. Minneapolis: Fortress.

Goldingay, John. 2015. *Do We Need the New Testament? Letting the Old Testament Speak for Itself.* Downers Grove: InterVarsity.

Hankle, Dominick D. 2010. "The Therapeutic Implications of the Imprecatory Psalms in the Christian Counseling Setting." *Journal of Psychology & Theology* 38: 275–80.

Hays, Christopher B. 2005. "How Shall We Sing? Psalm 137 in Historical and Canonical Context." *Horizons in Biblical Theology* 27: 35–55.

Kameeta, Zephania. 1986. *Why, O Lord? Psalms and Sermons from Namibia.* Geneva: World Council of Churches.

Kitz, Anne Marie. 2014. *Cursed Are You! The Phenomenology of Cursing in Cuneiform and Hebrew Texts.* Winona Lake: Eisenbrauns.

Laney, J. Carl. 1981. "A Fresh Look at the Imprecatory Psalms." *Bibliotheca Sacra* 138: 35–45.

LeMon, Joel M. 2010. "Saying Amen to Violent Psalms: Patterns of Prayer, Belief and Action in the Psalter." In *Soundings in the Theology of Psalms*, edited by Rolf Jacobson, 93–110. Minneapolis: Fortress.

Lewis, C. S. 1958. *Reflections on the Psalms.* New York: Harcourt, Brace & World.

McCaulley, Esau. 2020. "What the Bible Has to Say about Black Anger." *The New York Times,* June 14, 2020. https://www.nytimes.com/2020/06/14/opinion/george-floyd-psalms-bible.html.

Mihăilă, Alexandru. 2012. "The Prayer against the Enemies: A Hermeneutical Problem in the Orthodox Exegesis." *Sacra Scripta* 10: 223–41.

Nehrbass, Daniel Michael. 2013. *Praying Curses: The Therapeutic and Preaching Value of the Imprecatory Psalms*. Eugene: Pickwick.

Park, Hyung Dae. 2007. *Finding Herem?: A Study of Luke-Acts in the Light of Herem*. Library of New Testament Studies 357. London: T&T Clark.

Pemberton, Glenn. 2012. *Hurting with God: Learning to Lament with the Psalms*. Abilene, TX: Abilene Christian University Press.

Scharbert, Josef, ררא. [1974] 2003. *Theological Dictionary of the Old Testament (TDOT)*, 11 vol., edited by G. Johannes Botterweck and Helmer Ringgren. Grand Rapids: 1:406–18.

Silva, Larry. 2001. "The Cursing Psalms as a Source of Blessing." In *Psalms and Practice*, edited by Stephen Breck Reid, 220–30. Collegeville, MN: Liturgical Press.

Thompson, John L. 2007. *Reading the Bible with the Dead: What You Can Learn from the History of Exegesis That You Can't Learn from Exegesis Alone*. Grand Rapids: Eerdmans.

Tisby, Jemar. 2019. *The Color of Compromise: The Truth about the American Church's Complicity in Racism*. Grand Rapids: Zondervan.

Trimm, Charlie. 2020. "Praying for the Peace or Destruction of Babylon? The Intersection of Enemy Love and Imprecatory Psalms in the Old Testament." *Criswell Theological Review* 17: 13–33.

Volf, Miroslav. 2019. *Exclusion and Embrace: A Theological Exploration of Identity, Otherness, and Reconciliation*. 2nd ed. Nashville: Abingdon.

Wang, David, and Charlie Trimm. 2013. "C. S. Lewis and the Imprecatory Psalms." In *The Christian Mind of C. S. Lewis*, 135–49. 2013 Biola Faculty Integration Seminar. La Mirada, CA: Biola University.

Zenger, Erich. 1996. *A God of Vengeance? Understanding the Psalms of Divine Wrath*. Louisville, KY: Westminster John Knox.

Zubeck, Pam. 2014. "Updates on Mikey, Klingenschmitt." *Indy Blog* (blog). December 1, 2014. http://www.csindy.com/IndyBlog/archives/2014/12/01/updates-on-mikey-klingenschmitt.

Chapter 6

Aquinas on Anger

Matthew R. Boulter

In our contemporary culture in the West, most people regard anger as an emotion. Yet *emotion* (in its current usage) is a modern concept. Indeed, as one commentator writes:

> Thomas never wrote about emotion. He wrote about appetites, passions, affections, *habitus*, virtues, vices, grace, and many other subjects that relate to the contemporary category of emotion, but the word "emotion" has no direct parallel in the Latin vocabulary of the thirteenth century. (Lombardo 2011, 15)

In this essay however I will present the concept of *the passions*, or, as it occurs more frequently in the *Summa Theologiae*, "passion" (singular, and best translated into English without the definite article[1]), as tantamount to that of *emotion*, since this category includes the treatment of such phenomena as love, hatred, delight, sorrow, pain, hope, despair, and fear. Also in this list appears the emotion or the passion (in addition to others) of *anger*.

While all these phenomena are regarded by us contemporaries as emotions,[2] one must also remember, as we will see below, that for Aquinas anger is not only a passion, but also a vice. Hence he treats anger at two distinct *loci* in the *Summa*: anger as passion is treated in questions 46–48 of the *Prima Secundae* (known as "the Treatise on the Passions") and anger as a vice in question 158 of the *Secunda Secundae* (immersed in a long list of questions dealing with the cardinal virtues).

In this essay I hope to address the concept of *anger* in Aquinas by first treating Thomistic passion in general, then his view of anger as a specific passion, and finally Thomistic virtue and vice in general and anger as a vice in particular.

THOMISTIC PASSION IN GENERAL

For Aquinas, human psychology—conceived in Aristotelian terms largely on the basis of the Stagirite's *De Anima*—is rooted in metaphysics at the broadest possible scale. To see this one must note that in *Summa* I.5,[3] the angelic doctor establishes that being is convertible with the good (everything that exists is good, and everything that is good exists in reality), and that the good, by definition, is that which is desirable, or "appetible." Hence all existing things (at least in the realm of the sub-lunar)—rocks, plants, animals, humans—are characterized by desire or appetite: they all strive toward their perfection/fulfillment/*telos* in and as the good (Aquinas 2012a, I 1–70, Q. 5, 43–52). Further, in accordance with Aquinas' (adoption of Aristotle's version of the) tripartite schematization of the human soul, the particular version of desire which rational animals manifest is triple: with plants we are marked by *natural* appetite (in the nutritive or vegetative part of the soul); with brutes we are characterized by *sense* (or sensual) appetite in the middle (or appetitive) portion of the soul; uniquely as humans (again among sub-lunar creatures) we manifest *intellectual* appetite in the highest, or rational, part of the soul. Aquinas names this last "level" of appetite "will" (*voluntas*).

Yet it is not the highest part or "level" of the soul in which the rational animal experiences passion, for it is the *sense* appetite (in the middle portion of the soul, shared with nonrational animals) that, when apprehending an object imbued with intention, "may respond with a passion" (Lombardo 2011, 25). According to Aquinas:

> A passion is . . . [a] movement of the sense appetite, a passive power, from dormancy to act, in response to the apprehension of an object to which the sense appetite is inclined. (Aquinas 2012b, I–II 1–70: 22.3–3, 226–29; 41.1, 377–78; 45.2, 402–3)

In line with the earlier point about the metaphysical structure of the passions (as a special case of desire), Aquinas insists (in opposition to the Stoics but with Augustine) that the passions are necessarily, in and of themselves, ontologically good. If a person is vicious, say he is an alcoholic or a sex addict or a tyrannical ruler, this is not the fault of the passions. For the passions have a very strict and limited "sphere of competence": their "function is not to decide upon a course of action; the function of the passions is to respond to stimuli and prompt the human person to act according to the face value of those stimuli" (Lombardo 2011, 41).

It is the role of *reason* to "decide upon a course of action":

The passions defer to the judgement of reason, because only the rational appetite naturally tends toward conformity with reason. When rational analysis concludes that acting on a certain prompting of the passions is not conducive to the attainment of our final end, the passions have not failed to offer reliable guidance: they have provided precisely the sort of first-order response and motivation that is their sphere of competence. (Lombardo 2011, 41)

Aquinas organizes or classifies the passions according to their respective objects. These objects, however, are not simply identical to physical objects in the world, that is, to concrete, hylomorphic particulars of form and matter. Rather, they are formal or intentional objects (Lombardo 2011, 49). In other words, the object of any passion is "the object as it is apprehended through an intention" (Lombardo 2011, 49).

On the basis of these objects Aquinas identifies eleven basic types of passion: love, desire, joy, hate, aversion, sadness, hope, daring, despair, fear, and anger. These eleven specific passions, in turn, are subdivided into two overall classes of passion—the concupiscible and the irascible—which are *also* based on a kind of distinction between objects. The concupiscible "power" attends to objects of pleasure or pain and comes to *rest* in them (Lombardo 2011, 52). Here, in the case of the concupiscible powers, the relation between the faculty or power[4] of the soul and the object is relatively unmediated and direct: it is a simple matter of pleasure or pain *in the object itself*. A five-year-old child wants a piece of candy; a gardener runs away from a threatening wasp.

On the irascible side of the divide, however, things are a bit more complicated. For here, the object to which the soul or the power attends is tinged by some kind of obstacle or barrier to the state desired; the irascible power of the soul thus seeks a kind of *utility*, as opposed to a pleasure (or avoidance of pain), simply speaking. So for example, if St. George (of the medieval legend) "concupiscibly" desires the virgin princess for her beauty, he does so even as he "irascibly" desires to eliminate the dragon, it being a barrier or obstacle to his more immediate desire for (something like) pleasure in the form of the beautiful princess. To state it differently, if George longs to *rest* in the arms of the princess (the object of his concupiscible desire or passion) then he must eliminate the dragon. The dragon is not the object of his desire, even of his irascible desire. His *only* object of desire—both "concupiscibly" and "irascibly"—is the princess. Yet she is seen under different "aspects" (Lat. *species*), and so we can say that the one concrete particular that is the princess actually becomes two *intentional* objects for George. One might say, then, that the concupiscible passions fix upon an object of appetitive *pleasure*, while the irascible passions attend to an object of appetitive *utility* (Lombardo 2011, 52n10). One can now see why Aquinas characterizes the irascible passions as "second-order," in the sense that they are derivative of the more "first-order" passions for rest in an object, for example an object which is pleasurable (Aquinas 2012b, I–II 1–70: 23.1, 231–33; 25.1, 245–47; 40.1, 367–68).

Many readers will discern a slight (even subconscious) degree of aversion or distaste for these terms (in their English substantival forms), "concupiscence" and "irascibility." Especially in terms of the former, such negative connotations ought to be eliminated and ignored in the present context. While "concupiscence" does, indeed, derive from a technical—and pejorative— meaning assigned to it by Augustine, and while "irascibility" does derive from the Latin root "*ira*," or "anger," these terms (in their Latin, adjectival forms) were nevertheless simply adopted and carried over from William of Moerbeke's translation of Aristotle's *epithumetikê* and *thumetikê*.

Marie-Dominique Chenu, O.P., the towering twentieth-century commentator on Aquinas, makes the point well:

> The passions of the wise are not extinguished, but on the contrary maintain their full force. In the ideal order, both emotional and spiritual pleasures should attain their full intensity in ways radically different from the seductions of cheap excitement. True delight never experiences the bitter deception of sensual excess that fails to satisfy for long. True pleasure is not a useless and dubious accompaniment of indifferent acts, but rather the sign of . . . happiness. In such happiness, the freedom of the sons and daughters of God is expressed. (Chenu 2002, 106)

Not only are the irascible passions, like Plato's *thumos* (White 2002, 109), "second-order," they also fixate on an object that is "arduous" (Lat. *arduum*). This simply means that the object is "hard to get" or difficult to obtain. Being difficult to obtain, it will require the overcoming of some obstacle or barrier in order for the agent to acquire it.

> The irascible passions concern the interests of the concupiscible passions in the face of some difficulty: namely, the attainment of future goods (hope and despair), the avoidance or overcoming of future evils (daring and fear), and the elimination of present evils (anger). (Lombardo 2011, 62)

And yet one should keep in mind that it is not the *obstacle or barrier* which is the object of the passion; it is not the case that the passion simply or directly wants to eliminate the barrier. Rather, the passion, here as in the case of the concupiscible passions, takes as its object the that which it desires (or seeks to avoid). It is just that the object is now regarded under a different aspect: as *arduus*, or difficult to obtain (or repel), due to the intervening obstacle or barrier.

THOMISTIC ANGER AS A SPECIFIC PASSION

Within the "Treatise on the Passions" (comprising questions 22–48 of the *Prima Secundae*), Aquinas dedicates three questions to the topic of anger (QQ. 46–48), for a total of sixteen distinct articles. In this section of my essay, I will limit myself to what I take to be the highlights of Aquinas' treatment of anger.

While Aquinas offers a strict definition of anger nowhere within these three articles, he does come close with the following statement: "When a man is angry, he wishes to be avenged upon someone," someone who, it turns out, is a "noxious person" (Aquinas 2012b, I–II 1–70: 46.2, 409).

In the lengthier-than-usual *respondeo* section of article II ("Whether the Object of Anger Is Good or Evil"), Aquinas has an interesting discussion of the object(s) of anger. Consider the cases of the passions of love (treated in QQ. 26–28) and hatred (QQ. 29), both of which are simpler than anger, since they each have a single "directionality" of object. In the case of love, "we wish for some good to be in [the loved one]," whereas hatred desires "an evil" [*malum*] to be in, or inflicted upon, a "noxious person [*hominem novicum*]."[5] Love desires something the good for the good (person); hate desires the bad for the bad (person). Love's object involves a "double good," you might say, whereas that of hate a "double bad."

In the case of anger, however, things are more complicated, for here there are always "two directionalities" in view, for "when a man is angry, he wishes to be avenged on someone."

Hence the movement of anger has a twofold tendency: viz., to vengeance itself, which it desires and hopes for as being a good, wherefore it takes pleasure in it;

and to the person on whom it seeks vengeance, as to something contrary and hurtful, which bears the character of evil. (Aquinas 2012b, I–II 1–70: 46.2, 409)

Here, in the case of anger, there is a contrariety within the desires outcome of object: something good (vengeance) inflicted on someone bad, or at least perceived to be bad (a "noxious person").

THOMISTIC VICE IN GENERAL AND ANGER IN PARTICULAR

Thomistic Virtue in General

Before we can discuss what Aquinas regards as vice as such, we must say some things about *virtue*, for Aquinas sees vice as a lack of virtue (just as, at a more general level, all evil is seen as the privation of the good).[6] Vice, that is, is defined in terms of virtue.

Aquinas thinks that, at is most fundamental, virtue is a *habitus* (Aquinas 2012b, I–II 1–70: 55.1, 483). Derived from the Latin *habere* (to have), Aquinas states:

> If to have be taken according as a thing has a relation in regard to itself or something else . . . a habit is a quality; since this mode of having is in respect of some quality . . . and of this the philosopher says that habit is a disposition whereby that which is disposed is disposed well or ill, and this, either in regard to itself or in regard to another . . . [and] thus health is a habit. (Aquinas 2012b, I–II 1–70: 49.1, 432)

This term *habitus* translates the Aristotle's *hexis*, treated extensively in the *Nicomachean Ethics*. With Aristotle, Aquinas would indeed recognize that this concept denotes more than merely what is contained in the English "habit," for he speaks of it as a certain disposition, as a certain "power" (Lat. *potencia*) of the soul (Aquinas 2012b, I–II 1–70: 56.1, 491–92).[7]

In line with the tripartite schematization of the human soul (discussed above), Aquinas follows Aristotle in recognizing both intellectual virtues (in the mind, or the rational level of the soul) and moral virtues (in the appetitive or sensate level of the soul). Unlike the case of the will (which, as per above, is for Aquinas necessarily rational) and the passions (necessarily nonrational, or "arational" in an important sense), however, both "levels" of virtue may be said to be rational. That is, even the moral virtues come under the sway of reason for Aquinas. Unlike the passions, that is, they are *not* "pre-rational." To state this a different way, the virtues are the product of reason, or of a process of habituation that is inherently rational (even if not reducible, "all the way down," to reason alone).

Examples here will help. Aquinas says that "Fortitude is assigned to the irascible power, and temperance to the concupiscible power. Whence the Philosopher[8] says that *these virtues belong to the irrational part of the soul* (*hae virtutes sunt irrationabilium partium*)." Aquinas makes an important distinction here (in the *respondeo* section of Q. 56 A. 4), namely between (on the one hand) the two kinds of passion (concupiscible and irascible) as parts of the sense appetite (dealt with in the first half of this essay) and (on the other hand) the two kinds of passion *as participating in reason* (*inquantum participant rationem*). It is *in this second mode of consideration* that the passions are regarded as the subject of moral virtue.

Since for Aquinas (following Aristotle) both the passions and the moral virtues reside in the appetitive (or "middle level") of the soul, there is obviously a close relationship between the passions and the moral virtues, and

Aquinas addresses this relationship in Question 59 of the *Secunda Secundae*. After clarifying that moral virtue is not identical to passion (A. 1), he clarifies that "moral virtue can be with passion" (A. 2). He then registers what I take to be an exception to a "rule" stated above: not *all* moral virtues, in fact, reside in the appetitive portion of the soul. Justice, he says, "pertains to the will," which, as we have seen, is for Aquinas "located" in the rational part of the soul (A. 4).[9] Indeed, justice alone among the moral virtues may (in a sense) be without passion. Besides this exception, for Aquinas "the more perfect a virtue is, the more it does cause passion," again underlining a point about the passions above: that they are, in Aquinas' opinion, necessarily good (Aquinas 2012b, I–II 1–70: 59.5, 527–28).

Before moving to a consideration of vice, one more point about Thomistic virtue in general should be noted: as is the case for Aristotle, it "observes the mean" (Aquinas 2012b, I–II 1–70: 64.1, 563–65). On this point he simply carries over the Stagirite's doctrine of the mean (Aristotle 2011, II.7, 36–38).

As we will see below, Aquinas regards anger as a vice, residing in the irascible power of the appetitive soul. But first, what *is* a vice?

Thomistic Vice in General

In question 71 of the *Prima Secundae*, Aquinas argues that vice is contrary to virtue by appeal to Augustine (in the *sed contra*). Yet, in typical fashion, he goes on to "reason out" this deliverance of authority (in the *respondeo*). This line of reasoning about vice completely relies on the prior grasp of virtue, which he characterizes as "a disposition whereby the subject is well disposed according to the mode of its nature . . . to that which is best. . . ." Vice, together with sin and malice, is "found to be contrary to virtue" (Aquinas 2012c, I–II 71–114: 71.1, 1–2).

It is for this reason—that vice runs counter, or in opposition, to the full flourishing of a thing as dictated by its purpose—that it is, for Aquinas, contrary not just to virtue, but also to nature (Aquinas 2012c, I–II 71–114: 72, 13–27).

Note that, following Aristotle, Aquinas normally conceives of particular vices as standing in opposition not only to a particular virtue (every virtue is also a mean) but *also* to another, equal and opposite, particular vice. For example, the vice of prodigality stands in opposition *both* to the virtue/mean of liberality, but also to the equal and opposite vice of covetousness (Aquinas 2012c, II–II 92–189: 117–19, 189–217).

Thomistic Anger as a Specific Vice

Finally we arrive at the treatment of one vice in particular, that of anger.[10] Yet a bit of necessary prolegomena still remains, for the manner in which Aquinas handles and treats his vast catalogue of virtues and vices is highly ramified, with various tributaries flowing out of the main trunk of the river, as it were. In fact, one is hard pressed to deny that Aquinas' text in his discussion of the virtues and vices—as with his *Summa* generally—is rather dry and stultifying. (This is especially evident when one compares it to the more "spiritual" style of medieval writing one finds in, for example, Aquinas' colleague at the University of Paris, St. Bonaventure, whose writing is vivid, dramatic, and rhetorically pleasing.)[11]

And yet, what it lacks in thrill, it compensates for in clarity. The ramification, which for the most part is intended to function like a schema of *genus* and *species* (and could probably be schematized in a way similar to the biological hierarchies of the plant and animal kingdom, and so on, of Charles Linneaus), includes "general virtues" and "capital vices," each of which lead to more specific instances. For example, temperance (one of the four cardinal virtues, also known in English as "moderation"), as a "general virtue," has as its "subvirtues" (among others) honesty (Q. 145), sobriety (Q. 149), chastity (Q. 151), and the subject matter of question 157, "clemency and meekness." Anger, which is a vice resulting in a failure of clemency and meekness, is itself a "capital vice," having as its "subvices" what Aquinas (following Gregory the Great) calls "the seven daughters of anger," which are: "quarreling, swelling of the mind, contumely, clamor, indignation, and blasphemy" (Aquinas 2012c, I–II 92–189: 158.7, 520).

Hence, we can say that anger is a capital vice, which stands in opposition to that virtue of "clemency and meekness," which is itself a "subvirtue" or specific instance of the general virtue of temperance. It is to be expected, then, that the issues connected to anger as a vice amount to a matter of *extremes*. Indeed, this does turn out to be the case, as we read in the *respondeo* section of Q. 158 A. 6: "[anger] precipitates the mind into all kinds of inordinate action." But inordinate action of what kind?

After reminding us that, "properly speaking" (*proprie loquendo*) anger is a passion of the soul, from which the term "*vis irascibilis*" comes (Aquinas 2012c, II–II 92–198: 158.1, 512),[12] and that (appealing to "the Apostle" in Eph 4:31) under certain circumstances it is a sin, Aquinas goes on to specify two ways in which anger can be evil (*mala*). First, with respect to its object, which as we saw above is vengeance on an evildoer. If the character of the vengeance is in accord with reason in every respect, it is called "zealous anger." Otherwise it is called "vicious anger" (. . . *nominator ire per vitium*)

(Aquinas 2012c, II–II 92–198: 158.2, 514).[13] Among the ways of deviating from wisdom, Aquinas gives several examples:

> For instance if [one] desire the punishment of one who has not deserved it, or beyond his deserts, or again contrary to the order prescribed by law, or not for the due end, namely the maintaining of justice and the correction of defaults. (Aquinas 2012c, II–II 92–198: 158.2, 514)

The second way in which anger can be vicious is, as mentioned above (below?), is with respect to excessive degree (Aquinas 2012c, II–II 92–198: 158.2, 514). Again, this makes sense in light of the fact that anger is a privation of temperance or moderation: its specific form of viciousness pertains to its excess or extremity. In the opposite case, that is, a deficient level of anger, Aquinas identifies the vice of negligence (Aquinas 2012c, II–II 92–198: 158.8, 521–22).

Finally, Aquinas teaches that anger is not a mere vice, it is a *capital* vice, meaning that "many vices . . . arise" from it (Aquinas 2012c, II–II 92–198: 158.6, 519). Anger can spawn sub-species of vice in each of the two ways that he spelled out above in defining anger as a vice in the first place: its object and its degree (Aquinas 2012c, II–II 92–198: 158.6, 519–20). In both cases "[anger] is sin when it sets reason aside" (Aquinas 2012c, II–II 92–198: 158.2, 513).[14]

CONCLUSION

At the beginning of this essay I registered a certain "mismatch" between our contemporary (or modern) idiom and that of Aquinas' culture, in the attempt to talk about phenomena such as anger, fear, sadness, joy, love, and so on. Indeed, despite the medieval etymological provenance of the term *emotion*, this term is scarcely used by Aquinas in the context this article has been treating. Hence it is perhaps tempting for a contemporary reader to dismiss Aquinas' account of things as hopelessly outdated, useful for merely antiquarian purposes.

Yet, upon deeper reflection, nothing could be further from the truth. As Nicholas Lombardo points out in *The Logic of Desire*, Aquinas' account of the passions, regarded as thoroughly embodied and hence anything but merely cognitive, coheres nicely with the contemporary accounts of Peter King, Susan James, and Eileen Sweeny (Lombardo 2011, 4; King 2002, 229; James 1997, 30; Sweeney 1998, 215). Even Martha Nussbaum, whose more "cognitive-evaluative" view mental judgments over bodily movements or sensations, admits that "feeling" often accompanies emotion (Nussbaum

2003, 11), admitting at least partial (if tacit) agreement with Aquinas. These more recent approaches, which displaced more cognitive accounts (Bedford 1957), saw a return to the nineteenth-century view of William James, who identifies "emotion with bodily feeling" (Lomardo 2011, 10).

When one combines this contemporary thinking about emotion with the rise of virtue ethics in the late twentieth and early twenty-first centuries (often associated with Alasdair MacIntyre's *After Virtue*), one can appreciate the contemporary relevance of Aquinas' account of human psychology (the passions) and ethics (virtue theory), and anger within them.

NOTES

1. Of course, the Latin language has no definite article.

2. The Latin etymology of "emotion" includes the prefix "ex-" ("out of") and the root word "motus" ("motion"). In some sense, then, an emotion is a "outward movement" or a "movement out of something."

3. "I.5" here refers to the fifth question of the first "volume" of the *Summa Theologiae*, the *"Prima Pars"* ("First Part").

4. Aquinas makes frequent use of the latter term (Lat. *potentia*) when describing the dynamics of the soul.

5. In the latter case one might think of this as a "double negative": to negate a pernicious thing or reality is to bring about a state of affairs that is, overall, good.

6. This need to say a "word before" we address vice already hints at a key difference between anger-as-a-passion and anger-as-a-vice: the former being necessarily good and the latter being deformed, deficient, or somehow pernicious.

7. One compelling definition of *hexis* is that of Bartless and Collins: "ordered and stable states of the soul that mark us as the kinds of persons we are and permit us to act as we characteristically do." (Bartless and Collins 2011, 305–19 at 306).

8. For Aquinas, "the Philosopher" always refers to Aristotle, and in this context he cites *Nicomachean Ethics* III.10.

9. For a fascinating genealogy of the development of the concept of the will in western thought (including Aquinas' role within it), see Sorabji 2004.

10. Note that Aquinas *also* regards anger as a sin.

11. On the distinction between the "scholastic" and "spiritual" *genre* of medieval writing (embodied by Aquinas and Bonaventure, respectively), see Jean LeClercq 1974..

12. Aquinas 2012c, Q. 158 A. 1 (512).

13. Note that the English translation here has "sinful anger." Yet the Latin in this context has *vitium*, not *peccatum*.

14. The Latin here has *mala*, or evil. Yet throughout the context of his discussion of anger Aquinas uses "sin" and "vice" as if they were synonymous.

REFERENCES

Aquinas, Thomas. 2012a. *Summa Theologiae, Prima Pars 1–70*. Edited by John Mortensen and Enrique Alarcón. Translated by Fr. Lawrence Shapcote, O.P. Lander, WY: The Aquinas Institute for the Study of Sacred Doctrine.

———. 2012b. *Summa Theologiae, Prima Secundae 1–70*. Edited by John Mortensen and Enrique Alarcón. Translated by Fr. Lawrence Shapcote, O.P. Lander, WY: The Aquinas Institute for the Study of Sacred Doctrine.

———. 2012c. *Summa Theologiae, Secunda Secundae 92–189*. Edited by John Mortensen and Enrique Alarcón. Translated by Fr. Lawrence Shapcote, O.P. Lander, WY: The Aquinas Institute for the Study of Sacred Doctrine.

Aristotle. 2011. *Nicomachean Ethics*. Translated by Robert C. and Susan B. Collins. Chicago: The Univ. of Chicago Press.

Bartless, Robert C., and Susan B. Collins. 2011. "Glossary." In *Aristotle's Nicomachean Ethics, a New Translation*. Translated by Robert C. and Susan B. Collins. Chicago: The Univ. of Chicago Press.

Bedford, Errol. 1957. "Emotions." *Proceedings of the Aristotelian Society* 57 (1957): 28–304.

Chenu, Marie-Dominique, O.P. 2002. "The Virtuous Life." In *Aquinas and His Role in Theology*. Translated by Paul Philibert, O.P. Collegeville, 105–21. Minnesota: The Liturgical Press.

James, Susan. 1997. *Passion and Action: The Emotions in Seventeenth-Century Philosophy*. Oxford: Clarendon.

King, Peter. 2002. "Late Scholastic Theories of the Passions: Controversies in the Thomist Tradition." In *Emotions and Choice from Boethius to Descartes,* edited by Henrik Lagerlund and Mikko Yrjösuuri, *Studies in the History of Mind 1*, 101–32. Dordrecht: Kluwer.

Leclercq, Jean, O.S.B. 1974. *The Love of Learning and the Desire for God: A Study in Monastic Culture*. Translated by Catharine Misrashi, 2nd ed. New York: Fordham Univ. Press. Reprinted, 2017.

Lombardo, Nicholas. 2011. *The Logic of Desire: Aquinas on Emotion*. Washington, DC: Catholic Univ. Press.

MacIntryre, Alasdair. 2007 *After Virtue*, 3rd ed. Notre Dame, IN: Univ. of Notre Dame Press.

Nussbaum, Martha. 2003. *Upheavals of Thought: The Intelligence of the Emotions.* Cambridge: Cambridge Univ. Press.

Sorabji, Richard. 2004. "The Concept of the Will in Plato to Maximus the Confessor." In *The Will and Human Action: from Antiquity to the Present Day*, edited by Thomas Pink and M.W.F. Stone, 6–28. London: Routledge.

Sweeney, Eileen. 1998. "Restructuring Desire: Aquinas, Hobbes, and Descartes on the Passions." In *Meeting of the Minds: the Relations between Medieval and Classical Modern European Philosophy*, edited by Stephen F. Brown, 215–34. Turnhout, Belgium: Brepols.

White, Kevin. 2002. "The Passions of the Soul (Ia IIae, qq. 22–48)." In *The Ethics of Aquinas*, edited by Stephen J. Pope, 103–15. Washington, DC: Georgetown Univ. Press.

Chapter 7

Jonathan Edwards on Divine
Justice and Anger

Phillip A. Hussey

When people in North America hear the name Jonathan Edwards, their minds most likely gravitate to the famous—for some infamous—sermon preached at Enfield, Massachusetts (now a part of Connecticut), on July 8, 1741. Thanks to anthologies of early American literature, Edwards' sermon "Sinners in the Hands of an Angry God" represents for many the quintessence of "hellfire" preaching during the Great Awakening. Not without reason has it garnered such attention. Rhetorically, the sermon is a masterclass in the use of metaphor and illustration to create suspense and the feeling of personal horror. Edwards employs a variety of metaphors and descriptions—a "wide and bottomless pit," a fiery oven, "great waters damned for the present," a sword, a bow with an arrow "ready on the string" to be made "drunk with your blood," and so on—in order to depict the reality and intensity God's wrath. Of course, theologians and historians often register how this sermon does not represent Edwards' pastoral and theological agenda *tout court*. Within Edwards' vast sermonic corpus, the sermons on love certainly outnumber those on wrath. Take, for example, the series of sermons preached in 1738 (also in the context of revival) on 1 Corinthians 13, subsequently published under the title *Charity and Its Fruits*. These sermons represent an extended and moving account of divine love, both in its objective content and subjective appropriation. That said, it would certainly be misleading to distance Edwards from his imprecatory sermon(s) and then ignore them when interpreting his theology, as if he didn't mean what he said about divine wrath and hell. Although repugnant to much modern sensibility, Edwards never shied away from discussing and meditating upon God's wrath.

The purpose of this essay, therefore, is to present the main contours of Edwards' *theological* understanding of divine anger, or, in synonymous terms, divine vengeance/wrath. Beneath all of the vividly descriptive rhetoric, how does God's anger relate to God's nature and therefore character for Edwards? A surface reading of the Enfield sermon might suggest that God is not only hot under the collar, but bloodthirsty as well, delighting in punishing human beings in a similar way to how my son delights in eating fruit snacks, or, more sinisterly, to how a serial killer psychologically delights in perpetrating their crime. The broadness of this question and imprecision of these descriptions might be helpfully narrowed if we relate them to an old and thorny question in theology: is vindictive (avenging) justice a divine attribute? The question contains a corollary: is the manifestation of vindicatory justice necessary in the created order such that God would be "less glorious" without communicatively displaying it? According to Edwards, the manifestation of God's glory in creation consists in the "proper exercise and expression" of *all* of the divine perfections (*WJE* 8:428–37). Edwards even tells us that "[Hell] is a world prepared on purpose for the expressions of God's wrath" (*WJE* 8:390). But, as Edwards argues elsewhere, "'Tis true that God delights in justice for its own sake, as well as in goodness; but it will by no means follow from thence, that he delights in the creatures' misery for its own sake as well as [in their] happiness" (*WJE* 13:502). In order to make sense of these and other arguments pertaining to divine anger, I will explore the topic under three headings: (1) the divine perfections *ad intra*; (2) the divine perfections *ad extra*; and (3) Christology.

THE DIVINE PERFECTIONS *AD INTRA* AND DIVINE ANGER

Edwards, like many Reformed divines before him, equates divine anger (wrath) with vindictive (punishing) justice. Exercising vindictive justice functions equivalently to God's "glorifying his justice in punishing sin" (*WJE* 18:316). In other words, vindictive justice is a mode of God's justice as it meets sin, which, in turn, glorifies the divine perfection of justice. Time and again—from his early sermons (cf. *WJE* 10:525) to his final dissertation (cf. *WJE* 8:536)—Edwards indicates how sin requires (infinite) punishment precisely because of divine justice. This theological point is clearly evident in his Enfield sermon: "[Sinners] deserve to be cast into hell; so that divine justice never stands in the way . . . yea, on the contrary, divine justice calls aloud for an infinite punishment of their sins" (*WJE* 22:405–6). The concern at the moment, however, is not the manner in which a creaturely condition and action (i.e., sin) corresponds to the mode of expression of a divine perfection (i.e., justice). That will be treated in the next section. The question at hand concerns justice as a divine perfection *ad intra*. What about divine justice *per se* makes it "call," as Edwards puts it, for anything? Edwards' discussions in "Miscellanies" nos. 704 and 89 gesture toward an answer.

In "Miscellanies" no. 704, Edwards attempts to adjudicate the various issues at work within the supralapsarian and infralapsarian debate within Reformed theology.[1] An important feature of this debate pertains to the "end" in God's decree of predestination. In particular, certain proponents of supra-lapsarianism held to the position that God's intended (and ultimate) end in the decree of predestination is the manifestation of God's glory expressly in mercy and vindictive justice. Logically, not temporally, God decrees this *end* without consideration of the fall. In his analysis of the supra- and infralapsarian debate, Edwards isolates the consideration of the "glorifying [of] vindictive justice as a mere end" in the decree as particularly problematic, leading "to great misrepresentations and undue and unhappy expressions about the decree of reprobation" (*WJE* 18:316). On Edwards' interpretation, this makes it seem as if God considered the glorifying of vindictive justice on particular persons "as altogether prior in the decree to their sinfulness; yea, [to] their very being," with the consequence that the eternal decree of damnation occurs prior to the fall and creation of the human being. The mistake, at least for Edwards, rests on the improper conflation of *vindictive justice* with *justice*. "Vindictive justice is not to be considered as a certain distinct attribute to be glorified, but as a certain way and means for the glorifying an attribute." In particular, God's vindictive justice is a means of "glorifying [God's] justice, or rather his glorifying his holiness and greatness," which "has the place of a mere and ultimate end" (*WJE* 18:316). While God's vindictive justice includes the supposition of a sinful and created object, God's general decree to glorify God's justice—that is, God's holiness and greatness—"supposes neither their being nor sinfulness" (*WJE* 18:317).

Having clarified that vindictive justice is not a divine perfection but a mode of a divine perfection, we can now turn to the perfection of justice *per se*. In "Miscellanies" no. 89, Edwards explicitly relates divine justice to divine excellency. Excellency is a term of art for Edwards; it "may be distributed into greatness and beauty," with the former taken as "the degree of being" and the latter as "being's consent to being" (*WJE* 6:382). For Edward, consent is not merely a principle of volition but a mental activity involving the integrated action of affection, understanding, and will (cf. Bombaro 2012, 60–61). When consent occurs between "minds," Edwards refers to it as love because it entails both communication and union (cf. *WJE* 6:362). John Bombaro summarizes well the metaphysical contours of excellency in Edwards' thought: "'Excellency' or being consists, therefore, in *relations*. Beauty is proportion; proportion is excellence; and excellency is relational plurality or existence itself. Thus, to be is to be in relation. Excellency emerges, then, as the aesthetic expression of relations of consent—the principle components of ontological structures" (Bombaro 2012, 62). Recall from "Miscellanies" no. 704 that justice and greatness (as well as holiness) function as metonyms. By reason of parity, excellency may be distributed into justice and beauty. Justice, in this line of metaphysical reasoning, corresponds to the *degree* of agreeableness or disagreeableness to God's being. For God *in se*, the divine perfection of justice corresponds to God's *infinite* agreeableness or regard for God's own being. And Edwards defines God's holiness—a metonym for justice—in precisely these terms:

> GOD'S HOLINESS is his having a due, meet and proper regard to everything, and therefore consists mainly and summarily in his infinite regard or love to himself, he being infinitely the greatest and most excellent Being. And therefore a meet and proper regard to himself is infinitely greater than to all other beings; and as he is as it were the sum of all being, and all other positive existence is but a communication from him, hence it will follow that a proper regard to himself is the sum of his regard. TRINITY. (*WJE* 20:460)

Rather intentionally Edwards ends by emphasizing God's tri-unity. According to Edwards, God's beauty, excellency, and holiness are demarcated theologically (as opposed to strictly metaphysically) in accordance with God's tri-unity. God's consent to God's own being—that is, God's beauty—just is the *relations* between the Father, Son, and Spirit. Undergirding the entire metaphysical language of consent is God's triune love. Along these lines, Edwards appropriates the divine perfection of holiness to the Holy Spirit in particular, who is the bond of mutual love between the Father and the Son (cf. *WJE* 6:364; *WJE* 21:131).

When we put this entire picture together, the divine perfection of justice functions as a description of the mode and manner of God's triune love *ad intra*. "There is God's holiness," Edwards tells us, "but it is the same . . . with his love to himself. There is God's justice, which is not really distinct from his holiness" (*WJE* 21:131). In this sense, justice doesn't appear to be, strictly speaking, an "attribute" at all. The appropriateness of this conclusion is further corroborated when seen in light of the correlation between justice and beauty. Beauty pertains to consenting relations; justice pertains to the *extent* and *agreeableness* of these consenting relations. Divine justice, therefore, aesthetically describes God's being *ad intra*, in particular the harmonious, loving, and self-giving aspects of God's triune life.

We may summarize Edwards' understanding of divine justice *ad intra* in three axioms:

(#1) Divine justice is God's *perfect and infinite* regard to God's own being.
(#2) God's infinite self-regard is synonymous with the love that exists between the Father and the Son (and Holy Spirit, who is the bond of love).
(#3) Vindictive justice is not a divine perfection *ad intra*.

THE DIVINE PERFECTIONS *AD EXTRA* AND DIVINE ANGER

After considering the nature of justice as a divine perfection *ad intra*, it is now possible to think through the exercise of this "perfection" relative to the created order, or *ad extra*. Edwards makes the argument that God, in creating the world, must bring *all of the divine perfections* to their proper effects, effects which would otherwise lie eternally dormant without creation (e.g., *WJE* 8:428–29; *WJE* 18:97; *WJE* 23:1505–1). This should not be taken to mean that Edwards conceived of God as incomplete without the exercise of these attributes. God is perfectly *a se*, needing nothing from creation. "'Tis true," Edwards argues, "that there was from eternity that act in God within himself and towards himself, that was the exercise of the same perfection of his nature" (*WJE* 18:97). All of the divine perfections are contained "virtually" in God (*WJE* 18:97). In scholastic usage, this means that God knows, by simple intelligence, all of the operations and effects that God has the power (*virtus*) to generate, rather than those effects and operations existing in actuality, as if these effects constituted parts of God. Such an understanding functions hand in hand with divine simplicity, wherein God's attributes, though not really distinct in the simplicity of God's essence, may be distinguished virtually or eminently because they actually have a foundation in God and not just in our minds (see Duby 2017). With this caveat in mind, Edwards still insists that "God's regard to himself, and value for his own perfections, should cause him to value these exercises and expressions of his perfections; and that a love to them will dispose him to love their exhibition and exertment" (*WJE* 8:437).

Quite obviously for Edwards, there exists a strong connection between God's love for the divine perfections *ad intra* and their expression *ad extra*. On this point, it is important to remember that the love for the divine perfections *ad intra* cuts with a trinitarian edge for Edwards, such that the divine perfections are *positively* consented to (i.e., delighted in) within God's triune life. Although the details cannot be argued for in this essay, one important ramification of this for Edwards is that the eternal love of the Father for the Son "condecently" necessitates creation in order to communicate the divine perfections as they are manifest in the Son. As Edwards explicitly argues elsewhere, "[B]ut it was a condecent thing . . . & it was the will of G[od] to shew forth his own Glory & that in a Great degree so it was his Et[ernal] will greatly to shew forth his Love to his son . . . this was Gods Et[ernal] design & purpose & seems to be called by way of Eminency his decree" (Sermon 699. Heb. 2:7–8 [LL. 3v.–4r.]). The overall accent falls on union with and consent to the Son, thereby enabling the human creature to "affectively" love the Father, Son, and Spirit in an analogical manner to how they love each other, and, by extension, also enabling affective delight in the divine perfections as such. This form of creaturely delight is fairly well outlined in Edwards' treatise *Religious Affections*.

Given Edwards' understanding of divine perfections and the "condecent" necessity of creation outlined thus far, we can now turn directly the question of divine justice. How does the perfection of justice fit into this communicative picture, and, by extension, the mode of justice in the form of vengeance? Foremost, we need to recognize that the perfection of justice does not function as a control on God such that it *inclines* God toward a certain ultimate end in creating. As Edwards articulates in the opening introduction to *End of Creation*:

> But yet there is no necessity of supposing that God's love of doing justly to intelligent beings, and hatred of the contrary, was what originally induced God to create the world, and make intelligent beings; and so to order the occasion of doing either justly or unjustly. The justice of God's nature makes a just regulation agreeable, and the contrary disagreeable, as there is occasion, the subject being supposed and the occasion given: but we must suppose something else that should incline him to create the subjects or order the occasion. (*WJE* 8:412)

Clearly, the manifestation of divine justice *as such* cannot be the ultimate end for which God created the world. Given what we have already encountered regarding justice as a "perfection," how could it? Justice only describes God's mode of being God. Justice, for Edwards, might be agreeable to God as a *hypothetical* end upon the supposition of an object, though not as an ultimate end. But this, it seems to me, is equivalent to saying that God will *order* and *rule* the world in such a way that it analogically mirrors the perfection of God's being because divine justice, by definition, is God's excellency (i.e., the infinite consent by God to God's own being); therefore, God "cannot will to do anything but what is excellent" (*WJE* 13:253). The created order, in this sense, *necessarily* corresponds to God's regard for God's own being and perfections. Thus, we can now add two further axioms to Edwards' theological picture.

(#4) God creates the best possible world with the ultimate end in mind of communicating the Father's love for the Son, with the entailment that (#4a) the primary means of obtaining this end is through union of the creature with the Son so as to analogically share in God's triune love affectively and actively.

(#5) Divine justice requires that the world God creates necessarily correspond to God's being, with the entailments that (#5a) such correspondence includes the expression of *all* of God's perfections to their proper effects and (#5b) these effects are perceived by rational creatures.

Given Edwards' commitment to the expression of *all* of God's perfections in the created order, the question can be now phrased more precisely: in what sense must divine justice be expressed and recognized upon the supposition of creation? Edwards provides a tentative explanation of these matters in "Miscellanies" no. 348. In this early entry, Edwards begins by stressing, like he does so often, that the manifestation of the glory of the divine perfections is "a proper and excellent thing," and that the display of every perfection should be "proportionably effulgent" such that the creaturely beholder "might have a proper notion of God." Every perfection must be manifested as to answer God's "real and essential glory" (*WJE* 13:419). Based on this line of reasoning, Edwards unflinchingly asserts, "'tis necessary that God's awful majesty, his authority and dreadful greatness, and justice and holiness [should be manifested]; and this could not be except sin and punishment were decreed, or at least might be decreed" (*WJE* 13:419–20). But how does this square with Edwards' claim that *vindictive justice* is not an attribute, but a mode for the glorification of an attribute? Must the mode of justice as vengeance be displayed? Would God be "less" glorious without its expression? As Edwards goes on to explain, "the glory of [God's] goodness and love . . . would be faint" without sin and punishment; "nay, they could scarcely shine forth at all." In this way, the "sense of the good is heightened by the sense of evil, both moral and natural" (*WJE* 13:420). Most important, perhaps, God's loving communication would be incomplete without sin and punishment because "the creature's happiness consists in the knowledge of God and the sense of his love, and if the knowledge be imperfect, the happiness must be proportionably imperfect" (*WJE* 13:420–21). "The sense of the good," Edwards concludes, "is comparatively dull and flat without the knowledge of evil" (*WJE* 13:421). So, we must add a seventh and eighth axiom.

(#6) The necessary expression of God's perfections in creation includes *vindictive justice*.

(#7) God permits the fall in order to express *vindictive justice*.

In order to understand Edwards' reasoning here, we need to interpret the previous "Miscellanies" entry in light of his fuller thought. Three matters are key. First, Edwards believes "Even sin and wickedness itself . . . comes to pass because God has use for it, a design and purpose to accomplish by it" (*WJE* 18:581). God *permits* evil and, in so permitting, orders and disposes all states of events "for wise, holy and most excellent ends and purposes" (*WJE* 1:399). Although evil itself is disagreeable to God and God is not the efficient cause (i.e., "actor") of sin (cf. *WJE* 1:399), God allows sin and evil in keeping with God's perfect knowledge of all excellency (cf. *WJE* 13:253). Edwards explains this metaphysically in his notebook "The Mind," wherein he utilizes the language of consent and dissent, conformity and deformity. Primary beauty consists in consent among spiritual beings, foremost to God then to other creatures. Consent among spiritual beings is properly called love. The lack of such love—really disproportioned and disordered love—is deformity. As we observed earlier, this language directly relates to Edwards' notion of justice. "Injustice is not to exert ourselves towards any being as it deserves, or to do the contrary to what it deserves in doing good or evil, or in acts of consent and dissent" (*WJE* 6:364). In Edwards' more metaphysical register, the permission of evil functions equivocally to the permission of dissent (from God). And dissent from God, if that is a creature's "fixed nature, is a manifestation of consent to being in general; for consent to being is dissent from that which dissent from being" (*WJE* 6:363). Edwards refers to this matrix of dissent and consent as the "beauty of vindictive justice" (*WJE* 6:365).

This leads to the second point. For Edwards, the dissent of creatures—in keeping with the strictures of divine justice—evokes punishing justice. This should not be surprising given Edwards' theological position outlined thus far: sin is disagreeable to being; justice requires punishment for sin in proportion to the being offended; sin is against God, ergo sin is worthy of infinite punishment. But precision is needed here. Justice "requires" something, in Edwards' theological picture, only because the creature is "required" itself to love God as the supremely excellent Being. This is Edwards' principle of proportionate regard. Human beings were made to know and love God in an *analogical* manner to how God knows and loves within the triune life. To dissent from this—that is, to sin—means to fail to actively live in accord with the end for which one was made. Punishing justice, or divine anger, is God's "dissent" to "dissenting" being, and therefore, ultimately consent to God's own being. Thus, God's mode of justice as wrath corresponds to an inherently *moral* relation between God and creatures. And this relation takes the form of law: "The anger of God was the anger of One to whom it belonged to execute the law. The law of God is a fixed, unalterable rule for God's proceeding with the creature. The law threatened death, and it must be fulfilled. And as God was judge of the law, justice required that he should judge according to law" (*WJE* 17:340). For Edwards, any positive precept given by God already presupposes the *order* of justice. In the case of Adam, the command regarding the tree was not the "main rule" given, but presupposed "the great rule of righteousness written in his heart" (*WJE* 20:143). So Edwards says:

> [I]t presupposes the sum of the law of nature to have been already established and known by Adam, viz. that man owed God a supreme and perfect respect, and to be regarded above all other things, and that he ought to be entirely subject to him, and to improve his faculties and God's good creatures, that were given him, only in away agreeable to the will and designs of the Creator of all; and that if he refused, he deserved to be destroyed by his Creator. (*WJE* 20:142)

But Edwards doesn't simply assert that God exercises vindictive justice necessarily upon the supposition of dissent. Edwards further contends that an *increasing* sense of God's vindictive justice should "be kept up in the minds of creatures . . . in order to their right and just apprehensions of his greatness and gloriousness, and that perfect and becoming and answerable joy and happiness, in the spiritual sight and knowledge of him." This "sense," in fact, is "needful in order to the proper respect of the creature to God, and the more complete happiness in a sense of his love" (*WJE* 13:469). When worked out eschatologically, the damnation of the wicked in hell actively serves the happiness of the saints in heaven. As Edwards explains:

> The saints and angels in heaven before whom the wicked will be punished, will doubtless have a very great sight of the infinite greatness and awful majesty of God, against whom sin is committed, and so of the glorious excellency of that Savior and his dying love, that is rejected by sinners. . . .[T]his punishment is designed to raise their idea of God's power and majesty, to impress it with exceeding strength and liveliness upon their minds, and so to raise their sense of the riches and excellency of his love to them. (*WJE* 20:107)

This should not be taken to mean that the saints in heaven "find their own happiness increased by the torments of others" (Pauw 2002, 177). True, saints will see and sense the misery of the damned, but "It will not [be] because they delight in seeing the misery of others. Considered absolutely, the damned's suffering divine vengeance will be no occasion of joy to the saints merely as it is others misery or because that it is pleasant to them to behold others misery merely for its own sake" (Sermon 277. Rev. 18:20 [LL 5v.–6r.]). The saints delight in the "sense" of God's justice, not "torment" *per se*. As Edwards maintains, "'Tis true that God delights in justice for its own sake, as well as in goodness; but it will by no means follow from thence, that he delights in the creatures' misery for its own sake as well as [in their] happiness" (*WJE* 13:502). So it is with God, so it is with the saints.

Based on Edwards' aforementioned reasoning, three further axioms are required:

(#8) Vindictive justice enables the elect to "perceive" more clearly the love between the Father and the Son.

(#9) Sin (or dissent from Being) requires infinite punishment based on the principle of proportionate regard.

(#10) Infinite punishment is, strictly speaking, God's infinite dissent from dissenting being.

Now we arrive at the third matter needing attention: hell and reprobation.

Eschatologically, there are only two eternal states for rational creatures according to Edwards: heaven and hell. Heaven is a world of love where the saints commune with God in an ever-increasing union that "will come nearer and nearer to that strictness and perfection of union between which there is between the Father and Son" (*WJE* 8:443). Hell, on the other hand, is a "world of hatred," which God prepared "on purpose for the expression of God's wrath." God has no other use for hell but to "satisfy his hatred of sin and sinners" (*WJE* 8:390). In this way, as Edwards comments in his sermon on Ezekiel 15:2–4, the wicked are only useful in their destruction. The rationale is straightforward: if the human creature refuses to answer (actively) the ultimate end for which they were created, then God will act upon them "passively" in their destruction, and in so doing, glorify the subordinate end of justice. "When it is thus wicked men are useful only accidentally & not designedly" (Sermon 332. Ezekiel 15:2–4 [L 6v.]). Although Edwards clearly teaches sovereign election and reprobation, Edwards resolutely believes that God does not create *in order to* damn. Commenting on Roman 9:17—a *locus classicus* within Reformed exegesis on the divine purpose in reprobation—Edwards maintains, "This scripture will hardly justify our expressing ourselves so that God gives reprobates a being to that end, that he might glorify himself in their destruction" (*WJE* 24:1023). But, as many interpreters have noted, this seems to force Edwards into a theological quagmire wherein the elect are viewed as the primary objects of God's creation, while the reprobate are simply—in Thomas Schafer's memorable words—"ontological ciphers" (Schafer 1955, 53).

Schafer reaches this conclusion based on Edwards' metaphysical reasoning. Consent to God's Being involves an increasing union of love, whereas dissent from God's Being yields an "approach to nothing, or a degree of nothing" (*WJE* 6:335). Yet, according to Edwards, the dissenting human creature (i.e., the reprobate) is never annihilated. They asymptotically approach "nothingness" in an analogical manner to how the consenting human creature (i.e., the elect) asymptotically approaches the perfect union existing between the

Father and the Son. Thus, as we have already recognized, hell is eternal. God cannot bring an end to divine punishment based on the principle of proportionate regard. For this reason, Edwards could speak of the perfect execution of divine wrath without pity because divine wrath is not a *passion* in God, in the classical theological sense. Wrath is God's—given his definition of divine justice—proportionate response to the dissent of the human creature. Descriptions such as fury and fierceness only "denote the Greatest degree of Anger or wrath" and the "effects" of justice as it meets its object (Sermon 322. Rev. 19:15 [LL. 6r.–6v.]). Not only must the display of God's wrath be infinite in duration, it must be perpetually and increasingly perceived by both the saints in heaven and the damned in hell. God, in fact, "enlarges [the reprobates'] capableness of receiving misery or being made miserable, but he don't make 'em strong to bear misery" (*WJE* 18:197).

The terrain covered thus far certainly addresses the objectivity of God's wrath, but what of its subjectivity? How does Edwards conceptualize the reprobate's conscious experience of infinite punishment? The experience, as Edwards explains, is best described as hate: "Everything in hell is hateful" (*WJE* 8:390). The wicked hate God, hate Christ, hate angels, hate saints, and hate one another. "All those principles which are contrary to love," argues Edwards, "will rage and reign without any restraining grace to them within bounds. . . . And their hatred and envy will be a torment to themselves" (*WJE* 8:391). For Edwards, the enactment of wrath in hell will be by means of the unrestrained *wills* of the reprobate. Human creatures continually and increasingly dissent from God and from others in hell—the profound antithesis of union. Edwards' description of hell strikingly mirrors Søren Kierkegaard's account of sin and despair. Sin, for Kierkegaard, is fundamentally a *position* (not an act *per se*) before God, wherein the human creature, in their sin, wills to be a "self" apart from God. But this is an ontological impossibility because there is no such thing as a self apart from God. "Sin is: before God in despair to will to be oneself" (Kierkegaard 1980, 81). From this perspective, the human creature in hell eternally wills to possess their self apart from God and does so in full consciousness of God. The sinning is the punishment, and it is worked out phenomenologically at the level of the disordered will. This, it seems to me, parallels Edwards' account both of the rebellious will and its subjective expression in hell (cf. Vetö 2007, 199–259, especially 250–59). Theologically speaking, God's wrath is not experienced—for all of Edwards' vivid imagery—in a similar manner to how a human victim experiences torture—either physically or psychologically—at the hands of a perpetrator, as if hell was an infinite waterboarding session. Instead, God's wrath is experienced as God's dissenting presence, a presence that increases the knowledge that the damned have of their self as creature of God. And as God's dissent from the damned increases eternally, so does their dissent from God. That is the paradox.

Let's take stock by pulling all of the axioms together, along with three additional axioms incorporating Edwards' reasoning on hell and wrath.

(#1) Divine justice is God's *perfect and infinite* regard to God's own being.

(#2) God's infinite self-regard is synonymous with the love that exists between the Father and the Son (and Holy Spirit, who is the bond of love).

(#3) Vindictive justice is not a divine perfection *ad intra*.

(#4) God creates the best possible world with the ultimate end in mind of communicating the Father's love for the Son, with the entailment that (#4a) the primary means of obtaining this end is through union of the creature with the Son so as to analogically share in God's triune love affectively and actively.

(#5) Divine justice requires that the world God creates necessarily correspond to God's being, with the entailments that (#5a) such correspondence includes the necessary expression of *all* of God's perfections to their proper effects and (#5b) these effects are perceived by rational creatures.

(#6) The necessary expression of God's perfections in creation includes *vindictive justice*.

(#7) God permits the fall in order to express *vindictive justice*.

(#8) Vindictive justice enables the elect to "perceive" more clearly the love between the Father and the Son.

(#9) Sin (or dissent from Being) requires infinite punishment based on the principle of proportionate regard.

(#10) Infinite punishment is, strictly speaking, God's infinite dissent from dissenting being.

(#11) God's presence in hell takes the form of this infinite dissent.

(#12) God continues to sustain the existence of the damned and expands their "perception" of divine presence.

(#13) God's dissenting presence increases the dissent of the creature in hell in a directly proportional manner (i.e., their hatred of God and Christ).

The main problem for Edwards still lies with fact that (#6) [and therefore (#7) and (#8)] does not seem to follow from (#3). If vindictive justice is not a divine perfection, then why does it *have* to be expressed? Not only expressed but expressed in order to enable a *better* perception of God's love. Justice, by Edwards' own admission, doesn't demand this type of *ordering*. There seems to be a piece of the puzzle missing, without which Edwards would be endorsing a rather banal theodicy. And, in fact, there is just such a piece: Christology.

JESUS CHRIST AND DIVINE ANGER

Given axiom (#4), one would expect Edwards to coordinate the primary expression of divine justice with Christology. And so he does: "God's justice is more gloriously manifested in the sufferings of Christ for the elect than in the damnation of the wicked" (*WJE* 24:1024). Christ, in his passion, pre-eminently manifests "an infinite regard for the honor of God's justice" (*WJE* 19:577). Although there are obvious Anselmian overtones here, the overall picture is not rigidly Anselmian because divine justice is most properly about the *order of divine love*.[2] As witnessed in his sermon "Excellency of Christ," the passion uniquely reveals one conjunction of excellencies in Christ, "viz. his infinite regard to God's justice, and such love to those that have exposed themselves to it, as induced him thus to yield himself a sacrifice to it" (*WJE* 19:578). Of particular importance in this sermon is Christ's *humility* and *love*. For Edwards, justice is *more gloriously* manifested in Christ's passion because self-giving love is the foundational excellency of God's triune life. That is, love of this sort positively mirrors divine justice *ad intra*. Rather uniquely in Christ's passion, then, God's self-giving manifests itself in God's ability to reveal the disagreeableness of sin to God's being (i.e., vindictive justice), as well as the plentitude and perfection of divine love (i.e., divine justice *per se*) that is set in relief by it.

This coordination of Christology and justice also enables an understanding of Edwards' theologoumenon of the *felix culpa*, the happy fault. Traditionally, the phrase *felix culpa* functions as a shorthand for the theological position that human creatures receive greater benefits in Christ (chiefly his person) *as a result* of the fall. For Edwards, the *felix culpa* functions in a slightly different manner. It has less to do with the benefits associated with receiving Christ, and more to do with the *perception* of divine excellency as such—that is, the excellency of love which exists between the Father and Son. Thus, the fall functions so as to reveal two things: (1) that the communication of and con-sent to divine love (as revealed in Jesus Christ) is the proper *end* of the human creature; and (2) that to be a creature means to be sustained by God. With respect to the latter, Edward argues, "God's design was first to show the crea-ture's emptiness in itself and then to fill it with himself in an eternal, unalter-able fullness and glory." It is not that the fall *makes* the creature empty, rather it *reveals* the emptiness of the creature that exists apart from God's love. For Edwards, the creature needs to be brought to see "their own emptiness" in order to then "be brought to an entire dependence on the sovereign grace and all-sufficiency of God, to be communicated to them by his Son as their head" (*WJE* 20:192). And, as Edwards argues in *Original Sin*, the fall occurs no otherwise than from the withdrawal of God's supernatural presence from Adam (cf. *WJE* 3:380–84). Adam's *natural* principles—left ungoverned and to themselves—*necessarily* led to the fall. We may call this Edwards' entropic thesis: apart from God's supernatural love and grace, human creatures will inevitably sin, drifting toward self-sufficiency and self-love.

With this entropic thesis in place, it is now possible to see the manner in which Christ is the key to Edwards' claim about the necessity of manifesting vindictive justice. God designs the fall not only to reveal human insufficiency apart from God's love (i.e., that they are in fact *creatures*), but to reveal (in coordination) the sufficiency and perfection of God's love as it exists between the Father, Son, and Spirit. Christ's submission to the vindictive aspect of justice expresses the depths of God's self-giving love, as well as reveals the complete dependence of the creature upon God. To borrow a Barthian phrase, the No is always uttered for the sake of the greater Yes. So conceived, the "greatest manifestation of evil" and "dreadful nature of sin" appears in the crucifixion (*WJE* 20:199). At the cross, the full magnitude and reality of human dissent is revealed in that human beings actually reject and crucify the Lord of glory (cf. *WJE* 20:330). The cross also reveals the extent of God's dissent from sin, chiefly in the fact that only the incarnate Son can—as the only truly righteous one—restore dissenting creatures. At this juncture, it is imperative to recognize that God's dissent from sin did not render the Son himself odious to God: "Christ suffered the wrath of God for men's sins in such a way as he was capable of, being an infinitely holy person who knew that God was not angry with him personally, knew that God did not hate him, but infinitely loved him." Christ "became" sin, according to Edwards, in that he had in his soul "a great and clear sight of the infinite wrath of God against the sins of men, and the punishment they had deserved," and this in such way that "our sins were his tormenters" (*WJE* 20:329–30).

Most importantly, though, the cross reveals the glory of the love that exists between the Father and the Son. It is this *identical* love that the Son enacts, and therefore reveals, in his passion:

> Christ never did anything whereby his love to the Father was so eminently manifested, as in his laying down his life, under such inexpressible sufferings, in obedience to his command, and for the vindication of the honor of his authority and majesty; nor did ever any mere creature give such a testimony of love to God as that was: and yet this was the greatest expression of all, of his love to sinful men, that were enemies to God. (*WJE* 19:577)

The passion, in this sense, is not antithetical to God's love. It is the temporal unfolding of its perfection. Just so, the *necessary* manifestation of vindictive justice, in Edwards' larger reasoning, was never ordered toward the reprobate in hell but Christ at Calvary. Vindictive justice *reveals* the propriety of the creature's dependence on the Son's love and the worthiness of the Son as such. Though this does not resolve the difficulty latent in Edwards' doctrine of reprobation (i.e., that God actually reprobates), it certainly challenges any claim that Edwards bifurcates perdition and God's self-giving in Jesus Christ (cf. Holmes 2001, 211–53).

A FINAL (THEOLOGICAL) NOTE

Space does not allow for an assessment of the coherence of Edwards' entire theological picture. To do so would certainly require inclusion of elements hereunto untouched: divine causality, the determination of will, the atonement proper, and the presence of Christ in hell as the executor of divine wrath. My main intention was to outline the elements at work in Edwards' theology needed to put together an interpretive picture of divine justice and anger. I sought to show, chiefly, that the tension existing between Edwards' claims that (1) vindictive justice is not a divine perfection and (2) that it nevertheless *must* be expressed, needs to be adjudicated christologically. Such a re-orientation led directly to Edwards' notion of the *felix culpa*. Admittedly, Edwards' unwavering theocentrism on this point will prove unsavory for many: God wisely ordains the fall so that human creatures can *better* perceive the fullness of God's triune glory, in particular the Father's love for the Son. Or, to speak crudely, to reveal to human creatures how God's love *ad intra* works, and, in so doing, incorporate them into that love through union with the Son. On the face of it, this doesn't appear to be related to vindictive justice at all, especially not the *necessary* expression of it in the created order. Yet because human creatures are not divine persons, and cannot (ontologically) become divine persons, God's wise method for revealing the width and breadth and height of God's triune love includes setting it against the backdrop of creaturely dissent. As a result of the fall, human creatures learn, in fact, that they are creatures: not self-sustained, not self-sufficient, not self-governed. The futility (even inevitably) of the creature's self-making project is fundamentally exposed in Jesus Christ, the one in whom and by whom and for whom all things were created. Human creatures need to see (perceive) and believe (consent) that they are sustained only by the Son's love, apart from which they are deformed and deforming. "The light of God's beauty, and that alone, truly shows the soul its own deformity, and effectually inclines it to exalt God, and abase itself" (*WJE* 25:637). The true light of divine beauty is Christ crucified and risen.

Interestingly enough, Edwards' theological vision resonates with that of Karl Barth. Obviously, there are numerous divergences and, at times, significant ones; but in the supralapsarian elements of Barth's Christology, as well as Barth's articulation of sin as *das Nichtige* and explanation of the *felix culpa*, there exists strong parallels. Not without reason did Barth confess that his Christian thesis "bears a close resemblance to that of the well-known writings" of Leibniz (*CD* III/1, 388). The divergence, Barth contends, is christological. Leibniz could not and did not represent the *maxio ratio* of the best possible world as the divinity and humanity of Jesus Christ. Like Barth, Edwards believed this created order to be the best possible one, not in a Leibnizian sense, but simply because the best possible world is a creation internally structured around Jesus Christ. Barth's comments about the fall, then, could just have easily been written by Edwards: "The wisdom of God which allows [the fall] in order to make, not the episode itself, but the over-coming of it an occasion to magnify His grace and to reveal and actualize it—we have to say for the first time—as free grace in it, in accordance with His eternal will and purpose"; but never "necessary" in order to "excuse or exculpate the man who is responsible for it" (*CD* IV/1, 69). For me, at least, the vision is as compelling as it is offensive. The offense being that *God* creates and we are those *creatures*. Hence, to use the word creature is already to speak theologically, indeed christologically.

[Many thanks to Christina Larsen and Joshua Schendel for their comments on an earlier draft.]

NOTES

1. Within Reformed theology, the decrees of God are systematically broken down into general (e.g., creation and providence) and particular (e.g., predestination) categories. As Reformed theology developed after the Protestant Reformation—through codification and, most often, internal and external debates—there arose a controversy over how one should conceive the manner, order, and object of God's particular decree of predestination, which is commonly referred to as the infralapsarian and supralapsarian controversy. Infralapsarians often follow the historical order and structure predestination *infra lapsum* (below or subsequent to the fall), whereas supralapsarians often follow the teleological order and proceed *supra lapsum* (above or prior to the fall). The debate is more like a dispute among friends because the position was never fully confessionalized, and, as such, never resulted in a schism.

2. Here, Anselmian does not refer to a theory of the atonement *per se*, but the framework that undergirds it, especially with regard to the principle of proportionate regard. Nevertheless, there are divergences. Whereas for Anselm the contours of

justice take shape around honor vis-à-vis God's morally perfect being, justice cuts with a *trinitarian* edge for Edwards. That is, the honor of God's justice directly relates to the loving movement of the trinitarian persons.

REFERENCES

Barth, Karl. 1936–1977. *Church Dogmatics.* Edited by G. W. Bromiley and T. F. Torrance. 4 vols. in 13 pts. Edinburgh: T&T Clark.

Bombaro, John J. 2012. *Jonathan Edwards's Vision of Reality: The Relationship of God to the World, Redemption History, and the Reprobate.* Eugene, OR: Pickwick Publications.

Duby, Steven. 2017. "Divine Immutability, Divine Action and the God–World Relation." *International Journal of Systematic Theology* 19, no. 2 (April): 144–62.

Edwards, Jonathan. 1957–2008. *The Works of Jonathan Edwards.* 26 vols. New Haven: Yale University Press. [Abbr. = *WJE*]

———. Sermon 277. Rev. 18:20 (Mar. 1733). In *The Works of Jonathan Edwards Online.* Vol. 48, *Sermons, Series II, 1733,* edited by Jonathan Edwards Center. New Haven: Jonathan Edwards Center at Yale University. http://edwards.yale.edu/.

———. Sermon 322. Rev. 19:15 (April 1734). In *The Works of Jonathan Edwards Online.* Vol. 49, *Sermons, Series II, 1734,* edited by Jonathan Edwards Center. New Haven: Jonathan Edwards Center at Yale University. http://edwards.yale.edu/.

———. Sermon 332. Ezek. 15:2–4 (July 1734). In *The Works of Jonathan Edwards Online.* Vol. 49, *Sermons, Series II, 1734,* edited by Jonathan Edwards Center. New Haven: Jonathan Edwards Center at Yale University. http://edwards.yale.edu/.

———. Sermon 699. Heb. 2:7–8 (Mar. 1743). Box 11, Folder 816, Beinecke Rare Book and Manuscript Library, Yale University. Transcription provided by Kenneth Minkema, Director of the Jonathan Edwards Center at Yale University.

Holmes, Stephen R. 2001. *God of Grace and God of Glory: An Account of the Theology of Jonathan Edwards.* Grand Rapids: William B. Eerdmans.

Kierkegaard, Søren. 1980. *Sickness Unto Death: A Christian Psychological Exposition for Upbuilding and Awakening.* Edited and translated by Howard V. Hong and Edna H. Hong. Princeton: Princeton University Press.

Pauw, Amy Plantinga. 2002. *The Supreme Harmony of All: The Trinitarian Theology of Jonathan Edwards.* Grand Rapids: Wm. B. Eerdmans Publishing Co.

Schafer, Thomas. 1955. "Jonathan Edwards's Conception of the Church." *Church History* 24, no. 1 (March): 51–66.

Vetö, Miklos. 2007. *La pensée de Jonathan Edwards: avec une concordance des différentes editions de ses Œuvres,* nouvelle édition remaniée [new revised edition]. Paris: L'Harmattan.

Chapter 8

Anger, Humility, and Civil Discourse

Michael W. Austin

Anger is at the foundation of many personal and social ills. It can be a destructive force in an individual's soul, in our personal relationships, in our communities, in our institutions, and in conflicts between nations. Sometimes the result of this destructive force is nothing more than temporarily hurt feelings. At other times, it can lead to genocide and the deaths of millions. While anger is a consistent part of human life, a part that is at times at least encouraged in certain contexts, its value is questionable. As Dallas Willard strongly puts it, "there is nothing that can be done with anger that cannot be done better without it" (Willard 1998, 151). It is clearly the case that anger is a corrosive and destructive element in our civil discourse in the United States, as well as other places around the world. Whether it has to do with politics, theological disagreement, or even how to deal with a global pandemic at both personal and societal levels, anger seems to be the norm. It is almost as if disagreement *entails* anger these days. This is not true *logically*, nor need it be the case in daily life. Unfortunately, however, anger is often the characteristic response to disagreement. Willard helps reveal why this is the case: "The sense of self-righteousness that comes with our anger simply provokes more anger and self-righteousness on the other side" (Willard 1998, 151). Anger is not only destructive, it is also contagious.

Yet the case can be made from Scripture that there are forms of anger that are virtuous, and forms of it that are not. Paul writes that we are to "Be angry but do not sin" (Ephesians 4:27, NRSV), hinting at such a distinction. Proverbs instructs us that "One who is slow to anger is better than the mighty, and one whose temper is controlled than one who captures a city"

(16:32), and that "Those with good sense are slow to anger, and it is their glory to overlook an offense" (19:11). James writes that we ought to be "slow to anger, for your anger does not produce God's righteousness" (1:20). And Jesus himself warns us of the dangers of anger in the Sermon on the Mount (Matthew 5:21–26).

This is not just a Christian belief. Others agree that there are virtuous and vicious forms of anger. For example, Aristotle contends that "getting angry . . . is easy, and everyone can do it; but doing it to the right person, in the right amount, at the right time, for the right end, and in the right way is no longer easy, nor can everyone do it" (Aristotle 1999, 1109a27–30). Marcus Aurelius, the great Stoic philosopher, notes the destructive force of anger, both in our souls and our relationships with others. He says that "The soul of a man harms itself . . . when it turns away from another human being, or is even carried so far in opposition as to intend him harm—such is the case in souls gripped by anger" (Aurelius 2006, 2.16).

In this chapter, I will focus on vicious forms of anger, and argue that the virtue of humility can play a significant role in undermining them. In so doing, humility can help produce civil discourse that is in fact civil. Humility supports a certain approach to civil discourse that followers of Christ should develop and exemplify, namely, *rhetorical nonviolence*.

VICIOUS ANGER

It can be difficult to ascertain what *forms* of anger are virtuous, and how to determine whether any *particular instance* of anger is virtuous or vicious. Here, I will focus on clear cases of vicious forms and instances of anger, as they tend to corrupt our discourse with one another.

Willard offers a helpful analysis of vicious anger (Willard 1998, 147–51). He discusses anger in his interpretation of the Sermon on the Mount and argues that anger is often the root cause of much of the evil that we do. Anger does have an important role to play, as its primary function is to sound the alarm that my will for my life is somehow being obstructed. In that sense, anger is not sinful, though we might still be better off without it, according to Willard. The type of anger that concerns Willard is "much more than this and quickly turns into something that is inherently evil" (148). Anger at another, in his view, includes a desire to harm them, or at least the seeds of such a desire. Anger is a spontaneous reaction, but we can also choose to be angry, to feed anger and give it power over us and our actions. Anger that is indulged in this way "always has in it an element of self-righteousness and vanity . . . a wounded ego" (149). When we indulge it, "evil is quickly multiplied in heart-rending consequences and in the replication of anger and rage in the hearts and bodies of everyone it touches" (150). *Anger*, then, can be thought of as *a spontaneous emotional response to the thwarting of our wills that becomes vicious when it includes a desire or determination to harm others, and perhaps even malice towards them.*

Anger is dangerous in a variety of ways. It fuels and is fueled by prejudice. It can lead to fractured relationships, a fragmented soul, abuse, violence, and murder. But we often seek to justify our anger, seeing it as righteous. Perhaps we are easily self-deceived, blind to the ego-driven nature of much, even most, of our anger. In my experience, followers of Christ can also tend to misappropriate parts of the gospels to justify our anger, because we want so badly to justify it.

For some, the paradigm case of righteous anger in the gospels, often used as a justification for our own anger, is Jesus' cleansing of the temple. John's gospel offers the most detailed account:

> The Passover of the Jews was near, and Jesus went up to Jerusalem. In the temple he found people selling cattle, sheep, and doves, and the money changers seated at their tables. Making a whip of cords, he drove all of them out of the temple, both the sheep and the cattle. He also poured out the coins of the money changers and overturned their tables. He told those who were selling the doves, "Take these things out of here! Stop making my Father's house a marketplace!" His disciples remembered that it was written, "Zeal for your house will consume me." (John 2:13–17)

We see ourselves doing such actions, and we cannot imagine doing so without anger. We then assume Jesus was angry here as well. But it is *zeal*, not anger, that his actions brought to the minds of the disciples. Moreover, no one was reported as being injured or harmed. Only John mentions the whip of cords, likely made of rope, animal bedding, or fodder, and only John mentions the animals. It is therefore likely that the whip was used to shoo the animals away, and nothing more (Alexis-Baker 2012; Neufeld 2011, 61; Austin 2020, 93–97). In his study of the passage, David Rensberger concludes, "The traditional understanding of Jesus's action in the temple area as an act of violent fury cannot be sustained on a careful reading of the gospels" (Rensberger 2014, 189). The cleansing of the temple offers us a picture of virtuous zeal, not anger. If we are seeking biblical justification for our anger, this is not the place to find it. But if we are seeking ways to undermine our anger, the kind of anger that "does not produce God's righteousness," a good starting point is to cultivate and exemplify the virtue of humility.

HUMILITY AND ANGER

Humility can undermine human anger. In order to see how this is the case, we must first understand what humility is (Austin 2018). It is a central virtue for the Christian life. Humility is exemplified by Jesus and alluded to in many places in the Scriptures. It is also a virtue that is often misunderstood. Some think that humility involves what amounts to an irrational form of self-denigration, so much so that they lose sight of the Christian doctrine of human beings having inherent dignity because they are made in the image of God. Others discuss humility as nothing more than genuine self-knowledge. The former are mistaken about the nature of this virtue. The latter are closer to the truth, but are missing several crucial elements.

It makes sense to look to Jesus Christ for our understanding of humility, and any other virtue for that matter. He is our exemplar in all things, including the virtues. We can learn much about humility from a study of the life of Jesus as it is presented in the canonical gospels. The very beginnings of his life on earth as described in Luke's gospel are humble. As Richard Burridge observes, "Luke begins his portrait of Jesus among the pious poor and women, the meek and the lowly" (Burridge 2007, 232). But it is not only the birth story that is humble, Jesus exemplifies this virtue in several places in the gospels. Throughout the gospels, he humbly interacts with people that were ignored and undervalued in the Ancient Near East, including women, children, the sick, the poor, and others. His humility is on display when, prior to his crucifixion, he washes the feet of his disciples (John 13:1–20). Jesus even describes himself as humble in heart in Matthew 11:28–30.

But what is humility? How are we to understand this Christian virtue? A central passage in the New Testament for understanding the humility of Jesus and its implications for Christ-followers is Philippians 2:1–11:

> If then there is any encouragement in Christ, any consolation from love, any sharing in the Spirit, any compassion and sympathy, make my joy complete: be of the same mind, having the same love, being in full accord and of one mind. Do nothing from selfish ambition or conceit, but in humility regard others as better than yourselves. Let each of you look not to your own interests, but to the interests of others. Let the same mind be in you that was in Christ Jesus, who, though he was in the form of God, did not regard equality with God as something to be exploited, but emptied himself, taking the form of a slave, being born in human likeness. And being found in human form, he humbled himself and became obedient to the point of death—even death on a cross. Therefore God also highly exalted him and gave him the name that is above every name, so that at the name of Jesus every knee should bend, in heaven and on earth and under the earth, and every tongue should confess that Jesus Christ is Lord, to the glory of God the Father.

While there are many questions and issues here, which I have engaged in detail elsewhere, we can derive a definition of humility from this and other key passages of the Bible that is exemplified by Jesus and taught in various parts of the Scriptures (Austin 2018, 28–82).

Generally speaking, the ideally humble person is characterized by both a *proper self-assessment* and a *self-lowering other-centeredness*. He has knowledge of his personal limits, such as his own moral strengths and weaknesses, and the human limitations we all share, but his focus is not on himself. In this same vein, as C. S. Lewis puts it, "a really humble man . . . will not be thinking about humility: he will not be thinking about himself at all" (Lewis 1952, 99). He puts other persons (both human and divine) and values (e.g., justice and compassion) at the center of his life, rather than his own self.

One feature of Christian humility that is most salient here is the fact that it is a social virtue. That is, it is a virtue that is highly relevant to our relationships and interactions with others. Clearly we are to be humble before and in relation to God. But we also ought to relate to other human beings in a humble way. In the spirit of Philippians 2, this means that the humble person will have at least an initial preference for the satisfaction of the interests of others, over against her own. This will tend to motivate her to act, to do things for others, even things that are deeply sacrificial, for their good. She must use wisdom, and depend upon the guidance of God's Spirit, the Bible, and wise counsel from others, but the Christian life is to be marked by *kenosis*, or self-emptying. The Christian life is the sacrificial life. Humility is a crucial virtue for making this a reality.

So understood, the virtue of humility can be a powerful force not only for undermining vicious anger, but eliminating it. Recall Willard's observation that the self-righteousness that accompanies our anger provokes both self-righteousness and anger in those who are on the other side of the conflict. Clearly, humility is a corrective here. Humility and self-righteousness are diametrically opposed to one another. I cannot be both humble and self-righteous, insofar as these two traits conflict with one another. Self-righteousness makes no sense, when we consider the gap between our own righteousness and the righteousness of Christ. There is a wide moral gap between even the most righteous and virtuous human being and Christ. I might be able to generate a bit of somewhat reasonable self-righteousness when I am allowed to aim low and compare myself to a few other human beings intentionally selected to make me feel better about my own virtue, but certainly when Christ is the standard such pretentions are destroyed. With this in mind, having a low view of oneself, as counseled by humility, is rational. As Bernard of Clairvaux puts the point, humility "is a virtue by which a man has a low opinion of himself because he knows himself well" (Bernard of Clairvaux 1973, 30). Moreover, the humble person will not be concerned with making such comparative judgments, as he will be focused on others, not himself.

Given the above characterization of the virtue of humility, we can see that it sets the stage for the supreme virtue of love. One helpful way to understand the virtue of love, in the tradition of Thomas Aquinas, is as "*a disposition towards relationally appropriate acts of the will consisting of disinterested desires for the good of the beloved and unity with the beloved held as final ends*" (Silverman 2010, 59). Love, then, includes being disposed to act for the good of others, in an unselfish manner. Love takes into account the particular relationship. The way in which it is manifested is informed by that relationship. Love also involves unity with the beloved, among its final aims is to experience community with them. The humble person is other-centered. Love builds upon this to motivate not only acting for the good of others, but for the sake of a deeper relationship with them. When humility and love work in concert, I believe that they support a rhetorically nonviolent approach to civil discourse. It is to this idea that we now turn.

RHETORICAL NONVIOLENCE

Humility and love lead us to act in ways that put the interests of others ahead of our own, and to do so in a sacrificial way with unity as the final goal. Yet in our conversations with others, especially civil discourse about issues related to religion, morality, and politics, humility and love are all too often conspicuously absent. Rather than a love of truth, hope for furthering the common good, and a concern for unity, our discourse is marked by a desire for victory, the hope that we can shame or embarrass our rhetorical opponent while exalting ourselves and our viewpoints. Ultimately, and unsurprisingly, this leads to deep division rather than unity.

Examples of this are too easy to find. Get on your favorite social media platform and observe discussions about these topics. Or examine how our politicians, pundits, and many pastors interact with those who have an opposing viewpoint. We deflect, we show disdain for others, and we dehumanize them. For what? For having a different view than we do? For refusing to toe the party line at school, work, or church? Anyone who reflects upon the state of our civil discourse can easily see these problems. I have seen a professing Christian offer the following reply, on social media, to several plans and policies of "the left" (e.g., tearing down statues, transforming the United States of America, and renaming John Wayne Airport in southern California) with the following refrain: "GO TO HELL." It is easy to think that "these are merely words, they do not cause much harm," or "People need to be tougher," but the teaching in the Sermon on the Mount rejects such justifications and minimizing of the harm that angry words do. Concerning anger, Jesus says, "You have heard that it was said to those of ancient times, 'You shall not murder'; and 'whoever murders shall be liable to judgment.' But I say to you that if you are angry with a brother or sister, you will be liable to judgment; and if you insult a brother or sister, you will be liable to the council; and if you say 'You fool,' you will be liable to the hell of fire" (Matthew 5:21–22). It is clear that anger and words spoken in anger to others are taken very seriously here.

We all have witnessed, experienced, or engaged in discourse that is uncivil, insulting, or characterized by vicious anger. I have witnessed it, engaged in it, and been on the receiving end of it. People to the right of me politically have told me that I have imbibed "the liberal Kool Aid" because I take a moderate position on how we can reduce gun violence in the United States of America (Austin 2020). Others have questioned my commitment to Christ because my website does not have the word "Jesus" displayed prominently on its homepage. I have also experienced disdain from those on my political left, telling me that it is good that I live in Kentucky since I have such backward views about God and politics (though he misunderstood my views on both subjects). Honestly, this kind of thing used to bother me a lot, given my personality and emotional makeup. But over time I have learned to handle it better, minimizing the space I give such commentary in my life. To be sure, this kind of feedback should be expected, insofar as I sometimes write about controversial issues. But whether we are witnessing it, on the receiving end of it, or perpetrating it, such verbal behavior is out of bounds. As James 3:10 tells us, "From the same mouth come blessing and cursing. My brothers and sisters, this ought not to be so."

What if more of us who follow Christ set a different standard? What if we took the words of James to heart? What if we followed the example of Christ himself? "When they hurled their insults at him, he did not retaliate; when he suffered, he made no threats. Instead, he entrusted himself to him who judges justly" (1 Peter 2:23, NIV). Why was he able to respond in this way? There are many reasons, but among them is the fact that humility and love are central virtues in the character of Christ. They led him to eschew responding to insults and suffering at the hands of others with insults or threats. Instead, they led him, and ought to lead us, to adopt a practice of rhetorical nonviolence.

What is rhetorical nonviolence? In order to see what it involves, we will first briefly examine what nonviolent action refers to in general, and then apply it to our verbal interactions with others. Ronald Sider offers the following definition of nonviolent action: "Nonviolence is not passive nonresistance; nor is coercion always violent. Nonlethal coercion (as in a boycott or peaceful march) that respects the integrity and personhood of the 'opponent' is not immoral or violent. By 'nonviolent action,' I mean an activist confrontation with evil that respects the personhood even of the 'enemy' and therefore seeks both to end the oppression and to reconcile the oppressor through non*violent* methods" (Sider 2015, xv). This is consistent with the words of Jesus, when he instructs his followers, "Do not resist an evildoer" and to turn the other cheek (Matthew 5:39). A close study of the Greek word translated as "resist" here reveals that Jesus is not prohibiting all forms of resistance. Rather, he is prohibiting *violent* resistance. This is because the term *antistenai* "means to resist violently, to revolt or rebel, to engage in armed insurrection" (Wink 1998, 100). Nonviolence is not passivity, as Sider points out. It is a form of activism that rejects violence as a means to achieving its goal. While a defense of nonviolence as a Christian doctrine, as well as a defense of its effectiveness, is beyond the scope of this chapter, there is much good evidence, past and present, for both its truth and effectiveness (Sider 2015; Sprinkle 2013; Ackerman and Duvall 2000). In the United States, the civil rights movement as it followed the leadership of Martin Luther King Jr. is in many ways a paradigm case of a faithful and effective nonviolent movement. King and others actively confronted evil in their pursuit of justice, suffering and even dying for it. There is more to do, unquestionably, but it is also unquestionably the case that great progress was made due to this nonviolent movement. Of course, nonviolent resistance is not always effective, but for Christ-followers it is faithfulness, not effectiveness, that should be our key concern.

If we apply the foregoing to how we speak to one another, we can understand *rhetorical nonviolence* as *verbal behavior that reflects, in both content and tone, a respect for one's opponent as a person made in God's image, rejecting insult and vicious anger, with a goal of coming to know and apply the truth in unity.* Humility is necessary here, because only by it can we approach those we disagree with in a spirit of openness and willingness to being corrected. In humility, we put truth and the good of our verbal opponent at the center, rather than ourselves, our reputations, and our desire to win. We may, of course, be right, and we must resist what seems to us to be false. We should not be passive, because "Christocentric nonviolence says that we should fight against evil, we should wage war against injustice, and we should defend the orphan, the widow, the marginalized, and oppressed. And we should do so aggressively. But we should do so nonviolently. In other words, Christocentric nonviolence does not dispute whether Christians should fight against evil. It only disputes the *means* by which we do fight" (Sprinkle 2015). This applies to our discourse as well. We can be right, resist what is false, fight for truth, goodness, justice, and beauty as we engage in debate and dialogue with others. But we can interact with others—both fellow Christians and those who do not share our faith—in ways that reflect humility and love, rather than vicious forms of anger.

It is right to do this, first and foremost, because in so doing we follow the example of Christ who refused, when reviled by others, to revile in return. But I have found that it is also effective, that the words of Proverbs 15:1 are actually true: "A gentle answer turns away wrath, but a harsh word stirs up anger" (NIV). This proverb is true both in real life and in our online interactions. In the past year or so, I have tried to adopt this approach of rhetorical nonviolence. I have not done so perfectly, but I have made significant progress. I have seen several benefits to this approach, apart from knowing that it is a way I can express love for God and others. My experiences in working at this have made a difference, not just in the tone of my interactions with others when we disagree, but also in the substance. It is incredible to see how a response to someone's adversarial tone, or even an angry or insulting one, can change the dynamics of a conversation. I have seen this for years in the classroom and in-person discussions, but it also works in social media interactions. Instead of firing back, so to speak, we can ask a question, see if there is common ground, or simply ask someone why they believe what they do, in a genuinely curious way. Instead of being opponents or enemies, we become partners in the quest for truth.

I am not advising we *always* do this. Rhetorical nonviolence can take other forms as well. Sometimes, it may mean simply not responding at all. If someone is consistently antagonistic, fails to respect boundaries, or engages us in verbally abusive ways, rhetorical nonviolence does not counsel us to passively receive such verbal assaults. There are times when it may be wise to simply block someone on social media, or suspend and even end in-person relationships.

There are more benefits produced by rhetorical nonviolence. In my experience, it opens the door for better conversations, softens my opponent's heart as well as my own, and refocuses the conversation on the substance of our discussion. If we truly desire and seek after truth, then this approach can help us get there.

REFERENCES

Ackerman, Peter, and Jack Duvall. 2000. *A Force More Powerful*. New York: St. Martin's Press.

Alexis-Baker, Andy. 2012. "Violence, Nonviolence, and the Temple Incident in John 2:13–15." *Biblical Interpretation* 20: 73–96.

Aristotle. 1999. *Nicomachean Ethics*, 2nd ed. Translated by Terence Irwin. Indianapolis: Hackett.

Aurelius, Marcus. 2006. *Meditations*. London: Penguin Books.

Austin, Michael W. 2018. *Humility* and Human Flourishing: A Study in Analytic Moral Theology. New York: Oxford University Press.

———. 2020. *God and Guns in America*. Grand Rapids: Eerdmans.

Burridge, Richard A. 2007. *Imitating Jesus*. Grand Rapids: Eerdmans.

Clairvaux, Bernard of. 1973. *The Steps of Humility and Pride*. Trappist, KY: Cistercian Publications.

Lewis, C. S. 1952. *Mere Christianity*. New York: Macmillan.

Neufeld, Thomas R. Yoder. 2011. *Killing Enmity: Violence and the New Testament*. Grand Rapids: Baker Academic.

Rensberger, David. 2014. "Jesus's Action in the Temple." In *Struggles for Shalom: Peace and Violence across the Testaments*, edited by Laura L. Brenneman and Brad D. Schantz, 179–90. Eugene: Pickwick.

Sider, Ronald J. 2015. *Nonviolent Action: What Christian Ethics Demands but Most Christians Have Never Really Tried*. Grand Rapids: Brazos Press.

Silverman, Eric J. 2010. *The Prudence of Love*. Lanham, MD: Lexington Books.

Sprinkle, Preston. 2015. "A Case for Christocentric Nonviolence." Paper presented at the Annual Meeting of the Evangelical Theological Society. Accessed at https://www.prestonsprinkle.com/blog/2015/11/a-case-for-christocentric-nonviolence.

Sprinkle, Preston. 2013. *Fight: A Christian Case for Nonviolence*. Colorado Springs: David C. Cook.

Willard, Dallas. 1998. *The Divine Conspiracy*. San Francisco: HarperSanFrancisco.

Wink, Walter. 1998. *The Powers that Be*. New York: Galilee Books.

Chapter 9

Anger and the Law— Free from Passion?

Tammy W. Cowart

Aristotle is often quoted as saying that the law should be "reason free from passion." Indeed, in the American legal system, courtrooms are traditionally austere, regimented, and composed places, where lawyers, witnesses, and judges rise and sit and follow rules for standing, sitting, and speaking. In addition, our law schools teach a focus on case law and the *ratio decidendi*— rationale for the decision, as opposed to emotion. Even the images of Lady Justice portrayed in courthouses around the country show her wearing a blindfold with a blank expression on her face—seemingly devoid of emotion and passion. Our US legal system simply does not encourage displays of anger.

However, the icon of the goddess Justitia, the Roman Goddess of justice, "is never depicted without her unsheathed sword" showing her power and authority (Jay 2003, 97). Historical interpretations of her icons indicate that her sword represents the rigor of justice and her willingness to punish, while other interpretations are that her sword represents cruelty, harshness, and unwillingness to compromise (Curtis and Resnik 1987). Lee (2012) writes that Justitia's sword shows the state's power to inflict violence. "All sovereigns claim . . . that their violence goes forth in the name of Justice" (Curtis and Resnik 1987, 1734). Thus, at least historically there is some room for reason *and* anger or passion in the law. History shows us how anger and passion can influence the law and have caused societal shifts. Two recent examples are the #MeToo movement and the Black Lives Matter movement. This essay will examine these recent examples of anger and its influence on the law, as well as the underlying principles of Christian anger and how it endorses and constrains the display of anger in public life. This essay will also discuss the role of passion and anger in perceptions of justice and the legal system. History shows that passion and anger can be a catalyst for change in the legal system, perhaps more effectively than "reason free from passion," as Aristotle suggests. The trajectory of cultural, organizational, and legal changes started by the #MeToo movement and Black Lives Matter movement will be addressed as well.

CHRISTIAN ANGER

In Christian morality, anger is regarded as a threat to our common humanity (Muldoon 2008). Paul advises us to get rid of anger in Ephesians 4:31. The failure to do so can lead to bitterness, which destroys the soul according to Hebrews 12:15. Much of the admonition against anger stems from the judgmental aspects of anger. If anger is used foolishly, it can warp our sense of self as we consider and compare ourselves to others. It can make us feel as though we occupy a moral high ground as judges of others. Historically, the effects of anger and personal revenge led human societies to establish laws and develop legal systems (Muldoon 2008). Despite the warnings against anger in Scripture, anger is not always wrong. The type of anger that is expressed in response to violations of God's law is a righteous anger.

In the Protestant Reformation, Martin Luther willingly displayed his anger with the Catholic Church. He disagreed with the Catholic Church first over indulgences, papal authority, and the financial excesses of the church. He was completely confident that he was right and had no reservation in expressing that opinion to others. He is quoted as telling his adversaries, "You are idiots and swine"; and "Listen, you ass, you are a particularly crass ass indeed, you are a filthy sow" (Eire 2017). Carlos Eire (2017) writes that "recent scholarship has revealed that all of the churches created by the Protestant Reformation worked hard to do away with the abuses that made Luther and other reformers so angry, and that the Catholic Church followed suit. In the long run, ironically, Luther and all Protestant reformers succeeded in forcing the Catholic Church to listen to its faithful inner reformers and clean up its act." The changes that came from Luther and his anger against the Catholic Church led to the creation of new churches. Largely because of his efforts, the Bible was translated into German, so Europeans could read it for the first time ("Martin Luther" 2019). Since Christians had churches that did not require people to speak through priests, it also gave Christians an understanding that they had a direct line to God. Luther's passionate and sometimes angry pursuit of the injustices of the Catholic Church were monumental events for legal and societal changes for Europe and the world.

Finally, godly anger is always under control. A gentle answer turns away wrath, but a harsh word stirs up anger (Prov. 15:1). In Martin Luther King Jr.'s famous speech he said, "Let us not seek to satisfy our thirst for freedom by drinking from the cup of bitterness and hatred." Nussbaum (2016) argues that King believed in nonviolence and that anger can be an impediment to justice because it impedes the generosity and empathy that are needed to create a future of justice. Nussbaum calls King's philosophy "revolutionary non-anger" but describes it as an example of "transition anger"—a controlled redirection of anger toward positive social change. She writes, "Martin Luther King, Jr., followed Gandhi, espousing both nonanger (or at least a quick Transition to nonanger) and nonviolence. It appears that King, less saintly than Gandhi, both experienced anger (or at least expressed it in speeches) and encouraged it to a degree in his audience—but always with a quick move to the Transition" (Nussbaum 2016, 212). Is controlled anger then the key to the ability of a Christian to effect change in the law? It is this last characteristic that gives us context to examine the role of anger in the law.

ANGER IN THE LAW

James Madison wrote in the Federalist Papers that reason and not emotion should control the government (Maroney 2011, 634). Thomas Hobbes said that judges should be "divested of all fear, anger, hatred, love, and compassion" (Hobbes 1904). In fact, a common conventional view is that an emotional judge is a bad judge. This view comes from the idea that the law is based on reason and not emotion, since emotion is thought of as a primitive type of reaction. The idea of removing emotion from the law dates back to the Stoics and the Enlightenment era and the ideals of individual worth and the ability to reason. From this, reason and emotion were assumed to be dichotomous and inconsistent (Maroney 2011). Aristotle also assigned emotions to the nonrational part of ourselves, since emotions can prevent us from making rational decisions (Rapp 2018).

We find these principles of dispassion inherently imbedded in the American legal system. For example, the United States Court of Appeals for the Federal Circuit has a webpage for Courtroom Decorum Policy that requires that the dignity of the court must be respected at all times ("Courtroom Decorum Policy" n.d.). Moreover, it requires everyone to rise when the judges enter, restricts anyone from speaking other than the judges or counsel, and prohibits "exaggerated gesticulating." The same principles are repeated in courtrooms across the country.

Why is this so? Anger in particular seems to "threaten fairness, impartiality, and decorum" (Maroney and Gross 2014, 144). Yet, anger is powerful and confrontational, and the ability to display anger can actually increase its intensity. Although dispassion is a requirement for courtroom decorum, it is difficult to maintain in the legal process. Litigation is often emotional by nature when it involves broken families, victims of criminal actions, deaths, injuries, and lost fortunes. This often emotional process affects parties, witnesses, jurors, lawyers, and judges. Indeed, some believe that victim impact statements should be suppressed because they evoke inappropriate emotions in the context of criminal sentencing since they appeal primarily to hatred, vengeance, and even bigotry (Bandes 1996). However, Maroney writes that emotion "plays a critical role in moral judgment" (Maroney 2011, 647) so the discouragement of litigants and parties to display emotion might actually hinder the legal process.

Surely then there is a place for morally legitimate anger in the law. Solomon (1989, 365) writes, "If one had no sense of injustice, one could have no sense of justice." Without an expression of anger, our sense of injustice is diminished tremendously, and we might feel like we just endure life (Muldoon 2008). Nussbaum (2016, 172) has identified a historical tradition that "political justice requires angry emotions." However, Nussbaum argues that "anger is always normatively problematic" (2016, 5) and that only a transition anger can be applied appropriately to redress wrongs. Transition anger does not focus on status or payback but commits itself to a focus on the future and strategies for attaining justice (Nussbaum 2015). She points to Martin Luther King Jr.'s influence on the civil rights movement, Mahatma Ghandi's campaign for Indian independence, and Nelson Mandela's efforts to defeat apartheid in South Africa as examples of using transition anger to accomplish revolutionary justice (Nussbaum 2016).

Social contract theory is grounded in the idea that "actions are morally right and just because they are permitted by rules that free, equal, and rational, people would agree to live by, on the condition that others obey these rules as well" (Shafer-Landau 2015, 194). From this standpoint, free, rational and equal people will agree to abide by morally justified rules or laws as long as other people agree to do the same. Moreover, according to a Kantian approach, when laws are good, they guide us toward what is fair. However, sometimes the state does not enforce the law or rules that seem to be part of the social contract for a group of free, rational, and equal people. Conversely, the state may not punish the actions of violators of the law or rules that are assumed to be part of the social contract with free, rational, and equal people. In these instances, social contract theory could explain why breaking the law is morally acceptable. Moral laws must "mirror the rules that free and equal people would accept" (Shafer-Landau 2015, 204). When groups of people are disenfranchised for the benefit of others, those groups may feel justified to react in anger if they believe that there is no benefit to a society under the law. Shafer-Landau (2015) writes that when people are oppressed by society, they may remain oppressed, openly resist the injustice, or resort to violence. Indeed, Solomon (1973) says anger often is the sort of normative or moral judgment we choose when we believe we have been wronged or experienced injustice. Perhaps a sense of injustice has led to displays of morally legitimate anger with the #MeToo movement and Black Lives Matter. We can examine the responses that have been a catalyst for change.

HOW MORALLY LEGITIMATE ANGER INSPIRES LEGAL SYSTEM CHANGES

Rachael Denhollander and the #MeToo Movement

The courtroom was silent when Rachael Denhollander approached the podium and was invited by Judge Rosemarie Aquilina to read her victim impact statement. Rachael Denhollander made national news as the first person to publicly allege that respected Michigan State University doctor Larry Nassar had sexually abused her. Her detailed report began a tidal wave of similar abuse allegations, resulting in the conviction of Nassar on seven counts of first-degree criminal sexual contact and a sentence of 175 years in prison (Lee 2018).

Yet, it was Rachel Denhollander's victim impact statement, during the sentencing phase of the trial, that garnered the most attention. Her thirty-six-minute impassioned statement earned a standing ovation from the gallery and was one of the catalysts for the #MeToo movement. However, she was also criticized for her relentless pursuit of justice for Nassar and asked to leave her church by fellow church members (Bruinius 2018). She claims that the cost for her and her family was high—that because of her pursuit of justice, she lost friends and her church (Lee 2018). Her display of controlled anger during the sentencing phase of the trial most certainly was a factor in Nassar's sentencing and a factor in future systematic changes. As the last person to deliver a victim's impact statement during the trial, Denhollander said to Nassar, "I pray you experience the soul crushing weight of guilt so you may someday experience true repentance and true forgiveness from God" (CNN 2018). She also said, "Larry, I can call what you did evil and wicked because it was. And I know it was evil and wicked because the straight line exists. The straight line is not measured based on your perception or anyone else's perception, and this means I can speak the truth about my abuse without minimization or mitigation" (CNN 2018). Denhollander's statement seemed to exemplify the controlled, righteous anger—transition anger—that is not retributive and focused on payback, but focused on the future. She has followed through with that approach since the trial. Denhollander is now a victims' rights advocate in sexual abuse cases and frequent public speaker around the country. She was a recipient of the Arthur Ashe Courage Award in 2018 and named "Inspiration of the Year" by *Sports Illustrated* (Quarterman 2020).

Because of the victim's impact statement of Rachael Denhollander and over 150 other survivors of Larry Nassar's abuse, Michigan State University created a $500 million settlement fund. Survivors were eligible for awards of $250,000 to $2.5 million each (North 2019). Nassar's trial and subsequent reports of sexual harassment and abuse began a tidal wave of reports as part of the #MeToo movement that gained national headlines.

The #MeToo movement was ignited in late 2017 after a tweet from actress Alyssa Milano used the hashtag #MeToo to encourage her followers to share their experiences of sexual harassment and abuse (Segura 2018). The movement itself actually began much earlier in 2006, when activist Tarana Burke, a sexual assault survivor herself, began an organization to help survivors of sexual violence. Her decades of work went viral within days of Milano's tweet. Burke says, "Jesus was the first activist that I knew, and the first organizer that I knew, and the first example of how to be in service to people" (Segura 2018). While Burke speaks more of reconciliation and collaboration than anger, the fallout from the #MeToo movement has been extraordinary.

A group of Hollywood women started the Time's Up Legal Defense Fund to help sexual harassment survivors with legal representation. Since it launched in 2018, it has raised over $24 million and connected over 3,600 people with attorneys (North 2019). Public figures like Harvey Weinstein, Bill Cosby, Kevin Spacey, Matt Lauer, and others have been fired and in some cases convicted. The #MeToo movement even spawned a #ChurchToo movement, which has focused on sexual assault and violence by religious leaders, in churches, and in religious communities (Colwell and Johnson 2020). Scandals have stretched across denominations and affected prominent religious leaders.

As a result of the #MeToo movement, ten states have introduced harassment training requirements. Several states have extended the length of time during which employees can file harassment claims, and about a dozen have voted to limit the use of nondisclosure agreements in cases between an employer and employee. Another issue involves the limits of protections provided by federal sexual harassment laws, which only apply to employers and employees. This means that millions of independent contractors, like Uber drivers, domestic workers, and farm workers, are not covered by sexual harassment laws at all. Several states have expanded their state sexual harassment laws to include independent contractors. A bill has been introduced in the House of Representatives called the Be Heard Act and if passed, it would limit some types of nondisclosure agreements at the federal level.

Changes in the legal system spread even further than those reported in the headlines. The Equal Employment Opportunity Commission (EEOC) reported that in 2018 the EEOC filed forty-one sexual harassment claims, which represented a 50 percent increase over 2017. In addition, the EEOC recovered $70 million for sexual harassment victims in 2018, up from $47.5 million in 2017 (EEOC 2018). These statistics represent larger shifts in society and what women will—and will not—stand for anymore when it comes to sexual harassment in the workplace. Women have used their transition anger to effect changes in society. Their righteous anger and outrage caused significant changes at the federal and state level of government.

George Floyd and Black Lives Matter

On May 25, 2020, George Floyd, a forty-six-year-old black man who'd recently moved to Minneapolis, was detained by police on suspicion of passing a counterfeit $20 bill. After police questioned him, they decided to take him to the police station. According to court documents, Floyd protested and tried to avoid getting into the car. Ultimately, he was pinned face down on the ground and handcuffed by police. Minneapolis police officer Derek Chauvin pressed his knee against Floyd's neck for more than eight minutes, while cellphone video recorded Floyd pleading for his mother and saying that he could not breathe. When paramedics finally arrived, Floyd was nonresponsive. He was later pronounced dead (Jimenez 2020).

Unrest soon erupted in Minneapolis and around the country. People filled the squares and streets of at least 140 US cities, with people marching in the streets and holding signs of "I Can't Breathe" and "Black Lives Matter" (Al Jazeera 2020). Some protests lead to rioting and looting, with windows being smashed, stores being looted, and cars or other property set on fire. One report estimates the cost of damages to businesses and property owners in Minneapolis alone to be over $500 million (La Jeunesse 2020). Other protests were entirely peaceful and even included prayer vigils. In Atlanta, 300 people attended a public prayer vigil with a diverse group of ministers to "raise awareness of the critical need for a dramatic change in the manner in which our cities are policed" (Ross 2020). In Houston, members of the Fifth Ward Church of Christ flashed signs of justice, peace, and love at passing motorists as part of a peaceful sit-in. Protests continued in major US cities and even Europe, with calls for societal changes ranging from criminal justice reform to defunding the police.

According to a poll of registered voters by the *New York Times* and Siena College, 59 percent of all voters (and 52 percent of white voters) believe that George Floyd's death was part of a pattern of "excessive police violence toward African Americans" (Herndon and Searcy 2020). In battleground states, 54 percent of respondents said criminal justice system treatment of black Americans was a bigger problem than rioting that took place during some demonstrations (Herndon and Searcy 2020).

The widespread angry protests have resulted in legal changes in local, state, and national levels (Sloan, Pritchard, and Foreman 2020). Aunt Jemima will change the logo of its syrup and pancake mix. Its parent company Quaker Oats has acknowledged that the black woman in a handkerchief hat on the logo was based "on a racial stereotype" (Hsu 2020). The United States Army will conduct promotion and conduct hearings without photographs to address the number of black officers passed over for promotion compared to their white counterparts (Rempfer 2020). The Washington Redskins have decided to change their team name after years of criticism. Musical groups such as the Dixie Chicks and Lady Antebellum have changed their names to the Chicks and Lady A, respectively (Frank 2020). Mississippi lawmakers have voted to retire the state flag, a confederate symbol for more than 126 years (Pettus 2020). On the federal level, the George Floyd Justice in Policing Act passed the House of Representatives. It would restrict police chokeholds, set up new training procedures, and create a national database of police incidents involving use of force. It is unlikely to pass the Senate, and President Trump has vowed to veto the bill if it reaches his desk (Foran, Byrd, and Raju 2020). Other bills are in the initial stage at both the state and federal level. Nonetheless, it was the righteous anger of the protesters around the country that sparked the proposal in Congress.

CONCLUSION

Law is full of dispassion and decorum, but with a constant adversarial undercurrent. It is truly an odd paradox in many ways. It is a very structured environment with rules and regulations. Dispassionate judges may sit on an elevated bench and pronounce judgments with little emotion. Parties and lawyers air grievances with restraint, all in the pursuit of justice for their personal causes.

Yet, Solomon (1989) writes that emotions like anger ascribe responsibility and require that someone is to blame. Jesus did not call Christians to be dispassionate spectators quietly observing social injustice to ensure that the sun does not set on our anger. Martin Luther King Jr. once said, "For evil to succeed, all it needs is for good men to do nothing" (Eire 2017). In reading scripture, Christians often feel that anger is a sin and should be avoided. Christian psychology has historically categorized positive and negative emotions, with anger, envy, and pride being labeled as negative emotions (Solomon 1989). While this approach is essentially correct, we must remember how Jesus himself displayed anger in the temple in John 2:17. He acted out of a sense of justice and not vengeance. Even though Aristotle argued that anger and vengeance are tied together, it is possible to be angry and not feel the necessity for vengeance (Solomon 1989, 368). Thus, righteous anger is not a sinful attitude for Christians if pursued for justice and not out of vengeance.

Indeed, righteous anger of Christians throughout history has caused great changes in the law. We have herein examined the Protestant Reformation and actions of Martin Luther, which gave Christians the translated Bible and freedom from Catholic doctrines. We can also consider the Civil Rights movement, during which the protests, marches, and sit-ins roused the nation and inspired the passage of the Civil Rights Act of 1964 and the end of Jim Crow laws. The #MeToo movement, started by activist Tarana Burke, was propelled into the national psyche with the angry cries of so many women who felt disenfranchised by a system created by men. Increases in EEOC filings and new state laws have followed. Now, the Black Lives Matter movement and others like it are presenting an opportunity for white and black Americans to participate in something that could be revolutionary. As stated above, companies, artists, and teams are changing their advertising logos. Changes to police practices are proposed in many states and at the federal level.

Is there a role for Christians to play in responding to social injustices, and if so, how do we respond? The Bible says in Micah 6:8, "What does the Lord require of you but to do justice, to love kindness, and to walk humbly with your God?" We should note that the scripture does not instruct us to quietly observe justice or to simply think on justice. It requires us to *do justice*. The scripture prods us as Christians to do justice, and if that requires some righteous anger, then we are in pretty good company with the likes of Jesus, Martin Luther, Martin Luther King Jr., and Rachel Denhollander.

REFERENCES

Al Jazeera. 2020. "A Timeline of the George Floyd and Anti-police Brutality Protests." Accessed July 16, 2020. https://www.aljazeera.com/news/2020/06/timeline-george-floyd-protests-200610194807385.html.

Bandes, Susan. 1996. "Empathy, Narrative, and Victim Impact Statements." *The University of Chicago Law Review* 63: 361–412.

Bond, Sarah. 2017. "Were Pagan Temples All Smashed or Just Converted into Christian Ones?" *Forbes Magazine*, October 7. https://www.forbes.com/sites/drsarahbond/2017/10/07/were-pagan-temples-all-smashed-or-just-converted-into-christian-ones/.

Bruinius, Harry. 2018. "Churches Struggle with Their #MeToo Moment." *The Christian Science Monitor,* April 20. https://www.csmonitor.com/USA/Politics/2018/0420/Churches-struggle-with-their-MeToo-moment.

CNN. 2018. "Read Rachael Denhollander's Full Victim Impact Statement about Larry Nassar." *CNN.com,* January 30, 2018. https://www.cnn.com/2018/01/24/us/rachael-denhollander-full-statement/index.html.

"Courtroom Decorum Policy." n.d. United States Court of Appeals for the Federal Circuit. Accessed July 15, 2020. http://www.cafc.uscourts.gov/argument/court-decorum.

Colwell, Kelly, and Sheryl Johnson. 2020. "#MeToo and #ChurchToo: Putting the Movements in Context." *Review and Expositor* 117, no. 2: 183–98.

Curtis, Dennis E., and Judith Resnik. 1987. "Images of Justice." *The Yale Law Journal* 96, no. 8: 1727–72.

EEOC. 2018. "EEOC Releases Preliminary FY 2018 Sexual Harassment Data." US Equal Employment Opportunity Commission. Accessed July 12, 2020. https://www.eeoc.gov/newsroom/eeoc-releases-preliminary-fy-2018-sexual-harassment-data.

Eire, Carlos. 2017. "Martin Luther: The Wrath of God: Carlos Eire." *First Things.* Accessed July 16, 2020. https://www.firstthings.com/web-exclusives/2017/10/martin-luther-the-wrath-of-god.

Foran, Clare, Haley Byrd, and Manu Raju. 2020. "House Approves Police Reform Bill Named in Honor of George Floyd." *CNN*, June 26. Accessed July 17, 2020. https://www.cnn.com/2020/06/25/politics/house-police-reform-legislation-vote/index.html.

Frank, Allegra. 2020. "What's in a Name?" *Vox*, July 9. https://www.vox.com/the-highlight/21308236/redskins-name-racism-aunt-jemima-dixie-chicks-fair-and-lovely.

Herndon, Astead, and Dionne Searcey. 2020. "How Trump and the Black Lives Matter Movement Changed White Voters' Minds." *New York Times*, June 27.

Hobbes, Thomas. 1904. *Leviathan.* Edited by A. R. Waller. Cambridge, UK: Cambridge University Press.

Hsu, Tiffany. 2020. "Aunt Jemima Brand to Change Name and Image Over 'Racial Stereotype.'" *New* York Times, June 17. https://www.nytimes.com/2020/06/17/business/media/aunt-jemima-racial-stereotype.html?searchResultPosition=2.

Jay, Martin. 2003. *Refractions of Violence.* New York: Taylor and Francis.

Jimenez, Omar. 2020. "New Police Body Camera Footage Reveals George Floyd's Last Words Were 'I Can't Breathe.'" *CNN.* July 15. https://www.cnn.com/2020/07/15/us/george-floyd-body-cam-footage/index.html.

King, Martin L., Jr. 1963. "I Have a Dream." Speech. Lincoln Memorial, Washington, DC, June 28. American Rhetoric. https://www.americanrhetoric.com/speeches/mlkihaveadream.htm.

La Jeunesse, William. 2020. "George Floyd Protests Could Be Most Expensive Civil Disturbance in US History, Experts Say." Fox News. June 29. https://www.foxnews.com/politics/george-floyd-protests-expensive-civil-disturbance-us-history.

Lee, Morgan. 2020. "Why Christians Have a Reputation for Smashing Statues." *Christianity Today,* July 9. https://www.christianitytoday.com/ct/2020/july-web-only/statues-taking-down-christian-history-iconoclasm.html.

———. 2018. "My Larry Nassar Testimony Went Viral. But There's More to the Gospel Than Forgiveness." *Christianity Today*, January 31. https://www.christianitytoday.com/ct/2018/january-web-only/rachael-denhollander-larry-nassar-forgiveness-gospel.html.

Lee, Rebecca. 2012. "Justice for All." *Vanderbilt Law Review* 65: 217–29.

Maroney, Terry. 2011. "The Persistent Cultural Script of Judicial Dispassion." *California Law Review* 99, no. 2: 629–81.

Maroney, Terry A., and James J. Gross. 2014. "The Ideal of the Dispassionate Judge: An Emotion Regulation Perspective." *Emotion Review* 6, no. 2: 142–51. https://doi.org/10.1177/1754073913491989.

"Martin Luther." 2019. Biography.com. September 20. Accessed July 17, 2020. https://www.biography.com/religious-figure/martin-luther.

Muldoon, Paul. 2008. "The Moral Legitimacy of Anger." *European Journal of Social Theory* 11, no. 3: 299–314.

North, Anna. 2019. "7 Positive Changes That Have Come from the #MeToo Movement." *Vox*, October 4. https://www.vox.com/identities/2019/10/4/20852639/me-too-movement-sexual-harassment-law-2019.

Nussbaum, Martha C. 2015. "Transitional Anger." *Journal of the American Philosophical Association* 1, no. 1: 41–56.

———. 2016. *Anger and Forgiveness: Resentment, Generosity, Justice.* Oxford: Oxford University Press.

Pettus, Emily Wagster. 2020. "Mississippi Retires State Flag in Quiet Ceremony." *Time*, July 2. Accessed July 17, 2020. https://time.com/5862506/mississippi-retires-state-flag-confederate/.

Quarterman, Ted. 2020. "Where Is Rachael Denhollander, the First Woman to Speak Out Publicly against Larry Nassar, Now?" *True Crime Buzz*, June 26. https://www.oxygen.com/true-crime-buzz/netflix-athlete-a-where-is-rachael-denhollander.

Rapp, Christof. 2018. "Dispassionate Judges Encountering Hotheaded Aristotelians." *Aristotle on Emotions in Law and Politics Law and Philosophy Library*, 27–49. https://doi.org/10.1007/978-3-319-66703-4_3.

Rempfer, Kyle. 2020. "Army Ditches Officer Promotion Photos as Part of an Effort to Eliminate Unconscious Bias." *Army Times*, June 25. Accessed July 17, 2020. https://www.armytimes.com/news/your-army/2020/06/25/army-ditches-promotion-photos-as-part-of-an-effort-to-eliminate-unconcious-bias/.

Ross, Bobby Jr. 2020. "Protests and Prayers." *The Christian Chronicle,* June 11. https://christianchronicle.org/protests-and-prayers/.

Segura, Olga. 2018. "#MeToo Founder Tarana Burke: 'Jesus Was the First Activist That I Knew." *Sojourners,* September 24. https://sojo.net/articles/metoo-founder-tarana-burke-jesus-was-first-activist-i-knew.

Shafer-Landau, Russ. 2015. "The Social Contract Tradition: The Theory and Its Attractions." In *The Fundamentals of Ethics*, 192–205. New York: Oxford University Press.

Sloan, Steven, Justin Pritchard, and Tom Foreman, Jr. 2020. "Massive, Peaceful Protests across US Demand Police Reform." *ABC News,* June 6. Accessed July 17, 2020. https://abcnews.go.com/US/wireStory/ turning-grief-change-movement-targets-racial-injustice-71104375.

Solomon, Robert C. 1973. "Emotions and Choice." *The Review of Metaphysics* 27, no. 1: 20–41.

———. 1989. "The Emotions of Justice." *Social Justice Research* 3, no. 4: 345–374.

Chapter 10

Racism and the Spiritual Discipline of Righteous Anger

Jason Cook

TWO WARRING IDEALS

To be black and Evangelical in America is to embody a peculiar form of double consciousness.[1] We stand between the "two unreconciled strivings" for collective racial equality on one hand, and on the other hand for personal sanctification that holds individuals accountable for their circumstances (Du Bois 2020, 10). We mediate the "two warring ideals" of emotional expressiveness inherited from the black church tradition and the rationalism of the white Protestant theological tradition (Du Bois 2020, 10). Our emotional landscape is profoundly shaped by a collective memory of past and present injustices against African Americans, along with a compelling history of impassioned protest, both religious and secular. Yet Evangelical moral sensibilities have been informed by a rationalistic pragmatism that obscures the importance of taking seriously the emotional terrain of black people weary from racism. Black Evangelicals intuit the appropriateness of anger at unrelenting racial injustice. But our white sisters and brothers intuitively undermine the spiritual value of negative emotions, especially anger. Our shared faith prioritizes meekness and forgiveness. We should be "slow to anger; for the anger of man does not produce the righteousness of God" (James 1:20). Moreover, prudence advises us to avoid anger because it alienates our white brothers and sisters. So, we carry the burden of figuring out what to do with our inescapable anger. Shall we let it fester into silent bitterness? Do we vent our pain and risk alienation from our fellow Evangelicals? Should we keep traveling between two communities—a black (perhaps secular) community

137

willing to acceptour indignation and a white Evangelical community that regards our righteous anger as problematic? Or must we finally abandon white congregations altogether?

Discerning how to cope with anger provoked by racial injustice is a practical necessity. For black Christians who worship in predominantly white Evangelical traditions, this necessity is complicated by an underdeveloped theology of anger that fails to accommodate the experience of oppressed people groups in general, and black Americans in particular. The question we must wrestle with is whether the righteous indignation of oppressed peoples can be faithful to the logic of the gospel.[2] Anger, both righteous and unrighteous, is a significant theme in scripture. A biblical theology of righteous anger demonstrates that the trajectory of the gospel does indeed accommodate faithful anger. More than that, indignation at injustice plays a significant role in God's work of redeeming creation. Nevertheless, the anger of the oppressed is not inherently righteous. Nor is the appropriateness of indignation limited to marginalized peoples. Rather, indignation is a spiritual discipline that believers should cultivate according to the pattern of righteous anger modeled in scripture by God and his prophets.[3]

In what follows I develop a biblical theology of righteous anger as a framework for understanding how divine anger directed against injustice can discipline our experience of anger provoked by racism and other forms of institutionalized injustice. I begin by evaluating common objections to human anger and their relevance to institutions of judicial anger. Then I suggest how righteous anger can be understood as a spiritual discipline. I address concerns about biblical portrayals of divine anger. Finally I conclude with a reflection on the relationship between righteous anger and love.

THE PROBLEM OF HUMAN ANGER

Human anger is problematic for interpersonal relationships and social institutions. Among individuals, anger erodes friendships, estranges families, and cements hostility between enemies. By escalating disputes, it frequently leads to emotional abuse, physical violence, and even death. Anger directed at society more broadly manifests in mass shootings, strikes, protests, terrorism, and ultimately war. In either case, dealing with anger is an acute moral concern for Christians because of Christ's teaching to love our persecutors and because he models forgiveness toward those committed to violence against him (Matt 5:44; Luke 23:34).

Furthermore, coping with anger is a practical concern because it is an unavoidable feature of our common life. Anger is an ever present feature of public discourse, expressed, documented, and amplified on various media platforms. Regardless of race, we know what it feels like to be the target of another's anger. Christians who are victims of social injustice carry the added burden of dealing with the simultaneous presence of righteous indignation and morally unjustified anger. Coping with indignation is further complicated by emotions adjacent to anger such as hatred, bitterness, and a desire for revenge. In practice we may have difficulty establishing clear boundaries between indignation and these adjacent emotions. Thus, conversations about the potential legitimacy of anger often become clouded.

Because we generally experience the effects of anger as destructive, Christians often regard anger as a negative emotion to be avoided. But we should not take our aversion to anger for granted. It may be that the problem of human anger lies with a distorted humanity rather than the anger itself. In order to make such an evaluation, we can begin by defining anger as "an emotion characterized by hostility and the expression of frustration"[4] (Psychology Dictionary 2020a). This definition accounts for the *internal* emotional experience of anger and the *external* expression of that emotion (Brother John 2017, 11). The following critique addresses common objections to anger.

First, anger is irrational. The irrationality of anger may refer to a faulty basis for becoming angry. For example, anger may be aroused as a result of unreasonable expectations, faulty perception, or inaccurate information. The irrationality of anger may also refer to the lack of correspondence between the apparent irritant and the intensity or direction of the response. While anger may lead to apparently irrational behavior, anger is more precisely nonrational. It follows an emotional logic rather than the rational logic idealized by modern Western societies. Highly rationalized societies make few formal accommodations for anger to play a constructive social role (Brother John 2017, 26). Instead, anger should ideally be stripped of its emotional content and expressed in objective terms.[5] Such societies often marginalize even justifiable anger, especially in the public realm.[6]

Second, anger is violent. Anger-induced violence may be physical or psychological. Though often directed outward toward others, people experiencing anger may even inflict violence upon themselves when other avenues of expression seem unavailable. Violence in all of its manifestations destroys. It destroys relationships, bodies, communities, physical objects, and the natural environment. By assaulting people directly or attacking the means by which they survive and make meaning, the violent expression of anger undermines life. Even repressed anger manifests in self-destructive ways. However, indignation can also direct its destructive force against moral apathy, unjust social norms, and exploitative institutional mechanisms.

Third, anger begets anger. The perceived threat of anger directed against you is one of the most compelling temptations to respond in kind. Even the outward expression of righteous indignation can set off a cycle of escalating anger. In this regard, some dismiss the potentially constructive role of anger on utilitarian grounds. Not only is anger a philosophically inferior emotion because of its irrationality and a morally inferior emotion because of its destructiveness, anger is counterproductive. This third objection takes for granted that the utility of anger is a more important criterion than the moral appropriateness of anger. In cases of indignation at injustice, this assumption tends to hold victims accountable for managing the reaction of victimizers when confronting victimizers about their unjust behavior (Srinivasan 2018, 133).

Considering these widely acknowledged negative characteristics of anger, we might wish to inoculate ourselves from anger. Such thinking regards anger as a disease. But neither scripture nor modern psychology regard anger as a dispensable emotion. To the contrary, they both present anger, along with the other so-called negative emotions as essential to life.[7] In the case of scripture, anger also plays a prominent role in the vindication of righteousness. Despite the limitations of the metaphor, inoculation suggests that exposure to a certain kind of anger might train us to resist the destructive influence of objectionable manifestations of anger when we encounter them in ourselves. In order to understand how this might work, we must first clarify the nature of the disease by considering the relationship between anger and justice.

THE FALLIBILITY OF JUDICIAL ANGER

Both in scripture and in contemporary societies, those with sanctioned authority enjoy greater freedom to externalize their anger. Brother John of Taizé observes that in scripture, human "anger is expressed almost exclusively by individuals possessing authority, either political (notably the king) or familial (the father of head of household). They express anger above all to affirm their authority in a situation where it has been called into question or held in contempt" (Brother John 2017, 23).[8] In modern societies, this official expression of anger is exercised by governments through judicial (and military) institutions. Judicial anger necessarily affirms the authority that legitimizes it. The laws enforced by democratic judicial systems are established on the basis of a broadly accepted conception of justice. Although such systems may warrant critique in particular cases, they are not arbitrary. Consequently, one of the critical functions of judicial anger is to preserve a (more or less) just social order established by the governing authorities. In practice, this leads to the possibility of official anger becoming decoupled from justice.

The concentration of means to enforce official anger through institutionalized violence means that victims aroused to anger by socially sanctioned injustice poses limited options for coping with their anger. Those options include suppression, lament, subversion, civil disobedience, and revolt. One of the tragic ironies of such unsanctioned anger in modern Western societies is that it is inherently counterproductive. This is particularly evident in the phenomenon of rioting. Martin Luther King Jr. famously observed that "a riot is the language of the unheard" (King 1968). Yet he also expressed his conviction that "a riot merely intensifies the fears of the white community while relieving the guilt" and is consequently counterproductive (King 1968). When the oppressed members of a society lack official channels to effectively protest their unjust treatment, they may eventually resort to means that are emotionally charged and violent. Because this threatens the established order, the government is compelled to respond in officially sanctioned anger. From the perspective of those sympathetic to the government and the modern preference for objectivity, a riot can never be justifiable because it is an (apparently) irrational, violent, counterproductive expression of anger. Furthermore, the alleged illegitimacy of the outward expression of anger is often employed by those in power to delegitimize the just basis for the indignation.

Implicit in my assessment of anger and power is a critique that although we tend to regard unsanctioned anger as problematic, we often to fail to recognize that institutions enforcing the legally ordained standard of justice are powerful mechanisms of anger. However, the internal anger experienced by humans must be translated into objective, unemotional, rationally defensible laws and policies for these institutions. Because of this, we tend to have a higher tolerance for anger mediated by sanctioned authorities (unless we are its victims).

Even though anger is often regarded as problematic because of its irrationality, violence, and tendency to provoke more anger, the above discussion reveals that such a view is inconsistent with how we commonly regard institutionalized mechanisms of judicial anger. If we were to apply the same criteria to our judicial systems, we would find that they wouldn't bear such scrutiny unscathed. First, the policies that regulate institutional anger are not objective. They attempt to codify just standards that apply in a variety of situations, some of which cannot be anticipated. They are passionately debated, composed, and enacted by people on the basis of their limited knowledge, relationships, biases, and personal interests. They must be enforced on the basis of feasibility and available resources by people who are chipper, grumpy, distracted, or bored. My point is not to denigrate a particular legal system, but rather to note that institutions established to preserve a just society are subject to all the potential absurdity and wisdom of persons who experience internal anger as a nonrational emotion.

Second, institutions are capable of far more violence than any angry individual. Institutions exceed individuals in the frequency, scope, and intensity of their violence. This is simply a matter of resources. Developed nations have invested massive amounts of resources to build prisons, weapons, and militaries, all of which are explicitly intended to carry out some form of violence against those who violate the social order. The amount of resources expended to build a nation's capacity to execute violence for the sake of justice and the stewardship of those resources may deserve criticism, but the simple fact of marshalling resources to preserve social order is not inherently unethical. In a world like ours, cultivating the power to enforce justice is prudent. But institutions, like individuals, must cope with the simultaneous presence of both morally legitimate and morally illegitimate inclinations in the administration of justice.

Third, in democratic societies, the operation of the legal system presumes opposition and legally incorporates certain forms of dealing with opposition into its procedures. The complex systems of voting to establish lawmakers and laws, along with the vast network of courts, provide sanctioned means for opposing unwelcome attempts by the state to impose its will in ways that will harm victims of the established order. These sanctioned mechanisms for expressing opposition toward judicial institutions tend to privilege those already in positions of power. The ubiquity and training of police forces further reveals the expectation that state-sanctioned anger will often provoke anger in turn. Again, my point is not to undermine the potential value of institutions authorized to enforce justice, but to demonstrate that our aversion to unsanctioned anger on the basis of irrationality, violence, and a tendency to provoke more anger is superficial.

What we find disconcerting about the expression of nonofficial anger is that it destabilizes the order in our lives. The unregulated expression of anger destabilizes interpersonal relationships, institutions, and even our own inner worlds. This helps account for the reason we have a greater tolerance for anger enacted by institutions. Institutional anger works to preserve the established order. To the extent that we benefit from this order, we may be hesitant to challenge it. To the extent that we prefer the existing order to anticipated alternatives, we may also be inclined to perceive challenges to these institutions as threats. The aforementioned scenario applies to many of who don't possess any institutional authority but enjoy the benefits of the status quo. We might call this privilege. This dynamic tends to pit the privileged against the unprivileged, those who unjustly suffer some form of sanctioned institutional violence with limited means to correct the injustice.

In light of this, we can return to the metaphor of inoculation. The disease we should want to avoid is not anger per se, but unjust anger. Anger is a physiological response to a perceived threat against one's life or something one cherishes. Thus, anger is a secondary function of desire or love. The legitimacy of internal anger should therefore be evaluated on the basis of accurate perception and the object of love. First, is what seems to be threatened actually threatened? Second, is the thing loved worthy of such love? Just anger is not ultimately about protecting authority. Instead, just anger is the proper internal response to an actual threat against something worthy of love. Conversely, unjust anger can be aroused through faulty perception, or more fundamentally, a misguided love.

The moral imperative for Christians is to cultivate righteous loves and then justly oppose actual threats to what is actually good. For Christians, the dilemma of anger in an unjust society is that anger will sometimes be a moral obligation that sets us in opposition to institutions that benefit us and that possess significant means of carrying out violence against us if we become a threat to the established order. In such cases expressing anger makes us vulnerable to violence. Yet, righteous anger at injustice is a moral obligation precisely because of its capacity to destabilize the existing order. [9] This destabilizing effect of anger provides the opportunity for injustice within institutions to be removed or, in extreme cases, for irredeemable institutions to be replaced altogether.

RIGHTEOUS ANGER AS A SPIRITUAL DISCIPLINE

If we recognize that righteous anger at injustice is a moral obligation, our anger can err in several ways. First, we may become internally angry when we shouldn't, as when unworthy loves are threatened. Second, we may fail to become angry when we ought to.[10] Third, we may express a righteous internal anger in an unjust manner. These errors may be understood as sin (*hamartia*), a departure from the standard of righteousness. In saying this I do not imply that such errors are inherently malicious or intentional. But to the extent that any of us tends to err in these ways, we demonstrate that "sin is part of the internal structure of our lives" (Foster 1998, 4). For Christians, our missing the mark of righteous anger reflects the incompleteness of our inner righteousness. Though we may desire righteousness, we cannot make ourselves righteous. The inner transformation we need so that we habitually practice righteous anger is a gift from God produced by his Spirit working in us (Foster 1998, 6–7).

It may seem strange to regard the practice of righteous anger as a spiritual discipline, but the terminology of spiritual disciplines, as traditionally understood, is helpful for three reasons. First, it draws our attention to the necessity of relying on the Spirit to work in us and transform how we experience anger. Second, it highlights the importance of cultivating the practice of righteous anger as a habit. Third, it suggests that the very pursuit of this habit is a means of receiving God's grace.

Practicing righteous anger, in its internal and external dimensions, is not a spiritual discipline in the traditional sense.[11] Indignation may at times be expressed through disciplines such as, prayer, service (on behalf of the oppressed), and confession of individual or corporate culpability for injustice. However, practicing righteous anger is a spiritual discipline in the same way that loving your neighbor as yourself is a spiritual discipline. People naturally experience and express indignation just as we naturally experience and express love, imperfectly. We cannot avoid indignation. The world and its inhabitants will grieve and anger us. We often grieve and anger ourselves. We will either repress our anger, express it inadequately, or learn to conform our anger to the pattern of the Lord.

In order to practice indignation (more) righteously, we must become familiar with the Lord's own anger and the righteous anger modeled in scripture by the prophets and psalmists.[12] Modern Western Christians may intuitively assume that we should avoid giving excessive attention to divine anger in scripture. Dwelling on the Lord's wrath produces cognitive dissonance with our image of a loving, forgiving God. We already find ourselves defensively trying to explain away God's anger to critics of our faith. We might even risk turning into those fanatics who seem to delight in announcing judgment upon unrepentant sinners. To the contrary, I believe that meditating on righteous anger in scripture is more likely to stimulate our humility, compassion, mercy, and a fervent anticipation of Christ's return. But in order for us to experience God's transforming grace through encounters with righteous anger in scripture, we must deal with the apparent problem of divine anger.

NEGATIVE DIVINE EMOTIONS

In a sense, the modern objection to God's anger in scripture is not especially modern. By the second century, Marcion of Sinope had already rejected the deity of the Old Testament as incompatible with the Father of Jesus represented in the Gospels. He characterized the Creator as "judicial, harsh, and mighty in war" (Mahar 2020). He regarded this deity as fickle, improvident, and consequently inferior to the Supreme God (Mahar 2020). On the other hand, "the Supreme God is susceptible to no feeling of rivalry, or anger, or damage, or injury. He inflicts no punishment and takes no offence, and is not feared, as a good being ought not to be an object of fear, as a judicial being, in whom resides the grounds for fear—anger, severity, judgments, vengeance, and condemnation" (Mahar 2020). Many Christians today would be unwilling to take the extreme position of identifying the God of the Old Testament and the God of the New Testament as two distinct deities. Nevertheless, Marcion's sentiments reflect the sensibilities of many contemporary Christians and non-Christians about the "ideal" temperament of a loving, sovereign God. Marcion, however, presented a profound distortion of righteous anger in scripture, a distortion we are even more vulnerable to today because of the peculiar biases in modern Western cultures. In addition, we often fail to recognize and critique the counterpart to divine anger in contemporary societies.

Scripture frequently employs affective language to describe God's response to the people he has created. We are generally comfortable with the attribution of positive emotions, such as love and joy, to God (John 3:16). We may be less comfortable with emotions like grief or regret that suggest divine vulnerability (Gen 6:7). However, we object most strongly to emotions that describe divine hostility: anger, jealousy, and hatred (Exod 20:5).[13] Here I am particularly concerned with the internal dimension of emotion. Even prior to the expression of hostility, it seems problematic to think that the Lord *feels* anger or hatred toward someone he created, even if that someone is guilty of injustice. We may be willing to accept a divine judge, but we prefer him to be dispassionate in dispensing justice. In other words, we prefer that he administer justice in the same manner as our secular institutions.

One of the mistakes we make in thinking about the negative emotions ascribed to God in scripture is to project our own experience of negative emotions onto him. When the Bible, particularly the Old Testament, refers to God's anger, we imagine God suddenly losing his temper, becoming irrational, and losing his ability to accurately evaluate the circumstances. In short, we imagine God *being* angry like us. Yet we have no direct access to God's internal experience of anger. Nor can we rely on physiological changes in his appearance to *see* what God is like when he becomes angry.[14] To say that God's anger is kindled is already to engage in theological metaphor, rather than description, and of course, our own experience of internal anger is an inadequate source for a theology of divine anger (Brother John 2017, 11). To understand what the writers of the Hebrew scriptures meant when referring to God's anger, it is important to recognize that people in the ancient world did not conceptualize their identity on the basis of an interior sense of selfhood (Walton 2018, 63). A person's identity was determined by their relationships and role within a community. This psychological orientation is evident in scripture's emphasis on externalized expressions of attitude rather than internal feelings. This is particularly so in descriptions of God (Brother John 2017, 19).

In the Old Testament, divine anger is commonly manifested as "an outburst of energy with destructive consequences" (Brother John 2017, 19). Yet outbursts of divine energy are not always attributed to anger. When the Lord appeared to the Israelites on Mount Sinai following the exodus, his presence was manifested with thunder, lightning, and a trumpet blast that made the whole mountain violently tremble (Exod 19:16–18). But there is no indication that the Lord was angry. However, when the Israelites violated their newly ratified covenant by worshipping a golden calf, the Lord became angry. "Now therefore let me alone, that my wrath may burn hot against them and I may consume them, in order that I may make a great nation of you" (Exod 32:10). God's (potential) activity is similarly destructive in both cases, however the activity is understood as anger when it is a response to a violation of the divinely established order (Brother John 2017, 21).[15]

THE CYCLE OF DIVINE WRATH

When scripture presents the anger of God, there is no indication of irrationality, confusion, or capriciousness on the part of God. To the contrary, God's anger is uniquely predictable within the ancient Near Eastern world. In addition to being fallible, pagan deities did not clearly communicate their expectations to their worshippers (Walton 2018, 64, 67). This subjected their worshippers to the anxiety of being unable to anticipate the disapproval of their gods. On the other hand, the God of Israel established a covenant with his people by which they knew how to maintain right standing with the Lord, what were the consequences of violating his covenant, and how to restore fellowship after a violation. To the ancient Israelites who took the Lord's covenant seriously, the Lord's anger should have been refreshingly predictable.

Furthermore, although the Lord's anger may be suddenly provoked, as in the incident with the golden calf, it is never impulsive. Scripture frequently refers to the outward manifestation of God's anger as wrath. The wrath of God, which brings about destruction on people and their physical environment, implements justice against unrepentant offenders, and is generally directed against nations rather than individuals (Baloian 1992, 99–100). The concept of divine wrath, particularly in the historical books of the Old Testament, functions to explain Israel's misfortunes as God's judgment for her infidelity (Judg 2:11–21).[16]

Whereas humans lose their temper and sometimes vent uncontrolled anger out of proportion to the provocation, God demonstrates a controlled, identifiable pattern in the external expression of wrath. This pattern, which Baloian terms the cycle of wrath, follows three stages and presumes a covenant relationship between God and the nation of Israel.[17] The first stage of the wrath cycle is the *warning of wrath to come*. In the golden calf incident, the Lord verbalized his indignation and his intention to destroy the people for their stubbornness and idolatry (Exod 32:7–10). But he relented after Moses interceded for them. The Lord's warnings are notably not destructive. He issues them to affirm the intensity of his displeasure with sin and to motivate people to repent from evil deeds (Lev 26:27–28; Jer 4:4; Jon 3:1–10). God's warnings are not threats intended to intimidate his enemies or to simply blow off steam. They are expressions of his commitment to just human societies. In the case of Israel, they also manifest his determination to grant Israel the blessings that are contingent on their covenant faithfulness. Furthermore, they demonstrate his preference to respond to sin with mercy rather than judgment.

The second stage is *pouring out wrath*. Leviticus characterizes the resulting misfortunes as the Lord's discipline (Lev 26: 18, 23, 28). God's wrath is never merely punitive.[18] It always aims at restoring justice to a society and, in the case of Israel, restoring covenant fellowship between himself and his nation. Consequently, he may relent from his wrath in response to appeals for mercy (1 Kgs 8:46–53).

The third stage is *deliverance from wrath*. Because wrath frequently takes the form of oppression by foreign nations, the final stage in the cycle often entails liberation from enemies for a remnant. The Lord comforts his people (Isa 12:1) and does good to them (Zech 8:14–15). Ideally the people who survive will refrain from their prior idolatry and injustice. If they begin to turn away from the Lord again, the cycle repeats until the eschatological day of the Lord, when God's wrath will permanently remove all wickedness and evil from the earth (Zeph 3:8–15). God's anger is certainly severe. But it is neither irrational nor uncontrolled. The Lord manifests his anger in a calculated manner that steers people toward the pursuit of fellowship with himself and justice in their relationships with one another.

IMPRECATIONS AND DIVINE VIOLENCE

Another feature of divine anger that often disturbs us is the violent character of divine wrath. How can a good and loving God justifiably employ violent and destructive means to discipline people he loves? Yet we find the threat of violence included in the covenant that regulates God's relationship with Israel (Lev 26:21–33). To examine this question, we must identify several degrees of violence in relation to the role of curses in ancient Near Eastern society.[19] "A curse's ultimate purpose was to inspire heavenly rage by soliciting supernatural powers to intercede in situations that were believed to be beyond mortal control such as injustices, disease, injury, or just plain bad luck" (Kitz 2007, 616). Imprecatory petitions called on deities to inflict three distinct degrees of violence, all of which ultimately lead to separation from life. The mildest is the wish for a difficult life (Kitz 2007, 620). For example, wild beasts destroying crops undermines the conditions for life and constitutes a form of indirect violence. The intermediate degree is the petition for a premature death, which might be caused by disease, famine, or direct physical violence (Kitz 2007, 620). The most extreme curse is for extinction, which entails "complete eradication of any article or living being associated with the unfortunate target" (Kitz 2007, 621). This is reflected in the biblical language of being "cut off" (Lev 20:1–5). Imprecatory petitions in scripture appeal to God to carry out some form of violence in order to vindicate the innocent victim of injustice.

One of the reasons modern Westerners find biblical imprecations, particularly the imprecatory Psalms,[20] so objectionable is that we tend to separate the practice of religion from the enforcement of justice in society. The latter responsibility belongs to secular institutions (e.g., police departments, legal courts, and militaries). We recognize the necessity of these institutions for maintaining a society that can withstand the destabilizing influence of criminals and hostile foreign nations. Because we live in a world subject to the corrupting influence of sin, we generally accept the violence committed by these institutions as unfortunately necessary to protect the common good. We are rightly wary of any religious institutions attempting to enforce their vision of a righteous society through violence. This aversion to religious violence informs our understanding of divine wrath. However, modern Western secularism is alien to the world of scripture.

For the people of the ancient Near East, our distinction between religious and nonreligious institutions would have been unintelligible (Walton 2018, 47). They understood the spiritual and earthly realms as intertwined and that deities primarily existed within a shared world (Walton 2018, 47). Furthermore, since deities had established the cosmic order, they were responsible for enforcing that cosmic order when humans violated it (Walton 2018, 58). However regrettable the presence of violence is in and of itself, God is the most legitimate and trustworthy authority to determine when and how to employ violence in his governance of the cosmic order. This derives from his status as the sole Creator and source of all life. No one values human life and flourishing more than God. No one loves human life as purely as God. No one understands more deeply the tragedy of human lives being destroyed. On the other hand, even the best of our modern secular institutions that wield the threat of violence to maintain an orderly society are flawed. They don't consistently value all lives. They rely on fallible individuals and limited resources to administer justice. Furthermore, their vision of a just society is subject to profound biases. So, we pray for wise and just leadership. But if we are willing to tolerate the use of violence by institutions subject to the foibles of the people who built them, how much more should we trust the Lord's discretion?[21]

LINGERING INJUSTICE

A third feature of divine anger that troubles both Christians and their critics is the apparent withholding of wrath against people or groups that seem to deserve immediate, harsh sanction for their heinous crimes and disregard for human life. Related to this is the ongoing suffering endured by victims of abuse and oppression. A thorough consideration of theodicy in relation to the topic of divine wrath is beyond the scope of this paper. However, I will note that this is not an especially modern critique of God's administration of justice. The biblical psalmists as well as God's own prophets complained of how long the Lord was taking to deal with the wicked (Jer 12:1, 4; Ps 10). The fact that neither Jews nor Christians edited such complaints out of our respective canons of scripture suggests that they are an important resource for helping us cope with lingering injustice. The fact that these complaints are uttered by such righteous men as Jeremiah and Job gives all of us permission to bring our frustration and indignation before the Lord. The fact that God's response to such complaints is ultimately that we must wait for the eschatological day of the Lord when he will finally deal with all evil is unwelcome evidence that he truly is slow to anger (Zeph 3:7–8).

From a modern, rationalistic perspective, divine anger is objectionable because the God who created the world and established its proper moral order fails to be a dispassionate enforcer of justice. Instead, this God is personally invested in the righteousness of human relationships and the justice of human societies. He exerts his sovereignty by actively directing historical events to hold human societies accountable for entrenched wickedness. Although he can be appealed to by the oppressed, he is slow to anger, and he forgives those who have committed horrible offenses when they repent. According to some inscrutable logic, he permits some wickedness and unjust suffering to remain until an unspecified time in the (perhaps) distant future when he will permanently remove all evil from the world and then renew the earth. Such a God is unfathomable to the secular mind because it cannot find any objective analog among humanity. Such a God is profoundly different in kind and degree from the best of human leaders and institutions. Furthermore, daring to trust such a God and to hope in his vision of righteousness is to make oneself vulnerable to the anger of those institutions who object to him because he poses a threat to their own authority.

RIGHTEOUS ANGER AND LOVE

The preceding account of righteous anger in scripture is suggestive rather than comprehensive. Nevertheless, it demonstrates the capacity for a biblical theology of righteous indignation to help oppressed peoples, particularly black Evangelicals, discern how to faithfully cope with the simultaneous presence of righteous and unrighteous anger. Black Evangelicals find themselves in a situation analogous to the psalmists and prophets who lament ongoing injustice as we anticipate the final removal of wickedness from God's world. God neither demands that they suppress their indignation, nor does he prohibit imprecations that insist on the vindication of the righteous. Instead he invites victims of injustice to participate in his redemptive work through lament, imprecatory petition, and prophetic warnings of God's judgment against unjust institutions. These biblical forms provide us with spiritually productive vehicles for voicing our indignation in a manner that accords with the gospel's trajectory toward the ultimate eradication of unrighteousness and injustice.

We must now return to our prior definition of anger as an emotion characterized by hostility and the expression of frustration. Christ exhorted his disciples to love their enemies and bless those who persecute them because he knew that love would convert some enemies into friends. To consistently love our persecutors requires spiritual discipline. It also requires us to understand who and what constitutes an enemy. Thus, loving our enemies does not require us to condone their unjust behavior any more than loving our friends requires us to condone their unjust behavior. The faithful manifestation of righteous anger for the Christian would be an emotion characterized by hostility directed against injustice and love directed toward the perpetrators of injustice. On the surface, this paradoxical expectation may seem unfeasible. Yet this is the narrow way that leads to faithful anger that does not fall into moral apathy on one side or bitterness and hatred on the other. Cultivating the habit of such righteous anger is a spiritual discipline enabled by God's grace that God will ultimately honor in an eschatological day of divine wrath (Rev 6:9–16).[22]

By comparing our own experiences of human anger with the biblical presentation of divine anger, we see that the most objectionable features of human anger are absent from God's anger. God's anger is not irrational, casually violent, or aimless. His anger is predictably opposed to idolatry and injustice. He employs violence to motivate repentance, and even that comes after warnings intended to make room for his mercy. Above all, his anger aims to reestablish fellowship between himself and his people because this relationship is the means by which he conveys his love and grace to us. God's anger is not some version of dysfunctional human anger on a cosmic scale. It is the complete and consistent opposition of his entire triune being to the entrenched habits of unrighteousness that oppose the flourishing of life. It is based on his perfectly accurate perception of the threat posed by recalcitrant wickedness and his righteous desire for fellowship with his creatures.

This is why meditating on the Lord's righteous anger can so radically discipline our own experience and expression of anger. His anger teaches us what truly deserves our anger and trivializes all our petty offendedness and unrighteous loves. It teaches us to confront entrenched wickedness with courage. It teaches us to patiently bear suffering and injustice. It teaches us to extend mercy to those who least deserve it. It teaches us to condition our anger with love. Finally, it teaches us to aim always at the flourishing of God's world and to anticipate the return of our Savior.

NOTES

1. Du Bois coined the term "double consciousness" to describe the experience of black Americans "always looking at one's self through the eyes of others, or measuring one's soul by the tape of a world that looks on in amused contempt and pity" (Du Bois 2020, 10).

2. Some object to the legitimacy of anger on the basis of pragmatism. Anger and its supposedly intrinsic desire for retaliation fail to actually repair the damage caused by the offense (Nussbaum 2016). However, pragmatism is not a distinctly biblical or Christian basis for evaluating the legitimacy of anger. God held his prophets accountable for faithfully communicating divine opposition to unrighteousness, not for the effectiveness of such messages in provoking repentance (Ezek 3:16–21).

3. The culturally situated character of all theology leads to theological development that reflects the priorities, concerns, and biases of the communities producing theology. Consequently, theologians belonging to oppressed communities have given more energy and creativity to the challenge of coping with anger aroused by entrenched injustice. Such theological development is all the more robust because it accounts for the lived (including the emotional) experience of marginalization that is permitted or sanctioned by the dominant culture. For black Evangelicals in predominantly white churches, this means being separated from the wealth of theological resources that can help us cope with our indignation at racial injustice because white churches tend to prioritize the perspectives of white theologians. This separation is not absolute. Theology that is attentive to the perspective of oppressed people is accessible. However, black Evangelicals in white congregations generally can't access these spiritual resources within the local congregations that should nourish the spiritual growth of all its members. This in turn can lead to a sense of alienation from one's own spiritual community.

4. Against the assertions of Aristotle, the Stoics and contemporary philosophers such as Nussbaum who insist that anger intrinsically includes a desire for revenge,

Srinivasan points out that this may have been true in the honor-shame culture of the ancient world, but cannot be taken for granted in contemporary society, which has been profoundly influenced by Christian ethics (Srinivasan 2018, 129). The assumption that anger inherently includes the desire for revenge also fails to account for the possibility of the offended party remaining committed to the well-being of the offender. Yet scripture presumes this dynamic in its presentation of God's anger toward his covenant people.

5. This inclination fails to acknowledge that the emotional content of anger, independent of an objective account for the cause of anger, is epistemologically significant. The emotional aspect of internal and external anger registers the intensity of the offended party's objection to her treatment in a way that performs a critical function for managing interpersonal interactions. Suppressed anger of the offended deprives the offender of the awareness of the negative impact of his behavior and removes a potential incentive for him to adjust his behavior. The fact that people may use anger to exploit others is no more relevant to its epistemological significance than the fact that people may use rational argument to deceive is relevant to the epistemological significance of reason.

6. Public anger may be more or less acceptable depending on who expresses it, who it is directed toward, and whether different subgroups within a society feel a sense of solidarity with either party.

7. In psychology, negative emotions are so designated because people experience them as unpleasant, not because they are ethically negative (Psychology Dictionary 2020b).

8. For examples, see Gen 30:1–2; Exod 11:4–8; 32:21–29; Num 24:10; Judg 9:30; 1 Sam 11:6; 20:30; 2 Sam 12:5; Esther 1:12. Two notable exceptions affirm the general pattern. When Shechem rapes Jacob's daughter Dinah, Simeon and Levi vent their indignation upon Shechem by persuading them to circumcise all the men of their community and then slaughtering them while they recovered (Gen 34). Similarly, David's son Absalom murders his half brother Amnon for raping Tamar (2 Sam 13:20–33). In both cases, the sons expressed their indignation because their fathers, the heads of their respective households, failed to demonstrate their anger over the offense. In a sense, they were acting on behalf of their fathers. Furthermore, in both cases the sons ultimately suffered sanction for overstepping the boundaries of their authority to exercise wrath upon offenders.

9. The willingness to accept this risk is characteristic of Jesus' earthly ministry (Matt 2:13; Mark 11:15–19; Luke 4:16–30; John 11:45–53).

10. Aristotle's understanding of moral virtue reflects a similar conception of anger. Concerning anger, the morally virtuous person occupies an intermediate position between those given to excessive anger (irascibility) and those inclined toward deficient anger (unirascibilitiy). He describes such a person as good-tempered. Aristotle does not clarify whether a good-tempered person is distinguished by the moderate frequency of their anger or the nature of causes that provoke their anger. The difference is significant because a person who is appropriately angered by injustice may nevertheless be frequently angry in a society characterized by entrenched injustice. Such is the lot of prophets, biblical and modern, to be mischaracterized as given to excessive

anger by those with a higher tolerance for injustice (Aristotle, *The Nicomachean Ethics* II.7.1108a.4–9).

11. The practice of righteous anger includes both indignation and refraining from unrighteous anger. Obviously, repression of anger is psychologically harmful. Refraining from unrighteous anger entails suppressing unrighteous impulses toward anger and the cultivation of a spiritual disposition that is humble, long-suffering, full of compassion, and ready to forgive offenders.

12. Prophetic anger is not inherently righteous. For example, the Lord rebukes Jonah for his anger provoked by the Lord's compassion toward Nineveh (Jonah 4:1–11). That said, scripture often portrays prophets as harshly expressing their indignation without divine disapproval in ways that grate against modern sensibilities. In such cases, we are confronted with the possibility that our objections are rooted in our culture's moral intuitions, rather than some objective, universal standard of righteousness.

13. Evangelicals are quick to point out that God's love is purer and thus superior to human love, but we reflect less on how the difference between divine and human emotion applies to negative emotions. For instance, what would it mean to say that God's anger is perfect or pure?

14. The most common terms for anger in the Old Testament are *'ap* (literally "nose, nostril"), *ḥrh* ("to kindle" or "to become hot"), and *'nap* ("to wheeze"). In its characteristically concrete fashion, the Hebrew terminology for anger describes the appearance of someone becoming angry.

15. Similarly, human anger is also a contextualized interpretation of one's automatic physiological response to circumstances. People first become physiologically aroused and then interpret their reaction as fear, surprise, anger, etc. on the basis of situational factors and past experiences.

16. Brother John argues that "'the wrath of God' becomes in practice little more than a technical term to describe the consequences of evil in the universe which is the handiwork of a Creator who is good and the source of goodness." He understands the biblical concept of divine wrath as an objective, externalized rendering of God's anger. Although he recognizes a personal character to God's anger as expressed through some of the prophets, his argument seems to support, perhaps unintentionally, a version of God the Father as a dispassionate judge (Brother John 2017, 51–53).

17. My presentation of the cycle of wrath is an adaptation of the stages presented by Baloian (Baloian 1992, 109–24).

18. Despite English translations, the Old Testament does not contain a Hebrew verb that means "to punish." Rather, the Lord "visits (*pqd*) iniquity" upon wrongdoers (Lev 18:25; Ps 89:32) and "judges" (*špṭ*) them (1 Sam 3:13).

19. In Leviticus 26, the negative consequences for breaking the covenant are examples of conditional curses (Kitz 2007, 616).

20. Although imprecations occur in many of the psalms, a relatively small number could fairly be designated as imprecatory psalms in the sense that imprecations are a major motif. Commonly recognized imprecatory psalms include Pss 7, 35, 55, 58, 59, 69, 79, 83, 109, and 137. More precisely, these are lament psalms that prominently feature imprecations.

21. People may object to a government's use of capital punishment, torture, military conflict, and other forms of extreme violence. However, governments also employ various means of making life difficult to deter and punish social deviancy. As indicated in the discussion of imprecations in the ancient Near East, I regard these as milder forms of violence. Ideally, such milder forms would be sufficient to deter most crime. Additionally, we may object to an institution's inadequate administration of justice without objecting to the right to use sanctioned means to protect the common good.

22. Righteous anger is also distinguished by its twofold expression of frustration. Whereas the prophets are called to express divine displeasure toward offending people and nations, the imprecatory psalms express frustration about injustice toward God. Similarly, righteous anger provoked by racial injustice may be faithfully expressed through lament and imprecation on the one hand, and on the other hand through prayers of prophetic confrontations with the unjust that verbalize and dramatize the offensiveness of injustice to the divinely established moral order.

REFERENCES

Baloian, Bruce Edward. 1992. *Anger in the Old Testament.* American University Studies. Series VII vol. 99. New York: Peter Lang.

Brother John of Taizé. 2017. *The Wrath of a Loving God: Unraveling a Biblical Conundrum.* Eugene: Wipf & Stock.

Du Bois, W. E. B. 2020. *The Souls of Black Folk.* London: Global Classics.

Foster, Richard J. 1998. *Celebration of Discipline: The Path to Spiritual Growth,* twentieth anniversary ed. San Francisco: HarperSanFrancisco.

King, Martin Luther, Jr. 1968. "The Other America." Speech at Grosse Pointe High School, Gross Pointe, MI, March 14). Accessed May 6, 2020. http://www.gphistorical.org/mlk/mlkspeech/.

Kitz, Ann Marie. 2007. "Curses and Cursing in the Ancient Near East." *Religion Compass* 1, no. 6: 615–27.

Mahar, Daniel. "Antithesis: Contradictions Between the Old Testament Deity and the New Testament God." The Gnostic Society Library. Accessed May 7, 2020. http://www.gnosis.org/library/marcion/antithes.htm.

Nussbaum, Martha C. 2016. "Beyond Anger." *Aeon,* July 26. Accessed July 17, 2020. https://aeon.co/essays/there-s-no-emotion-we-ought-to-think-harder-about-than-anger.

Psychology Dictionary. 2020a. "Anger." Accessed May 6, 2020. https://psychologydictionary.org/anger/.

———. 2020b. "Negative Emotion." Accessed May 6, 2020. https://psychologydictionary.org/negative-emotion/.

Srinivasan, Amia. 2018. "The Aptness of Anger." *Journal of Political Philosophy* 26, no. 2: 123–44.

Walton, John H. 2018. *Ancient Near Eastern Thought and the Old Testament: Introducing the Conceptual World of the Old Testament,* 2nd ed. Grand Rapids: Baker Academic.

Chapter 11

Anger in an Ethics of Love

Gregory L. Bock

Christian ethics is an ethics of love. It teaches that God's love is revealed in the life and death of Jesus of Nazareth and that his followers ought to imitate him and be known for how they love one another (John 3:16; Ephesians 5:1–2; John 13:35). If love is so important to the Christian life, what place is there for anger? Is anger morally permissible? Is being angry with one's neighbors (or enemies) compatible with loving them? Famously, Joseph Butler raises a similar question in his eighteenth-century sermon "Upon Resentment." He asks, "Why had man implanted in him a principle, which appears the direct contrary to benevolence?" (Butler 2017, 68). His answer is that anger is a divine gift that enables us to respond appropriately to sin and that as long as anger is not excessive, it is compatible with loving one's neighbors, even one's enemies. Butler is clear that he thinks anger and love are compatible, but he is less clear about whether he thinks the two are more deeply related. In fact, because of a missing distinction, Butler's readers might take him to believe that anger and love are at cross purposes.[1] In this paper, I reflect on Butler's insights and argue, with help from Nicholas Wolterstorff, David McNaughton, Rebecca Konyndyk DeYoung, and others, that anger should be in the service of love, of wanting what is best for oneself and others and responding appropriately within limits when this is not realized. Anger that is not loving in this way is not godly or righteous.

AGAPIC LOVE

In order to talk about an ethics of love, one must be clear about the meaning of love, and as difficult and cliché as this sounds, I will do my best to present a short exposition of the biblical idea of love in what follows and show that such love is both a matter of will and affection. The word for the highest form of love in the Greek manuscripts is *agape*. Agapic love is one of God's central attributes[2] and describes his caring relationship to the world (1 John 4:8; 2 Corinthians 13:11; John 3:16). It is other-regarding but also self-regarding (Matthew 22:39; 1 John 3:16). It includes feelings but is more than a feeling.[3] Jesus modeled it in the sacrificial way he lived and died, and he teaches his followers to love each other in the same way (John 13:34; John 15:12). The Apostle Paul describes it in the following way: "Love is patient and kind; love does not envy or boast; it is not arrogant or rude. It does not insist on its own way; it is not irritable or resentful; it does not rejoice at wrongdoing, but rejoices with the truth. Love bears all things, believes all things, hopes all things, endures all things. Love never ends" (1 Corinthians 13:4–8).

Nicholas Wolterstorff defines *agapic love* as care, and he defines *care* as seeking the good of others (2011, 93, 101–18). He explains this "seeking the good of others" in the context of Jesus' new commandment: that we ought to love others as he loves us (John 13:34; John 15:11–13), which means to love self-sacrificially. It means going to the cross metaphorically, sometimes denying oneself, sometimes taking great risks. For example, one person might choose to work on the frontlines in the healthcare field in order to care for patients during a pandemic. Another might sacrifice her own career plans to care for a sick child.

Wolterstorff says that what matters to Jesus is that we care for our neighbors, not whether we do so because of any particular affection or attachment we have for them (2011, 118).[4] However, this does not mean that love is purely a matter of obligation (in a Kantian sense) and involves no positive feelings or inclination, because feelings can motivate.

Wolterstorff identifies different motivations, such as attraction, solidarity, and compassion, and argues that it is possible to care for our neighbors in the way that Jesus requires and to be motivated by any one of these sentiments. Agapic love is not contrary to feelings of attachment.[5] In fact, God cares for us and feels these emotions, too. According to Ephesians 2:4–5 and John 3:16, it is because of God's great love that he initiates a plan of salvation through Jesus. Wolterstorff writes, "God's love for us is not only love as care but love as eros, attraction-love" (2011, 109). Wolterstorff continues: "The love that we should have for God and that is appropriate to have for self and neighbor is not only love as care but love as eros. Where there is worth, it is appropriate to be drawn to it, attracted" (109). In this, Wolterstorff explains that God's care for us is deeply emotional (93).[6] Miroslav Volf describes this in terms of delight. He writes, "God delights in us, and therefore God gives. Divine delight in creatures is a bit like our delight in our own children—we delight in their feats, their triumphs, or their good looks, but even more basically, we delight in the sheer 'that-ness' of their existences. That they *are* delights us. That we *are* delights God" (Volf 2005, 73).

In short, God's love is both passionate and volitional. He cares for us and seeks our good self-sacrificially, and he does so because he sees us as worthy of love and delights in us.[7] So, I offer the following definition of agapic love: *a holistic caring (heart, mind, and will) for self and others.*[8] It may be true that such love is exceedingly difficult for human beings to realize and that every act of love that we initiate can at best only approximate perfect love, but this is no reason to aspire to anything less.

THE ETHICS OF LOVE

Agapic ethics (agapism) enjoins us to love others as God loves us (John 13:34). In Matthew 22:37–40, Jesus lays out a hierarchy of commandments, saying that we must first love God and second our neighbors as ourselves. He adds that all other laws "hang on" these two.[9] Agapism takes this ordering seriously and makes love the fundamental moral value.[10] According to Timothy P. Jackson, it is a metavalue: "that virtue without which one has no substantive access to other goods, either moral or nonmoral" (2003, 10). Jackson says that agapic ethics is marked by three features: "(1) unconditional willing of the good for the other, (2) equal regard for the well-being of the other, and (3) passionate service open to self-sacrifice for the sake of the other" (2003, 10).

These features are both internal and external—being and doing. If agapism were simply understood as a principle of action, such as the principle of beneficence, then a deontological system like Kant's might suffice. Also, if agapism were simply concerned with the greater good, then utilitarianism might suffice, for such ethical systems also promote the good of others as central to their theoretical frameworks (Frankena 1973, 57). Nevertheless, as described above, a biblical love is much more than simply actions and consequences. It is not enough to simply do good to others and avoid harming them. If this were so, one could be a loving person by just paying one's tithe and controlling the urge to punch people, but actions are not the only subject of moral evaluation. Agapism also includes emotions in its analysis. William Frankena writes, "If one [construes agapism as the principle of beneficence], one must, of course, conceive of the principle of beneficence as asking us not only to do what is in fact beneficent but also to be benevolent, i.e., to do it out of love" (1973, 58). This sounds like Aristotle's virtue-theoretic account of feelings. Aristotle says, "But having these feelings at the right times, about the right things, toward the right people, for the right end, and in the right way, is the intermediate state and best condition, and this is proper to virtue" (1106b21–23). So, Frankena construes agapism along virtue-theoretic lines, for a virtue framework makes ethics more than just an analysis of right action and puts the matter in terms of dispositions, character, and feelings. He writes, "An [ethics of virtue] is concerned with being rather than doing—its basic instruction is, roughly, 'Be loving!' or 'Have love!,' or, more accurately, 'Love and (ultimately) love alone is a virtue'" (1973, 31).

Agapism makes love the cardinal virtue and makes the task of ethics the cultivation of this virtue. Jackson writes, "[Love] is a participation in the very life of God and, as such, the foundation of all virtues for those made in the Image of God" (2003, 14). The goal of the Christian life is to become more loving, to transform one's character by the love of God. This is difficult and takes time. It may start quickly with an awakening experience in which one encounters God's grace and mercy for the first time, but the road of spiritual development is long and difficult (James 1:2–4; Romans 5:3–5; Romans 7; Hebrews 12:1). New believers are called to a life of discipleship in imitation of Jesus, to emulate him in character, feelings, thought patterns, and actions. At first, they may only be able to replicate his actions externally. A mature believer may feel great joy at helping the needy whereas a new believer may only do so out of a sense of duty. A mature believer may have a generous, stable character whereas a new believer's character may be unreliable. It is only through much practice that progress is made.[11] Aristotle calls this pro-cess "habituation." He says, "We are completed through habit . . . we become builders, for instance, by building, and we become harpists by playing the harp. Similarly, then, we become just by doing just actions, temperate by doing temperate actions, brave by doing brave actions" (1103a25–1103b). The agapist adds to this the virtue of love: we become loving by doing loving actions. Frankena writes, "Before one is loving one can do only what the lov-ing man would do, but afterwards one can do it as he would do it" (1973, 32).

JOSEPH BUTLER ON RESENTMENT

So, if agapic love involves the heart, mind, and will, and an ethics of love is not only about doing the loving thing but also doing it lovingly, what room is there for anger? Or, as Butler frames it: "Why had man implanted in him a principle, which appears the direct contrary to benevolence?" (8.1).[12] I have worked out elsewhere the difficult task of interpreting Butler's eighth and ninth sermons "Upon Resentment" and "Upon Forgiveness of Injuries," so here I will just provide a short summary (Bock 2020).

The purpose of his two sermons is to show that resentment (anger) is compatible with benevolence (love) unless anger becomes excessive. He claims that resentment is actually a gift from God that serves the following functions. First, it is a useful guide to help us know right from wrong. When we get angry at others for wrongdoing, we realize that our emotional response would condemn us too if we did the same thing (8.16). Second, it is the proper response to "injury and wickedness: that which is the only deformity in creation, and the only reasonable object of abhorrence and dislike" (8.17). Nevertheless, God-given anger can be abused, and the abuse of it interferes with love. He writes:

> The chief instances of abuse are: when, from partiality to ourselves, we imagine an injury done us, when there is none: when this partiality represents it to us greater than it really is: when we fall into that extravagant and monstrous kind of resentment, towards one who has innocently been the occasion of evil to us; that is, resentment upon account of pain or inconvenience, without injury; which is the same absurdity, as settled anger at a thing that is inanimate: when the indignation against injury and injustice rises too high, and is beyond proportion to the particular ill action it is exercised upon: or lastly, when pain or harm of any kind is inflicted merely in consequence of, and to gratify, that resentment, though naturally raised. (8.11)

In short, our capacity for anger is God-given and good in its divinely intended place, but it can be abused in five different ways: (1) when no wrong has actually occurred, (2) when the wrong is exaggerated, (3) when the wrong was unintentional, (4) when anger is disproportionate, and (5) when anger becomes retaliation.[13]

He argues that anger and love (benevolence) are compatible and gives two examples: parenting and friendship. He does not explain these examples and only says that in each case the two emotions "lessen" but "do not necessarily destroy each other" (9.13). What does this mean in the example of parenting? It does not mean that parents can simply choose to do the right thing for their children while feeling ill-will toward them because in the same sentence, Butler identifies love as a passion, not just an action (9.13). In other words, it is not enough to show that parents can fulfill their duty to their children while resenting them inside. Rather, he thinks that one can have both feelings at the same time toward the same person, even though he admits that the two passions will "lessen" one other. I imagine that Butler means only that a mild form of resentment is compatible with loving one's children, perhaps the kind of resentment one might feel upon hearing about a wrong committed against a stranger by a stranger. In the same sermon, he says that a person "ought to be affected towards the injurious person in the same way any good men, uninterested in the case, would be; if they had the same just sense" (9.19). In other words, the anger should be objective, and the angry one should not take the wrong personally. An example of mild anger in parenting might be when one's child gets in a bit of trouble at school. The parent could address the infraction in a heart to heart conversation over smoothies after school, perhaps saying, "I'm very disappointed in you. But I love you and I know you are going do better next time, right?"

David McNaughton claims that readers of Butler should distinguish between resentment and indignation.[14] Indignation is anger at wrongdoing.[15] Resentment, on the other hand, is personal (Butler 2017, 175). He writes, "One can feel indignant on anyone's behalf, whereas one can typically resent only injury to oneself or those with whom one is closely identified. One who resents is often typically aggrieved, feels betrayed, or has their feelings hurt, in a way that one who is merely indignant is not" (175).[16] On this account, resentment means taking things personally, and taking things personally means having ill-will or a "hostile attitude" toward the wrongdoer (xxx). This is incompatible with love. Applied to Butler's parenting example, parents can be indignant about their children's behavior and still love them, but if the parent resents the child, perhaps when the child is impudent or impertinent, then this lessens love and may totally obstruct it.

Can one be indignant, in McNaughton's sense, with a wrong committed against oneself? In other words, can one be wronged without taking it personally? McNaughton thinks so. He says, "I can only resent wrongs done to me . . . but I can be indignant about any wrong done to anyone (including, of course, myself)" (Butler 2017, xxix). Describing Butler's view, McNaughton writes, "one can feel [indignation] on one's own behalf, or on behalf of others. It is only in the former case that it is liable to be excessive" (175). This means that righteous anger is not only directed at wrongs done to others but also at wrongs done to the self; however, it is much harder to remain righteously indignant when the self is involved, and this is where Butler's notion of forgiveness is relevant. Forgiveness is what makes it possible to be indignant about wrongs done to the self. Forgiveness is what love does when resentment interferes with it, when anger gets in the way of Jesus' command to love one another. For Butler, forgiveness is the forswearing of excessive resentment (Bock 2020, 103), and what qualifies as excessive is what is found in his list of five abuses. From here on, I will adopt McNaughton's conceptual distinction and identify resentment with bad anger—of taking something personally—and indignation with righteous anger, which is anger directed at appropriate targets and constrained within limits.

McNaughton's distinction fits well with Butler's five abuses. In what follows, I will apply McNaughton's concepts to the abuses and illustrate them with examples. The first abuse is when no wrong has actually occurred. Butler writes: "when, from partiality to ourselves, we imagine an injury done us, when there is none" (8.11). When we take wrongs personally, we show "partiality to ourselves," and, as Butler describes, this can confound a proper understanding of the situation, such as when there is no harm or ill-will. An example of this is when two friends misunderstand one another and neither friend meant what the other one took them to mean. In such a case, resentment obscures the details and causes one to misinterpret the actions of the other as hostile. In parenting, this might occur when young children express their displeasure at the food they are served at the dinner table. Parents are likely to take this personally, but there is no real injury. A child does not yet understand social etiquette and when to keep their opinions to themselves. Parental love requires great patience.[17]

The second abuse is as follows: "when this partiality represents it to us greater than it really is" (8.11). Again, the source of the abuse is "partiality to ourselves," but in this case, there is a wrong committed; however, the reaction is overblown. For example, one can imagine a father returning home from work with the stresses of the day on his shoulders and encountering his son's bicycle in the driveway, blocking his car. One can imagine a father exploding with violent emotions, especially if this is not the first time this has happened. Although the child's action may be an example of disobedience and carelessness, an outburst like this would be excessive. Of course, the bike or the car could be damaged by the child's negligence, but this hardly justifies inflicting emotional trauma on the child.

The third abuse is when the wrong is unintentional, when the suffering or inconvenience inflicted is accidental. In such a case, preoccupation with oneself leads the one who suffers the effects of the action to resent the person who is nothing but the occasion of misfortune. To resent innocent people, especially the ones we ought to love, is to fail to have one's feelings track reality. Of course, being the victim of an accident and having one's desires thwarted can be frustrating, but such experiences are a part of life. Love is not irritable, and it endures all things.[18] To be a good parent, one must overcome regular inconvenience with love. For example, a father might be working in his study, writing a chapter for a book, and is interrupted by his young son with updates on a Minecraft game. These interruptions can be aggravating, especially if the dad is under a writing deadline. Nevertheless, while the aggravation might be understandable, resenting his son is not justified. There is no ill-will; in fact, from the son's perspective, quite the opposite is true: he loves his dad so much that he wants to share his happiness with him. How tragic it would be if the father lets his work shatter this special moment.

The fourth abuse is when anger is disproportionate. This is anger directed at an appropriate object, but the reaction is excessive, such as punching a wall. In parenting, the occasion for this anger may be in witnessing one's child being harmed, such as by a bully on the playground or by an illegal tackle on the soccer field. It is one thing to correct the offending child on the playground or notify the referee, which is compatible with being indignant and wanting what is best for everyone. It is quite another to lose one's head on the sidelines in a profanity-laced tirade.

The fifth abuse is when anger becomes retaliation, when someone seeks to harm someone else in retaliation for what was done to them, not for the sake of the other, but to protect one's pride or reclaim one's lost status vis-à-vis the other.[19] It is the application of pain to satisfy the injury sustained to one's ego. In the case of parenting, retaliation is never acceptable. Parents should seek the well-being of their children, not their children's humiliation or harm, and a parent's ego defenses should not come into play. Retaliation runs contrary to parental love. However, we must distinguish between retaliation and discipline. Discipline is the application of harsh measures for instructional or training purposes. Just as coaches might make their players run extra laps at the end of practice, so parents might apply penalties in response to disobedience. These measures are applied for the good of the child and should always be conducted with gentleness and restraint. Parents who do not discipline or discipline too harshly are rightly questioned about whether they, in fact, love their children because not only is proper discipline compatible with parental love, but also love requires it. Moreover, discipline is compatible with feelings of anger, but this anger must be tempered if it is not to transform what would be appropriate, loving discipline into retaliation.

THE DEEP CONNECTION BETWEEN ANGER AND LOVE

A casual reading of Butler might produce the impression that while anger and benevolence are compatible, the two are at cross purposes.[20] On this misreading, anger is a natural human emotion but not a holy one. God may tolerate it but does not condone it and certainly does not require it. Christian ethics, one might say, enjoins us to keep anger in its place so that it does not interfere with what one is supposed to do, which is to love one's neighbor. Of course, this interpretation of Butler is in error; he does not believe that anger is unholy or sinful in its original form because he explicitly says it is a divine gift whose target is "injury and wickedness" (8.17), but it is unclear whether he sees any deeper connection with love. In fact, there is reason to think that he makes no connection because he says that anger "lessens" love (9.13). How can one lessen the other if one is an expression of the other?

If love is as central to Christian ethics as I argue above, then there must be a deeper connection. First, the doctrine of sin should be understood in relation to love. Sinful acts are an absence or failure of love, a violation of Jesus' love command. "Injury and wickedness," the targets of anger on Butler's account, are not just the breaking of arbitrary rules or rituals. Second, good anger then should be targeted at trespasses of this kind and should seek the restoration of the victim and the repentance of the wrongdoer. Moreover, anger should be felt and expressed in proper amount, neither too little or too much, just as much as agapic love requires.

DeYoung's analysis of anger in the context of the seven deadly sins can be helpful in further elucidating the connection to love. She distinguishes between good and bad anger. Good anger is anger that is directed at the right target and is not excessive. The right target is injustice. She writes, "The end that moves the rightly angered person is the good of justice, a desire for things to be made right between persons" (DeYoung 2009, chap. 6). As she says, "You don't get angry unless you *care*" (chap. 6). On her account, anger does not simply spring out of a preoccupation with personal entitlements or equality for equality's sake or power for power's sake. Instead, anger should be motivated by care for oppressed individuals. She writes, "Anger, when it is a *holy* emotion, has *justice* as its object and *love* as its root" (chap. 6). This fits with how Cornel West describes the connection between justice and love: "Justice is what love looks like in public."

DeYoung calls bad anger *wrath*, which she describes as "self-regarding and selfish." Wrathful people think too highly of themselves, exaggerating their own self-worth. Their anger is focused on wrongs done to themselves, and their anger may go wrong in one of several ways. First, they may take out their anger on an undeserving person. For example, DeYoung says, "An older child receives the pent-up explosion of the parent worn down by two hours of dealing with an aggravatingly whiny two year old" (2009, chap. 6). Second, anger may go wrong in how it is expressed. It may be directed at a true injustice, but its manifestation may be out of proportion. Acts of violence are examples of this. Third, anger can go wrong by staying angry too long. Resentment can fester for years in the hearts of parents and spouses. This long-term anger corrupts the heart and destroys loving relationships.

DeYoung ties wrath to a lack of humility and a desire to be in control. She writes, "Our bad anger thus shows us to be trying—and failing—to be God. We are wrathful when we can't control things that hurt us and keep them at bay" (2009, chap. 6). She notes that, indeed, we should fight against injustice, and anger can be effective in motivating us to make the world a better place. However, the injustice in the world must always be kept in perspective. Ultimately, God is in control; we are not. She writes, "In wrath, we ultimately want our own way. In gentle self-mastery, we pray, 'Thy will be done'" (chap. 6). This humility means that we understand the limits of our power and control, and we surrender what we cannot control to God, which is an act of loving God.

Anger is a loving, necessary response to wrongdoing. Andrew D. Lester makes a strong case for the necessity of anger. He writes, "Anger is not opposed to love, but is in the service of love" (Lester 2003, chap. 12). Christians should get angry when they hear about injustice, and they should be motivated to address it. Lester correctly describes three ways that love will manifest in the face of injustice: "speaking the truth in love, compassionate resistance, and nonviolent confrontation" (chap. 12). Christians who do not speak the truth, compassionately resist injustice, or nonviolently confront evil cannot be said to fully love their neighbors or enemies.

CONCLUSION

According to agapic ethics, right and wrong are understood within a framework of love. Right action is loving action, and not only action, but also affection and cognition. It is not enough to act for the well-being of others; love also requires caring deeply about them. And this deep care produces anger when those who are loved are harmed. However, anger can go wrong, and when it does go wrong, it is uniquely destructive. Therefore, right anger will be felt, as Aristotle would say, in the right way, at the right time, and for the right end. For an agapist, these are determined by the perfectly loving person—Jesus Christ.

However, we must admit that this is quite a high standard, and few, if anyone can love like Jesus. Nevertheless, apapic ethics, as a virtue-theoretic approach, conceives of the moral life in terms of growth and habituation. It is not a matter of simply doing the right thing on any given day; it is a lifetime of development, and by the grace of God, we shall be perfected in the end. Until then, we are in training, and our merciful, loving God bears our moral training with patience, and we should, too.

NOTES

1. The missing distinction is McNaughton's resentment/indignation distinction, which I discuss below.

2. It is arguably his most central attribute, at least as he relates to us. In response to the counterclaim that God's main attribute is his glory, not his love, Miroslav Volf

writes, "We just need to say that God's glory, which is God's very being, *is* God's love" (2005, 39).

3. In other words, it is both passionate and volitional. Agape's strong volitional demands are evident in the conversation between Jesus and Peter in John 21:15–18. Jesus asks Peter if he "agapes" him, and Peter answers sheepishly that he only "philias" him (philia is the Greek word for friendship). In other words, Jesus asks if Peter is "all in," and Peter responds that he really likes Jesus; however, Peter confesses (because he has just been tested and found wanting) that his love is not much stronger than that. This shows that agape is a strong commitment. Nevertheless, agape is also a feeling, for in 1 Corinthians 13:3, the Apostle Paul says that love is more than just doing the right thing. He says that if he gives to the poor without having agape, then he "gains nothing."

4. Wolterstorff seems to stress the volitional side of love whereas the Apostle stresses the emotional dimension in 1 Corinthians 13:3. See notes 3 and 6.

5. Agapic love is not opposed to inclination and does not require a Kantian sense of acting for the sake of the moral law alone (Wolterstorff 2011, 116–18).

6. Wolterstorff (2011, 116–18) distinguishes between agape and eros and says that God loves us in both ways. On my interpretation of John 21:15–18; 1 Corinthians 13:3; and passages that describe God's love for us, agapic love is complete love— heart, mind, and will—not just will or action. Eros (and philia) are aspects of agape. However, whether eros is part of agape or is a separate form of love is irrelevant for this essay. My argument depends only on recognizing that God loves with both eros and agape, affection and volition, and that we ought to do the same.

7. For more on the dimensions of divine love, see Bock 2016 (235–36) and Pettigrove 2012 (74–95).

8. The difference between my definition of agapic love and Wolterstorff's is that I include eros in agape (see note 3).

9. See also Galatians 5:14. For a discussion on what it means for all others to hang on these, see Paul Ramsey 1950 (46–91).

10. Miroslav Volf says, "A genuinely Christian reflection on social issues must be rooted in the self-giving love of the divine Trinity as manifested on the cross of Christ; all the central themes of such reflection will have to be thought through from the perspective of the self-giving love of God" (1996, 25).

11. For more on spiritual disciplines, see Willard 1988.

12. All references to Butler's sermons are to the sermon and section number in Butler 2017.

13. For more on the abuses, see Bock 2020.

14. McNaughton's claim is not that Butler actually makes this distinction but that he should have, that such a distinction makes better sense of what Butler is trying to do and captures the psychological phenomena best. McNaughton thinks Butler only requires forgiveness in cases of resentment, not indignation.

15. In case it is not obvious in what follows, indignation is, in fact, a hot emotion. It is not a cold, rational courtroom-like judgment. However, it is tempered and avoids Butler's abuses.

16. This distinction is similar to Rebecca Konyndyk DeYoung's. She says, "When [anger] is good, anger is a passion for justice, motivated by love for others. We get angry when someone we care about is hurt or threatened. . . . Anger turns vicious, however, when it fights for its own selfish cause" (DeYoung 2009).

17. One of the characteristics of love in 1 Corinthians 13:4.

18. Two characteristics of love in 1 Corinthians 13:5, 7.

19. For more on anger's connection to status-injuries, see Martha Nussbaum 2016 (17–21).

20. No scholar I know actually holds this interpretation of Butler, but among the laity such an ethics of anger is quite prevalent.

REFERENCES

Bock, Gregory L. 2016. "Christian Love and Unconditional Forgiveness: A Response to Glen Pettigrove." In *The Philosophy of Forgiveness Volume I: Explorations of Forgiveness: Personal, Relational, and Religious*, edited by Court D. Lewis, 223–42. Wilmington, Delaware: Vernon Press.

———. 2020. "Understanding Joseph Butler's Sermons on Resentment and Forgiveness." In *The Ethics of Anger*, edited by Court D. Lewis and Gregory L. Bock. New York: Lexington Books.

Butler, Joseph. 2017. *Joseph Butler: Fifteen Sermons Preached at the Rolls Chapel and Other Writings on Ethics*. Edited by David McNaughton. New York: Oxford University Press.

DeYoung, Rebecca Konyndyk. 2009. *Glittering Vices: A New Look at the Seven Deadly Sins and their Remedies.* Grand Rapids, MI: Brazos Press. Kindle.

Frankena, William. 1973. *Ethics*, 2nd ed. Upper Saddle River, NJ: Prentice Hall.

Jackson, Timothy P. 2003. *The Priority of Love: Christian Charity and Social Justice.* Princeton, NJ: Princeton University Press.

Lester, Andrew D. 2003. *The Angry Christian: A Theology for Care and Counseling.* Louisville, KY: Westminster John Knox Press. Kindle.

Nussbaum, Martha. 2016. *Anger and Forgiveness: Resentment, Generosity, and Justice.* New York: Oxford University Press.

Pettigrove, Glen. 2012. *Forgiveness and Love.* Oxford: Oxford University Press.

Ramsey, Paul. 1950. *Basic Christian Ethics.* Louisville, KY: Westminster John Knox Press.

Volf, Miroslav. 1996. *Exclusion and Embrace.* Nashville: Abingdon Press.

———. 2005. *Free of Charge: Giving and Forgiving in a Culture Stripped of Grace.* Grand Rapids, MI: Zondervan.

Willard, Dallas. 1988. *The Spirit of the Disciplines: Understanding How God Changes Lives.* New York: HarperCollins.

Wolterstorff, Nicholas. 2011. *Justice in Love.* Grand Rapids, MI: William B. Eerdmans Publishing Company.

Index